DATE			

JUN - - 2022

Corrections in Ink

Corrections in Ink

a memoir

Keri Blakinger

ST. MARTIN'S PRESS
NEW YORK

Some portions of this text have been adapted from essays previously published in the *Houston Chronicle*, The Marshall Project, and *The New York Times*.

Epigraph excerpted from "Not Waving But Drowning" by Stevie Smith, from COLLECTED POEMS OF STEVIE SMITH, copyright ©1957 by Stevie Smith. Reprinted by permission of New Directions Publishing Corp.

First published in the United States by St. Martin's Press, an imprint of St. Martin's Publishing Group

www.stmartins.com

Library of Congress Cataloging-in-Publication Data

Names: Blakinger, Keri, author.
Title: Corrections in ink : a memoir / Keri Blakinger.
Description: First edition. | New York : St. Martin's Press, 2022.
Identifiers: LCCN 2022002306 | ISBN 9781250272850 (hardcover) |
    ISBN 9781250272867 (ebook)
Subjects: LCSH: Blakinger, Keri, | Women journalists—United States—Biography. |
    Drug addicts—United States—Biography. | Ex-convicts—United States—
    Biography. | Figure skaters—United States—Biography. | LCGFT: Autobiographies.
Classification: LCC PN4874.B553 A3 2022 | DDC 070.92 [B]—dc23/eng/20220127
LC record available at https://lccn.loc.gov/2022002306

Our books may be purchased in bulk for promotional, educational, or business use. Please contact your local bookseller or the Macmillan Corporate and Premium Sales Department at 1-800-221-7945, extension 5442, or by email at MacmillanSpecialMarkets@macmillan.com.

First Edition: 2022

10 9 8 7 6 5 4 3 2 1

To all the people I met inside,
and the ones still there today

Author's Note

This book is a memoir, drawn from my experience, recollections, letters, and voluminous journal entries, some of which have been condensed and edited for clarity. The events here are described as I remember them—though I have fact-checked my memory where possible, through government records and personal interviews. Some conversations are included verbatim based on notes and journals, but others I reconstructed to the best of my ability.

I have changed the names and some identifying details of people I met behind bars, including all staff and most prisoners. I made similar changes when writing about people described committing crimes or doing drugs. There are a few exceptions: I used the real names of people who are now dead, as well as the real names of prisoners I met in the course of my work as a reporter after my release. In many cases, their names have already appeared publicly in my stories. Finally—at their request—I have used the real names of both Stacy Burnett and her pet chicken.

Nobody heard him, the dead man,
But still he lay moaning:
I was much further out than you thought
And not waving but drowning.
—"NOT WAVING BUT DROWNING" BY STEVIE SMITH

Corrections
in Ink

Chapter 1

Ithaca, 2010

I have problems: I am out of clean clothes, I cannot find my glasses, my English paper is late, and my pockets are not big enough for all the heroin I have.

But, honestly, more than anything, I want a cigarette.

I'm only ten minutes from where I'm going, and it's cold outside. The sun is deceptive; it looks like a nice upstate New York morning, but really it's December and the wind is whipping up from Ithaca's gorges. I stop walking and push my fingers deep into my pockets in search of a Parliament.

In a minute, there will be police, with questions and handcuffs. By tomorrow, my scabby-faced mugshot will be all over the news as the Cornell student arrested with $150,000 of smack. I will sober up to a sea of regrets. My dirty clothes and late English paper—one of the last assignments I need to graduate—will be the least of my problems.

But that's all in the future. Right now, I just want that ciga-rette. *Where the fuck did I put them?*

When I woke up this morning in the stash house on Stew-art Avenue, the first thing I did was look at my day planner—I am over-organized as ever, even on the brink of disaster. Then, I answered the phone after my boyfriend called repeatedly. We got in a fight. I emailed one of my professors to beg for another extension and promised myself today would be the day I would finally finish everything I need to graduate.

Then I mixed up a spoon of heroin and coke and spent the next two hours poking my arms and legs, fishing around under the skin with a 28-gauge needle in search of relief. My veins are all shot out and scarred and hard to find, so my stabs at oblivion usually involve a few hours of crying as I bleed all over the floor, leaving behind the speckled blood spatter of a crime scene.

This time, I got extra-high, and that last shot was really just out of spite; my boyfriend had the nerve to accuse me of stealing from our heroin, and frankly, I'm pissed. I'm pissed at him, I'm pissed at myself, I'm pissed at every moment that's led me here, and I'm pissed that he's calling on repeat, screaming and threat-ening me while I'm just trying to get high, to get smashed, to get far away from the darkness I'm running from—or toward. Sometimes it's hard to tell the difference.

The phone goes off again, buzzing with the pop-punk notes of a New Found Glory ringtone bought with drug money.

You were everything I wanted, but I just can't finish what I started.

It's him, of course: Alex. He's been smoking crack all morn-ing, holed up with my skittish dog in our basement apartment beneath an unofficial adjunct sorority house up the hill in Collegetown. I can imagine him there, his tattooed arms prying the blinds open as he checks for the black bears and SWAT teams of his drugged-out hallucinations. He is fourteen years my senior, but I know how his face looks childish with terror when his dark eyes gape at what is not there and he begins muttering in his parents' native tongue. They are Greek, and he is whispering a tragic chorus.

Right now, it seems, he's more focused on his phone than on his fear, as he's been calling me again and again to demand that I come back immediately with our Tupperware of drugs. He wants me to bring the whole six-ounce stash so that he can check the weight and make sure I didn't steal any before we sell it.

Before leaving, I take out three or four grams and tuck it under the insole of my black suede sneakers. I like to be prepared. You never know when you might need more heroin. I leave behind the tiny digital scale, an array of baggies and needles, some assorted pills, and my backpack of schoolwork. But then the drugs kick in, and I accidentally nod out for an hour or so in the bathroom before I finally head out into the cold in a black, dragon-print hoodie that leaves me significantly underdressed for twenty-five-degree weather.

I'm a couple houses away—right next to the gorge where I tried to kill myself three years earlier—when I realize I can't find the smokes.

I was damaged long ago, though you swear that you are true, I still pick my friends over you.

Without even glancing down at my beat-up flip phone, I

send Alex straight to voicemail. Then, I whip the clear container full of heroin out of my oversized hoodie and put it down on the curb.

This—like so much else in my life—is probably not a good idea. But it'll only take a minute, and I need a damn cigarette.

I lose sight of everything else as I hunch over to empty out my pockets, pawing through ballpoint pens, mechanical pencils, gram-sized drug baggies, lint, and the assorted debris of my life.

When I look up, empty-handed, there's a cop walking toward me. Given the presence of the patrol car a few houses down, I'm guessing he drove—but he sure seems to have materialized out of thin air, a harbinger of bad things ahead breaking through the haze of my high.

Instinctively, I toss the heroin under the nearest car before I stand up, hoping he didn't see my roadside discus toss. I smile to show that everything is okay. *Of course it's okay, Officer! Why wouldn't it be?*

Then something happens—did I just nod out or black out?—and I'm still yammering away to this cop about the weather (which is not as nice as I'm claiming it is) when a middle-aged lady who works at the nearby flophouse comes plodding across the parking lot. She is large and largely unmemorable—except that she is holding the next two years of my life in her hands.

"Are you looking for this, sir?"

Shit.

Eying the contents of my Tupperware, the cop clears his throat and instructs me to empty out my pockets—which I know hold at least a $150 eight-ball of coke and ten or twenty of the deep-green eighty-milligram Oxys.

Welp.

I decide to make this arrest as painless as possible. I take out the coke with my left hand and as I'm handing it over, I take my right hand and pop the pills into my mouth and swallow them all dry. The cop threatens to pepper spray me if I don't spit them out—but it's too late because I've already eaten them all. It's enough to kill most people, but I've built quite a tolerance through nearly a decade of self-destruction.

Soon I'm handcuffed and in the back seat, bouncing around like one of those annoying little jumpy dogs. The policeman is standing outside doing paperwork, but when he notices the flurry of movement gently rocking the car, he glances over, disinterestedly asking if I'm okay.

"Okay" is not the word I would use to describe this situation.

But I nod and smile; I need him to turn back around so I can finish transferring the heroin from under my insole to a far less accessible spot—up my ass. I know I'm probably going to jail—at least for a few days—so I'll do anything to stave off the impending dopesickness.

As the pills really start to kick in, the day proceeds in snapshots of clarity surrounded by dense pillars of cognitive fog. The present fades to the past, and I am seventeen and alone, sitting on a cement step somewhere around Brattle Street in Cambridge, Massachusetts.

I came here for Harvard Summer School; my promising figure skating career fell apart and my parents realized there was something wrong. This seemed like a fix. They know about the eating disorders, the depression. They do not know about the suicide attempt. They do not know what to do. And neither do I.

So here I am—in far too public a place for this—staring down at a brown line of heroin laid out hastily across my copy of *Sons and Lovers*, a high school summer reading assignment that I will never finish. These are about to be firsts for me. Both my first line and the first time I will not finish my reading assignment.

I am tightly wound, a taut rubber band of perfectionism and self-destruction. And I am about to make things worse.

The rubber band snaps, and I'm back in the present, hand-cuffed in the Ithaca police station.

At some point, I remember nodding out in an interview room, while police pepper me with questions I don't remember answering. The next thing I know I'm staring up at a judge. She talks about me as if I cannot hear her, and the look on her face could be annoyance from being called in on a weekend or sheer disdain at the scabby, smelly junkie in front of her.

Time contracts, and the scene changes. Now I have Fritos all over my chest, and I'm alone in a room with a metal toilet but no toilet paper, a shower stall caked in vomit, a two-inch-thick mattress with holes in it, and two walls made of security glass. I think I'm in a holding cell in the county jail, and I'm guessing that I was just served lunch or dinner, which probably included the Fritos that I've nodded out on and made such a mess of.

Another flash, and I'm sitting at a metal desk in front of a jail guard, who's asking me intake questions I'm entirely too high to answer accurately. My hair is wet from a delousing shower, and I'm wearing a two-sizes-too-big jail-issued snap-up orange jumpsuit paired with flip-flops. Someone took a mugshot, but I don't remember it.

Everything goes black again, and this time when the world flashes back, I'm holding a blue plastic bin of jail-issue items as I stagger forward, following the commands of a sour-faced guard. I put my bin down on the bunk where I'm told. Before I can turn around again, she's slammed shut the metal bars, locking me into what I now realize is my own cell.

I've been too out of it to pay attention to my surroundings—and I've lost my glasses, anyway, further blurring the corners of this unfamiliar world. I only realize that I'm not entirely alone here when another girl wanders up to my cell bars. I am confused. *How are other people out and walking around? Why am I locked in my cell and everyone else is not?* She explains: *You are locked in because you are new and awaiting medical clearance. It could be a week before you get out to mingle.* But she has been here some time, and it's not her first stay. This is her milieu, and she knows how it works. When she starts peppering me with questions, I do my best to answer, but I don't really understand any of this.

No, I don't know what my charges are. No, I don't know if they're serious. No, I don't know if I've been arraigned. No, I don't know if I have a lawyer. But, I say, I do know this: *I am too high to remain upright any longer, and I have a very important question. I have drugs on me right now, and if you tell me how and when I can best do them without getting caught, then I will give you some.* She smiles slowly, a sly Cheshire cat in an orange jumpsuit.

You'll fit in just fine here.

I wish, for the me I was then, that I could add one more flash, much further forward. I wish that the me nodding out in a cold cinderblock cell could see ahead five years, or even ten. I wish that she could see herself getting out of prison, getting sober, finally finishing those college papers and getting a degree. Her last class will be about mass incarceration—and she'll get an A. That cop who arrested her will run up to her one day on the street and want to shake her hand, smiling in the face of an apparent success story. She'll get her first job as a reporter—here, in Ithaca. And she'll love it.

I wish that, instead of being so bitter and broken right now, she could be grateful for the opportunities and chances she'll have that not everyone will. I wish she could see how she'll grab at those chances and run with them.

I wish she could see the day in 2018, when she is crying alone on the bedroom floor—not because she is sad but because she did a thing and it mattered. She wrote a story about prisoners and how the prison system wouldn't give them teeth. But then the people in charge read her story and changed their minds and decided to give more prisoners dentures. And yes, sure, it's a little thing, in one corner of the world—but it made a difference to people who live where she is about to spend the next two years of her life.

I wish she could see who she will become, and the parts of

herself she will leave behind. The darkness that she will learn to live with, and the light she will learn to let in.

But I can't show her those things yet. She'll have to learn the hard way, on a thin plastic mattress in the Tompkins County Jail where—right now—she really, really wants a cigarette.

Chapter 2

A former national skating star and Lancaster Country Day School graduate is in jail in Ithaca, N.Y., after being arrested in December with heroin in her possession, police and news reports say.

According to a news release from Ithaca police, 26-year-old Keri Lynn Blakinger was arrested with nearly 6 ounces of uncut heroin—about 500 doses—in Ithaca on Dec. 19.

The drug was worth between $50,000 and $100,000, police said, although various news reports later estimated the drugs' street value at $150,000.

Police charged Blakinger, a dean's-list student at Cornell University, with criminal possession of a controlled substance in the second degree, a felony. She admitted to police that the drugs were hers, according to a report in the Ithaca Journal.

Police arrested Blakinger in a hotel parking lot after a man who lives near the hotel called 911 to report a man and a woman acting suspicious in the parking lot.

"She appeared uncomfortable, uneasy, having a hard time

standing still and of an altered state of mind," the neighbor told
police, according to reports.
—*excerpt from* Lancaster Intelligencer Journal, *March 2011*

The neighbor was not wrong. But as I read the story from inside my jail cell, I picked apart the tiniest of inaccuracies in the article: It wasn't $150,000! There was no man in the parking lot! I was not acting suspicious! I was ready to be outraged at something, someone, anyone other than myself.

That article was nearly the last in a string of media coverage that stretched out for months, like a trail of breadcrumbs leading back to a time before I'd ever seen the inside of a jail.

Early on, there was the straight news story from the *Ithaca Journal,* then the quick-turn blast in the New York *Daily News,* the anonymous crime brief in the Cornell student newspaper, and the blog entry from *The Washington Post* with the headline: ANOTHER IVY DRUG BUST. In a more salacious slant, Gawker wrote that I "posed in bikinis on Facebook" (what twenty-something didn't?) and "hung out in a notorious drug den" (okay, fair—it was my apartment).

When my hometown paper in Lancaster finally got around to the story in March, it can't have taken them long to comb through the archives—like I did every day in my own mind—and see how far I'd fallen. Splashed across the print edition, the article described me as a dean's-list student, an ex–Girl Scout, a former figure skater, and a writer for the student newspaper.

"In 1994, after winning the gold medal in beginner freestyle skating at the Keystone Winter Games, Blakinger—then only 9 years old—expressed a desire to compete in the Olympics," the article continued.

"A former Girl Scout, she was honored locally with the Young Poets Award in 2000 and received a Scholastic Writing Award the same year for a short-short story. She was a member of the Spanish National Honor Society and the debate club at Country Day, and she was a writer for the school's literary magazine."

All that's true: the skating, the good grades, the awards, the promise. But so is this: For as long as I can remember, I've had a dark side. I tried to kill myself for the first time in my mid-teens, lingering by the side of the Pennsylvania interstate in the gloaming as I waited for cover of dark and debated whether the churning wheels of semis speeding along Route 30 would make for a quick end.

Instead, my therapist—of all people—drove by and picked me up.

Before that, I dabbled with cutting, but instead settled on starving myself. I was obsessive and anxious. Overachieving and talkative. Driven, but not stable.

To anyone paying close attention, it can't have been any surprise where it all led.

I grew up in the suburbs of Lancaster, not far from the colonial row houses of downtown or the rolling cornfields a few miles out. It was a fifty-five-thousand-person city, but in the heart of Amish country—so you might pass by a drug deal on one street and a horse-and-buggy on the next. It was also the place where my parents had grown up, born and raised in walking distance from the brick house that hemmed in our upper-middle-class life. On my bedroom shelf was a black-and-white picture of them kissing when they were three; their mothers were best friends, so they'd known each other forever, even before that staged photo with the punny little caption: "A little DAB'll do ya'."

My dad's initials are DAB.

Harvard-educated and a lawyer, he was raised on athletics as a promising lightweight wrestler in high school and college. Throughout my childhood, he worked obsessively, getting up at 5 A.M. to hunch over paperwork in our living room before driving me to skating practice. Everywhere he went, he toted around a foot-thick briefcase so heavy he tilted to the side when he walked, like the Leaning Tower of Dad.

On the weekends, he did the errands and the yard work, listening to old Grateful Dead tapes in the car and baseball games on a portable radio he'd set out on the sidewalk. With his musical predilections and aversion to confrontation, he was the parent I would have most suspected of being a reformed pot head—but given his sporty background, he always swore he'd never tried it. He might have a few beers at night after my brother and I went to bed, but work, it seemed, was his real escape.

My mom was a Cornell-educated grade school teacher, a part-time reading instructor working in the same district where her mother taught before her. She was tiny, careful, and extremely organized, color-coding everything from weekly schedules to Christmas presents. She'd grown up middle class, but not rich—and was always conscious of making the most of everything, impressing upon us with almost religious conviction the value of working hard, avoiding cholesterol, excelling in school, and eschewing such brain-rotting vices as TV and video games. Both were largely banned in our house. Instead, she gave me and my brother standardized tests for fun and made sure I tried all the possible childhood activities: figure skating, piano, soccer, horseback riding, gymnastics, Girl Scouts—a smorgasbord of suburbia.

I sampled it all with the relentless drive of an Energizer Bunny and the perfectionist zeal of a little Hermione Granger. Doing it all, being constantly productive, was a badge of honor in our family; if nothing else, surely my parents instilled in me an impeccable work ethic. Even so, I was pretty sure that my younger brother, Andrew, was my mom's favorite. He was neater, less stubborn, and a little more even-keeled.

I, however, was ready to haul off and live life like a race. When I started kindergarten at a small private school, I skipped up to first grade in the middle of the year, then skipped another year in math. But like so many other things, I only remember this because I was told. In fact, my memories are sparse before third grade.

There are some things I haven't forgotten: One of my earliest memories is turning down food. My mom was—and is—a true believer in healthy eating, and when the pediatrician told her my cholesterol was high, she taught me how to go on a low-cholesterol diet. Starting sometime in nursery school, full-fat cheese, whole milk, and fried foods were all off the table, and I diligently refused them everywhere like doing so was a mark of distinction.

I am competitive enough to remember that I won a somer-
sault contest in some gymnastics class when I was about five—
and that I lost the cartwheel contest a year later.

I stayed out of trouble enough that I remember getting
yelled at once in second grade, when the teacher caught me
reading a book under my desk. I am stubborn enough that I
remember I did not stop, and got yelled at for it twice.

But I do not remember a single thing I did with my first
friend, the next-door neighbor. I do not remember birthday parties I had or attended, though surely there were many. I do not
remember riding bikes or playing on playgrounds, though these
things must have happened. And I do not remember how I got
hepatitis B when I was nine. The infection is primarily trans-
mitted through blood and semen, but on occasion also through
shared toothbrushes and razors. That year, my babysitter's husband died of liver disease, but there is nothing in my memory to
explain how I got hepatitis, or how my brother got it after me.
It may have been something entirely mundane and forgettable,
but I only know that I felt guilty afterward as if it were my fault.
I'd done something wrong, been dirty, failed to protect him. Not
measured up.

That year I began having trouble making friends at school.
It seemed I'd hit the age when mean girls are just learning how
mean they can be. The rest of elementary school, I spent a lot
of time crying in the bathroom as I learned it, too. I was smart
and athletic, but not in the *cool* way; at recess I played sports
with the boys or sat in a corner and read. I talked incessantly at
adults, but was completely at sea with my peers.

Admittedly, my unfortunate decision to wear pigtail braids

throughout all of fourth grade probably did not help anything. All the grade school fashion sense and social cues seemed cloudy to me, and the hours I spent devouring everything from Isaac Asimov to Shakespeare did not teach me witty retorts to cafeteria insults. In a war of words I was, somehow, ill-equipped. When put on the spot, I would panic, offer no meaningful response—and then I would block it out afterward, perpetually unable to see where I'd gone wrong because I couldn't remember.

By fifth grade, I discovered self-destruction. Sitting at the shellacked wooden table of the school cafeteria, I listened, rapt, as a skinny blond girl in the uniform plaid kilt and white polo explained how to make yourself throw up. Take a spoon, she said. Stick it down your throat. She had the whole table's attention, a gaggle of unpopular girls basking in our private little grade school miseries.

No one suggested this was a bad idea. Quite the opposite; we took it further. The discussion turned to cutting, then suicide. These were all things that had simply not occurred to me before, but the darkness appealed: Maybe I couldn't be popular, but I could be tragic. I couldn't be in the know, but I could have my own secret. I stuffed all that newfound knowledge away for future use; I was intrigued, but I wasn't there yet. But I remember the conversation so clearly I think I must have known that at some point I would be, and sooner rather than later.

By the end of that school year—with much persuading and many tears—I convinced my parents to let me switch to public school. Some of my similarly tormented friends had either convinced or tried to convince their parents to do the same, and I was inspired. I, too, wanted out. And surely, I thought, the kids in public school would be nicer.

They were, but by that point it didn't matter: The ice-cold world of figure skating was beginning to consume my life.

I'd taken my first lesson a few years earlier—maybe third grade or so—after my mother spotted a newspaper article about skating classes at the local ice rink. She clipped it out and showed it to me: Was I interested? I said sure.

The rink itself was an utter dump, a former iron works factory with no heat or bathrooms and a rust-lined roof that would drip bronzy spots onto the ice, as if warning us of its slow plans to collapse. Despite the utterly unwelcoming arena and my intense hatred of the cold, I fell in love.

Inside the ring of the plexiglass barrier was a different world. It was solitude, even on a crowded day. Life moved faster here. There were no parents, the skate-less elders relegated to rinkside.

Being small was an advantage. Social cues didn't matter—because the point was not to talk, the point was to skate. And on top of all that, I was better at it than the mean girls from school, who sometimes took lessons at the same rink. Whenever they showed up, I could jump, spin, and literally skate circles around my enemies.

But even as I found my footing on the slippery ice, I became increasingly unstable everywhere else—even the friendlier public school wasn't enough to save me from me. In sixth or seventh grade, I finally took the skinny blonde's advice to heart, though

I used my fingers and not a spoon. I started weighing myself, began memorizing the calorie counts on food, and learned to clean the vomit out of my braces. I'm not sure what was the final straw, the thing that pushed me over the edge from being miserable in one half of my life to being overtly self-destructive in all of it. Whether it was hormones or budding mental illness, I had simply become volatile. Not overnight, but in fairly short order.

One time in sixth grade I asked a friend at school one too many questions about Kurt Cobain, who had killed himself two years earlier. She got scared and told the guidance counselor, who told my parents. I'm not sure what I planned to do, but the questions weren't entirely idle; the thoughts that led me there were those that led me to the edge of Route 30 a couple years later.

In the meantime, as I dreamed of death, my choices for escape were limited: smoking did not appeal, and the purloined beers I occasionally swiped from my parents' liquor closet did not hold my interest. They had too many calories, and finding a time to steal the liquor closet key and clandestinely drink them was more effort than it was worth. Anything else seemed too risky, too much chance I could lose control. The first time I tried something more, I got caught: In seventh grade at the public school, I tried huffing glue and eating Tylenol 3's in the bathroom with two friends, a trio of experimental angst. Finally, I was not crying in the bathroom alone.

One of the girls—Allie—was brilliant and badass, in my world. She had piercings, dyed hair, and an older brother who might have gotten in trouble with the law. Given her own mother's seemingly laissez-faire parenting, she was appalled at the schedule, organization, and rules in my house. The other girl was mousy and brown-haired, and I did not know her well.

After a few days of secret lunchtime bathroom trips, she was the one who ran to the principal and confessed—and we all got in-school suspension for the whole month of December. I remember thinking that seemed unreasonable since none of the substances were illegal, and I hadn't even managed to abuse them correctly; despite my best efforts, I never felt high. Regardless, the thing I dreaded most was my parents' response—my dad's sad disappointment, my mother's stern embarrassment. She taught in the same district and worried that my mistakes would reflect on her.

The vice principal cautioned my parents that even if they grounded me—an almost meaningless action since I had almost no social life outside of school—they should still let me skate, as the ice seemed to be the primary force keeping me on a good path. Without it, I would have nothing to lose.

My parents agreed. But they insisted I transfer back immediately to the same private school I'd hated so much before, a place they thought I would be safe from trouble—as if that were an external force.

After many tears and much screaming, I made my reluctant return midway through the year, the prodigal child who apparently couldn't hack it in the rough-and-tumble world of suburban Pennsylvania public schools. I don't think anyone really asked questions; they all knew, the way kids know these things. Some of the characters had changed in the year and a half I'd been gone; there were now more uncool kids who'd transferred in, or maybe they'd fallen from the ranks of cool. We banded together—me, the one Black girl, a couple overweight kids, the girl with scoliosis, the tall redhead—and gave ourselves a tongue-in-cheek moniker: the Social Rejects Group-Club, a bunch of outcasts who didn't quite fit the regular middle school labels. We called ourselves SRGC and joked that we were so rejected we weren't even cool enough to just be a group or a club. So we were a group-club. For the most part, we had issues; one of my clearer memories of high school is when another girl in the group swallowed a bottle of pills in the dean's office, apparently trying to kill herself when he'd stepped out and left us there. I only realized what had happened when I saw the empty bottle. I panicked, but thinking of my own impulses for self-destruction, I felt fleetingly guilty when I summoned a teacher. My friend lived, but the episode prompted a frantic midday ER trip with the upper school principal, squeezed in before I left for skating practice.

There were all the same mean kids, and a few new ones, including a much taller guy who once picked me up and threw me hard enough that the circular snaps of my off-brand Adidas pants cut into my leg and left little round scars. That bothered me less than the wars of words—those at least I felt like I *should* be able to win and somehow couldn't. But *this* wouldn't have been close to a fair fight. Afterward I just sat down at my desk and went to sleep, saving my limited anorectic energy for more important endeavors.

Other than that, most of my memories of high school are sparse, not because I've forgotten them but because they never existed. I just wasn't in school that much: I was at the rink.

Chapter 3

Cleveland, 2000

The ice is cloudy below me, glistening like a frozen dream. I wish this moment could last forever. For a second, it feels like it will: My adrenaline is moving faster than time. This is the short program at the 2000 U.S. Figure Skating Nationals, and the music is about to start.

I'm wearing a simple blue sleeveless skating dress with Swarovski crystals on the front. My pairs partner is wearing black skating pants with a blue shirt. The lights are bright and the ice is cold.

As the cheers die down and we strike our starting pose, I look at my partner and whisper, "We made it." I still can't quite believe it; for almost as long I can remember, I've thrown my whole life at this. I love the ice—and at moments like this I think that maybe it loves me back.

I know I got here late. Not literally today, but in a larger sense. I didn't start skating until seven or eight; most of my rink friends had already begun by four or five. One girl I know got on the ice when she was two. I've been behind in a race for as long as I can remember, toiling to catch up.

When I was little, at that rusty dump of a rink in Lancaster, and my friends or frenemies wanted to horse around between jumps, I'd tell them no. I have to work, I'd say again and again, like a broken record. I watched the other mothers yell at their daughters for falling too much or for goofing off, sometimes lambasting in full-on shouts and sometimes in angry hisses like vipers at the edge of the rink, poking their pointy heads through every opening in the plexiglass boards.

I was proud that my mother was not like that; she was never the type to disagree—let alone raise her voice—in public. But she had expectations, and I did not want to disappoint.

And I did not—at least not on the ice.

After a year or so of lessons in Lancaster, I needed more ice time and better coaches. My parents started driving me forty minutes to Hershey, where the whole town smelled like chocolate and the street lights were shaped like Kisses. In a paint-chipped and aging arena that felt massive by my fourth-grade standards, I learned Axels and Lutzes, camel spins and laybacks.

Sometimes, my younger brother, Andrew, would get dragged along for the trip. Between practices and competitions in other states, I think he learned his way around the pinball machines at half the rinks in the northeastern United States. Just four years apart, we were close and often commiserated about my parents. But he never complained that he spent so much of his life playing under the fluorescent glare of rink lights, and never seemed to mind that I took up so much of the spotlight.

When I got a little better, my parents started driving me a few minutes farther to Harrisburg, where there were two surfaces and even longer practice hours. My dad—who did most of the driving at that point—would make work calls the whole way there and back on his bulky car phone, the hallmark of a 1990s workaholic. Aside from the added time, the price tag went up, too. Boots—one pair a year—were a few hundred dollars. Blades, sold separately, were a couple hundred more. Then there were the lessons ($50 to nearly $100), the practice time (around $10 per forty-minute session), the practice dresses ($50 and up) and the competition dresses (anywhere from homemade to $1,000). My parents never talked about these specific numbers, but I knew that it was expensive—and I knew that this was okay as long as I made the most of it.

Around my regular school day, I packed in all the ice time I could—5 A.M. sessions in Lancaster on Mondays, Sunday mornings in Hershey, and trips to Harrisburg after class. My first competitive season—fourth grade—I skated to a medley from the musical *Annie*. Fifth grade was *Oklahoma!*. Then came *Mary Poppins*, *Man of La Mancha*, *West Side Story*—my life measured in Broadway hits. Though I would have preferred something darker, my mom was enthusiastic about the song selections—and my first coach had rules about what age you had to be before you could skate to *Phantom of the Opera*.

The first time I ever won a competition was with that *Annie* program. It was the Keystone State Games, which sounds important but is, in fact, not. State Games are fairly meaningless in figure skating. I didn't start on the qualifying competitions—the ones that could, in theory, get you to the U.S. National Figure Skating Championships—until a couple years later. To me that was always the goal: Nationals. Sometimes I told people I wanted to go to the Olympics, but I felt like it was just a thing all skaters are expected to say. In truth, it seemed like an unrealistic goal. Nationals was still a long shot, but in the realm of possibility.

My entire middle school years were spent trying to learn a single jump: a double Axel. Named after a nineteenth-century Norwegian skating great named Axel Paulsen, the jump is unlike every other in that the skater takes off while facing forward, adding an extra half rotation. Lutzes, flips, and Salchows all start backward and land backward, an even number. Thus a double Salchow is an even two rotations. But because it takes off forward, a double Axel is 2.5.

Getting a double Axel is a watershed moment in a skater's career. Once you can land it, triple jumps will typically come soon after. But not everyone gets there. A double Axel is an obstacle that many skaters never clear, effectively dooming their competitive futures.

I started trying double Axels in sixth grade. For three years, I fell on them every single day. Hundreds of times. I would try, come up a half rotation short, fall, then circle around and try again. And again. And again, for hours. My entire middle school years were spent failing. In my head, I would calculate how many times I'd fallen, multiplying the number of falls by the number of days I trained per week and the number of weeks in a year. I knew that time was working against me, and every fall counted. I had the tenacity, but I didn't know if I really had the talent—and elite skating requires both.

Watching the lack of progress from atop the metal bleachers at the side of the rink, my parents must have wondered about the point of it all—though if they did, they kept it to themselves. My father saw me fall so often he developed a perfect sense of my timing, learning just how many lines of his legal papers he could read before looking up just in time to catch my next attempt.

Amid all those falls and failings, I realized that even if I got a double Axel, I didn't actually have the raw ability to make it as a singles skater. I knew in my heart I just wasn't good enough alone—so I threw my hopes into pairs.

There are two kinds of partnered skating: ice dance, the one little kids tend to describe as "boring" because it doesn't involve any jumps; and pairs, the one where the guy throws the girl around and it looks all dangerous and shit. It feels all dangerous, too; there's a certain wild thrill in being dangled upside down by a teenager on an eighth-inch-thick steel blade, or being hurled across the ice and expected to land on one.

With neat makeup and a bouncy ponytail, I looked the part of the prim, elite athlete—but moves with names like headbangers and death spirals appealed to me. There were risks involved, risks that not everyone was willing to take. Even if I lacked the talent to succeed in singles, I could make up for it with the willingness to endanger myself that was necessary to succeed in pairs.

On top of that, pairs didn't require all the triple jumps that singles skating did. Typically, one triple—maybe two—would be enough for a solid pairs career. It was certainly enough to get you to Nationals, and might even be enough to get you to the Olympics.

But first, you need a double Axel. And a partner.

My first pair partnership was not very serious, with a short country kid from outside of Reading, Pennsylvania, with brown hair in a bowl cut, a permanent devilish grin, and unexpectedly big jumps. We each still trained for singles, but skated together a few days a week in Harrisburg and competed for only one season as a team, traveling to Florida to vie for a berth at junior nationals in our homemade green and gold costumes with our underwhelming Egyptian-themed routine.

We did not make it. When we later parted ways during my eighth-grade year, I was not sad. My partner had spent much of our time together in unproductive pursuits: calling me fat, refusing to work, and passing it all off under the guise of his goofball personality. But I knew that pairs was my best shot at a future on the ice, and more than anything—except, perhaps, a double Axel—I wanted a good partner.

To get either of those things, I needed to step up my game: I needed to go to the University of Delaware. A little over an hour away, along winding and treacherous backroads, UD of the early 2000s was a figure skating mecca, one of the top training centers in the country. I knew of one other girl from the Hershey and Harrisburg rinks who'd begun training there—and she had triple jumps.

I'd been there a few times before. It seemed like an ordeal, like crossing the Atlantic in search of greatness; my mother and

I had geared up for the voyage and climbed in her silver 1988 Volvo and made a day of it. It must have been sometime in early middle school, because Tara Lipinski was still training there at the time. I watched her coach scream at her, alongside the other hollering coaches. The skaters all seemed so fast, and there were so many, so much better than I was. Twenty-five or thirty teens doing double and triple jumps, speeding in different directions amid the cold cacophony of Beethoven and bellowing coaches.

But Delaware was far, and at that point, I wasn't good enough to really merit making a full-time life of it. By the end of middle school—with still no double Axel in sight—it was clear that was the only way I was going to be. We found a nice coach who didn't holler—Tracey—and started going a few times a week. Before the start of my freshman year of high school, I convinced my parents to let me train there full-time. We all knew it was the only way to really make it further in the sport, but I was still shocked when they agreed so easily.

Most of the skaters who trained at Delaware were either home schooled or attended the one nearby public school that had become very accustomed to accommodating skaters' schedules, letting them leave en masse before lunch to go train. Some had moved from faraway places—Virginia, Florida, the Midwest, Israel—to live there, boarding with strangers hundreds of miles from their families. My mom said it was lucky we lived close enough that I did not have to do that but, as a fourteen-year-old, getting to stay home did not especially seem like an added bonus.

And so I became a commuter. Starting in ninth grade, I began leaving school between ten and one every day and making the trek to Delaware. My parents each drove one day a week, my grandma who lived nearby drove one day—listening to *Fresh Air* and *All Things Considered* the whole way—and a retired truck driver my parents paid covered the other two days. On Saturdays, I practiced in Harrisburg at 6 A.M., and on Sundays I skated in Lancaster. The old dump had been demolished, so I went to a newer dump across town.

In school, I went to each of my classes once or twice a week, showing up as the outcast who dipped in just long enough to ace all the tests, then dipped out to go to the rink. On the way there I'd change in the car, then skate three or four forty-minute sessions, do ballet, weight training, some off-ice cardio, and head home, doing homework with a flashlight on the drive back. I practiced jumps in the backyard, and stopped pretending to understand a normal childhood.

Aside from lessons with my main coach, Tracey, I began spin lessons with Scott, ice dance with Gary, and choreography with Jill. Every other Friday night, my dad would drive me an hour away to get my skates sharpened by a top-notch blades guru. In the summer, we drove to Baltimore once a week for lessons with a special spin coach.

I had already thrown my soul into it years earlier, but I guess that was the year that skating consumed me fully.

That was also the year I began starving myself in earnest. I'd toyed with eating disorders—mainly bulimia, some mild anorexia—before then, but in the winter of my ninth-grade year, I got more serious about it. They say that eating disorders are about control, but it is not that straightforward. They are also about self-destruction that feels just like success. I wanted to waste away, slowly and tragically—and in the meantime, I wanted to win. Or at least land a double Axel.

That was, it seemed, the one thing in life I just could not do.

Until, suddenly, I could.

Late one afternoon, in the Delaware rink, I circled around yet again and set up for another attempt in the back corner, near the Zamboni door. When I landed, unexpectedly upright, my head snapped down to peer at the landing: the mark my blade made on the ice that would reveal whether I had actually done all 2.5 of the required rotations.

I had.

I only landed one that day. But I landed two the next. And three the day after that. Then four, then five. I stopped counting when I got to ten. That year, I started pair tryouts to find an elite partner. My coach Tracey would set up trial sessions with unpartnered male skaters from across the country. Some came to Delaware for a few days, but others I met at a national try-out at the U.S. Olympic Training Center in Colorado Springs. There, for a few days, we all stayed in the athlete dorms, ate at the athlete mess hall, and tried imagining our futures with any of the would-be partners around us.

In general, there were a lot more girls looking for partners than there were guys; not surprisingly, figure skating suffers a dearth of male competitors. That meant that at the lower levels, at least, it was easier for boys to make it through qual-ifying competitions to junior nationals; sometimes they didn't have to do much more than show up, while girls had to duke it out through initial and final rounds. And when it came to pairs, that disparity meant ultimately the guy usually had the pick—pick of long-term training location, pick of coaches, pick of partners.

The partner I ended up with—Mark Ladwig—was from Fargo, North Dakota, far from any major training center. That made decisions easy, at least in terms of what rink we'd be based out of. He was four years older than me and a senior when we tried out. He moved to Delaware right after graduation and lived in a boarding home full of skaters waiting tables and coaching to pay for their dreams.

He was vaguely mischievous and sometimes cheesy, in an older brother sort of way. My family invited him to vacation on the Jersey shore, and we did pairs lifts together on the beach, turning heads. When he came along to a Fourth of July celebration at the country club, he recruited me and my younger brother to build sandcastles in the golf course sand traps. People often asked if we were related.

But even though we occasionally engaged in wholesome family activities outside the rink, it was a work relationship. Unlike with my first partner, there was no name-calling and very little goofing off; it wasn't junior nationals we were aiming for now, but the big leagues. Our first season, we planned to compete at the sixth of eight levels. Between all the on-ice pairs training and the off-ice lift practice that was required, Mark was the person I spent by far the most time with every day. Our futures and dreams were intertwined, but we weren't close. Friendly, but not friends.

We rolled our eyes at some of the other teams who dated, something we both agreed was a terrible idea. And we raised eyebrows at the ones who fought, flipping each other the bird and shouting obscenities across the ice.

To me, it wasn't Mark I wanted to shout obscenities at: it was the ice itself, a crisp manifestation of my best future with the cloudy swirl of my persistent failings running through it. It was a love-hate relationship, volatile as any teenage romance.

When it was good, it was great. When it was not, life lost its meaning.

It's hard to describe the feeling of skating—it's more than leaping and spinning while the wind whistles in your ears. At some point, after years of work, it all clicks, and the movements become more natural than walking, sleeping, or eating.

And in February 2000, as I stood on the ice at my first Nationals, at an aging rink in Cleveland, I thought: *Maybe it's really ice that runs in my veins now.*

Whatever the case, as the opening drumbeats of the Big Bad Voodoo Daddy's "Go Daddy-O" blasted through the speakers, slicing through the silence of the spectating crowd, I knew that now was not the time for philosophizing. Now was the time for skating.

But a split double twist, a side-by-side combination spin, a death spiral, double flips, a throw jump, and a footwork sequence later, it was all over. It was the best two minutes and fifteen seconds of my life. There would be more programs, more competitions, and even another Nationals in my future—but nothing is quite like the first time.

Chapter 4

Tompkins County Jail, December 2010

My first week in jail was a blur. Not a complete blackout—I
didn't wake up one day and wonder where I was or how I'd
gotten there—but I sure as hell couldn't outline any details of
the process.

For the first day or two, I alternately slept and snorted the
heroin I'd smuggled in. I wasn't even subtle about it; it absolutely did not occur to me that bringing drugs into a jail could
be another felony, or even that it was *possible* to catch another
felony when you were already locked up. Jail was the most serious consequence I could imagine, and the idea that there could
be worse things in store didn't really compute.

The evening of my arrival, I ripped a little strip off of my
legal paperwork and rolled it up into a straw, then snorted the
soft brown powder from the top of the metal cell desk, kicking
off the first step in a familiar cycle: get high, pass out, rinse,
repeat.

At some point—maybe my first morning in jail—the other women woke me up to point out my mugshot flashing by on the news.

"You're famous," one said, with a touch of irony and a raise of the eyebrows. Barely able to stand, I leaned my head against the cell bars and squinted at the pocked face glaring down at me from the TV. Had I been more sober, I might have felt ashamed or embarrassed. But if the thought did not occur to me, it also did not seem to occur to my new blockmates. Some seemed thrilled at the excitement of knowing a minor celebrity, a flash of something interesting in the monotony of jail life. Others were just too kind to point out how bad I looked.

They probably understood the seriousness of my situation better than I did.

When I got called out that day—or maybe the next— for my first court trip, I stuffed the remaining dope back up my ass, then mindlessly chucked the rolled-up paper under my bunk where any observant passerby could have seen it. A woman two cells over walked by and warned me not to be so careless, but the guards chose not to notice or to question why I was still so high. They just asked everyone else in the block to keep an eye on me and make sure I was still breathing as I nodded out again and again, knocking my head on the cell bars when I stood and falling asleep in improbable contortionist positions when I sat.

I knew I would have to come down eventually, and each line was only buying time, stalling my return to the jagged metal corners of reality. Eventually, I would get dopesick. There would be sweats and chills. All the things that usually happened when my dealer was dry or I just ran out of money: twitching, restless legs, ants under my skin, diarrhea, catatonic despair. Like the flu on steroids—but this time instead of an empty Collegetown drug den, the setting would be the floor of the county jail.

When you are dopesick you do not make good decisions. You miss exams or skip work. You sell sex on dark streets and shoot up in public places. It's not just that you are desperate to feel better, but also that everything seems foggy, and distinctions— like right or wrong, risky or safe—feel more fluid, at least until you're high again and can willfully ignore the difference. This is to say: Dopesick is not a great frame of mind for hard choices, like how to handle a legal case or whether you want to stay sober.

Short of getting more drugs smuggled into the jail—which was not out of the question—there were two alternative possibilities to that coming sickness: one, release. The other, medication.

In the first hours after my arrest, I'd harbored some delusional hope of getting out immediately. I knew I had a decent amount of drugs, but I wasn't sure if six ounces—enough to fill four or five cigarette packs—was a lot in the eyes of the law. I wasn't running a Scarface-scale operation, but in New York it really didn't matter. Anything over four ounces was enough to earn you football numbers, prison slang for the double-digit sentences that belonged on the scoreboard at the end of a game.

That's because the Empire State was once home to the notorious Rockefeller drug laws. Signed by Republican governor Nelson Rockefeller in 1973, those laws were an opening salvo in the War on Drugs and a way for an ambitious politician to look tough on crime. They made the minimum punishment for just having—not even selling—four or more ounces of hard drugs fifteen-to-life, even on a first offense. Other states rushed to follow suit, even though the new laws made the New York prison population increase fivefold and heightened racial disparities, filling the state's prisons and jails with even more Black and brown bodies.

It wasn't until 2004 that activists convinced the state to change the law. First, the legislature eased the harshest sentences, and five years later—just one year before my arrest—they mostly dismantled the rest of it.

Under the old law, I could have been looking at at least a decade and a half behind bars—with life on the back end.

But I didn't know that at the time. There was no one in my life who could explain that, or tell me how lucky I was; all I knew was that the women around me said I probably wasn't going to get out anytime soon. I was charged with an A-2 felony—a class of crimes that included predatory sex assault, use of biological weapons, and hard drugs over four ounces—and thus automatically not eligible for bail.

And if I wasn't getting out, that meant there was only one other way to avoid dopesickness without doing anything desperate: Suboxone. The six-sided orange pills nicknamed "subs" were a combination of two drugs—buprenorphine and naloxone—that would ease the pains of detox and make it almost impossible to get high. Basically, dope just wouldn't work; the rush would be muted, unsatisfying.

Usually, Suboxone is prescribed for long-term use, to help people stay off drugs and lower the risk of a relapse; it's after a period of sobriety—like jail—that heroin is at its deadliest, when you think you can do as much as you used to and don't realize that high you seek will now kill you. Sometimes, though, Suboxone is just prescribed in the short-term—only a few days at a time—to ease the symptoms of dopesickness down from a super-flu on steroids to a weeklong, uneasy discomfort.

Most jails don't stock it at all, but the other women told me that Tompkins County was different. They, apparently, weren't worried about accusations of "coddling" inmates, at least not for a few short days for detox. One problem: Getting it was no guarantee. Access to medical care was arbitrary, and the nurse, I was told, was known to play favorites. If she decided she didn't like you, you got Tylenol and a jar of Kool-Aid while you shat yourself and threw up for three days. But if you fell into her favor, you won access to the chalky orange pills and saccharine taste of salvation.

On my third day behind bars, my salvation showed up on the morning meds cart. I breathed out desperation and inhaled relief as the orange tab dissolved on my tongue and a nine-year fog began to recede.

The next day, I was cogent but still in a light haze when I was cleared to be in general population. I walked out of my cell into a brave new world I still did not understand.

The Tompkins County Jail was small, as far as county jails go. While big-city lockups like New York City's notorious Rikers Island could easily house more than 10,000 people, the single-story brick building outside Ithaca held roughly 100 at full capacity. Up a long, sloping hill north of town, it was just far enough to make visiting a hassle for poor families without cars. The building went up in 1986, and by the time I got there in 2010, it looked like an aging jail sent back home from central casting because the wrinkles were showing.

The cell walls had been painted over again and again, beige tones over blue ink graffiti from generations of unhappy inhabitants. In one block, the cement bricks in the waist-high privacy wall in front of the shower had been kicked so much they'd crumbled down to knee height. But the most visible sign of age felt theatrical, like a dark expressionist distortion of reality: the oversized clanging metal bars on the sliding gates at the front of each cell.

Jail architects did away with that kind of design more than a decade earlier, and the guards always told us it was because the bars on each cell made it too easy for people to kill themselves; bars, poles, anything desperate people could tie a makeshift noose to represented a risk. All the newer jails had isolating, solid doors instead of sliding gates. Those doors were supposed to be safer, but the old-fashioned gates meant we could always talk to each other. The guards could lock us all in, but we would never be entirely alone.

Our cells ran down the outside walls of the building, with long horizontal windows at the top where we could not see out of them. If we stood on our bunks to peer out, the guards would yell at us. We wanted to spy on the visitors in the parking lot or gape at the wild turkeys across the highway; they wanted us to sit the fuck down and shut up. The bunks themselves were metal, two to a cell. We tried to make the place homey by using chalky county-issued toothpaste to stick decorations to cement walls and metal bunks. Most people favored photos of their pets or boyfriends or children; I had no such images, so I pasted up a copy of the Stevie Smith poem "Not Waving But Drowning." In any case, our attempts at decor were against the rules—though I was never sure what was a real rule and what was an unwritten rule. In The Twilight Zone of jail, it didn't really matter. They were equally enforceable.

Each cell opened out into the common area for the cellblock, where there was a TV, a few metal tables, a shower, and an eye-in-the-sky camera looking over it all. Since officers still needed to see what was going on in each cell, every block also had long, eye-height horizontal windows along one wall that looked out into the hallway. That way, passing guards could peek in to keep tabs. Of course, the passersby weren't just guards; they were also GED teachers, lawyers, workers, male inmates, and the sheriff himself—and they could all ogle or glare. The cell bars did nothing for privacy, and with a cursory side glance, anyone walking by could accidentally (or intentionally) see us getting in the shower, changing a tampon, or taking a shit.

On one level, having a dozen leering men watch you take out a tampon as they stroll by on the way to rec is humiliating. But it's also subtly disorienting, a reminder that regular cultural norms don't exist here—simply going to the bathroom can turn into a shamefest, or pass unnoticed. Like so many other parts of jails and prisons, it seems this setup was not made with women in mind.

For everything I learned about my surroundings in those first few days, I did not actually know where I was. That is, I didn't know the difference between jail and prison. In the back of my mind I'd always realized I could end up in one, or both, but I didn't know the difference: Jails are short-term. Prisons are long-term.

Basically, jails are run by the county, and it's where you wait until your case is resolved. If your sentence is short enough—under a year if you're in New York state—you stay in jail to serve your time. There usually are not many educational or vocational programs, very little to do, and very few privileges. In part, that's because no one is expected to be there very long; if you get sentenced to a lot of time, you go to state prison. Prisons are bigger, tougher, and further away. That's the big leagues, for the long-timers.

No one explains this—or so many other things—when you come in. No one in charge tells you what happens next in your case, why you're being locked in a cell alone, or whether you'll get medical care. They don't tell you the rules, the unwritten rules, or the tricky caveats. They don't tell you how to get a lawyer, how to call your family, or when you get that fabled one free call. I would say there's some bizarre assumption that you know everything you need to know, but that's not it: it's simply that no one cares if you know. The system does not care if you understand it.

If you are lucky, the women around you do.

During the first few days after I came in, there were seven of us in the cellblock. We were early twenties to early sixties, first-time arrestees to "frequent flyers." Few of us had finished high school, and most were mothers, some single and some not. Our crimes ranged from DUI to burglary, but we'd all landed behind bars because of our addictions.

We were a fairly representative sample of women in jail anywhere except for one thing: We were all white. That was perhaps not surprising in a county that was a little over 80 percent white at the time. But it would have been an anomaly anywhere else; nationally in 2010, jail and prison populations were 39 percent white, 40 percent Black, and 19 percent Hispanic. In Tompkins County at about the same time, those figures were 73 percent, 22 percent, and 4.5 percent.

Black people were still over-represented, but the numbers—especially in the women's blocks—were so small it was easy to miss the disparities. There was one Black woman across the hall when I arrived, but for months at a time the entire female population was all white. As much as the class, income, and educational disparities were on full display, the racial demographics of mass incarceration were not so readily apparent at the Tompkins County Jail. That was a reality that took me far longer to realize.

After I emerged from my prolonged drug haze, Tawny the Cheshire Cat was the first of my new blockmates to introduce herself. She was in her mid-twenties, pretty, and looked vaguely like Katy Perry. She'd been in and out of jail before, and now she was waiting to see whether she'd get sent to rehab or prison after she'd failed out of drug court. Out in the free world, she had a boyfriend, kids, and a heroin problem. Behind bars, she was full of drama, alternately hyper, monopolizing the phone, or bickering over whether the floor was clean or whose coffee cup was on the table. People warned me she was only friendly because she wanted a good drug connection when it was all over, but even if it were true, I didn't really care. In the interim, at least, she was generally nice—and when she wasn't, her drama was a welcome distraction from my own.

Her bunkie, Lizzie, was the youngest one in the block—maybe twenty-one or twenty-two at the time. She was thin, with long blond hair and a baby face, and she rarely spoke, instead grinning in sheepish silence. It was hard to imagine how she'd ended up here—but when I asked her where she was from, she told me, "I'm migratory. I live near Ithaca in the winter and then I go down south in the summers because I'm usually on the run in the summer." I laughed; it seemed so incongruous with who she was now.

Over time she told me much of her family had some brush with the law in their pasts, but for her the trouble came from heroin. She had a sister still running wild, a husband already in prison, and a small son waiting at home. By her account, though, she'd already been sober more than a year when she got sent back to jail for a probation violation simply because she missed an appointment. Looking back, I think she was telling the truth, but at the time I didn't quite believe it.

At the end of the cellblock were Summer and Susan, sharing the cell nearest to the shower. Summer was only in her late twenties but always acting like the mother hen, shushing loud outbursts of laughter and constantly pointing out suspected germ hotspots. When she was sent to state prison in March, in a show of maternal concern she wrote me a letter explaining every step of the transfer in intricate detail so I would know what to expect if that's where I ended up.

Susan, the one who'd told me ironically that I was famous, was a sixty-year-old lesbian with cropped gray hair, a pagan necklace, a dry wit, a few college degrees, and a background in the merchant marine. By the time she ended up in the county jail she'd racked up enough drunk driving charges that she absolutely knew she was going to prison.

On the opposite end of the block was Brandy, a loud woman in her early twenties. She was like an animated jailhouse rulebook; I learned all the rules by watching her break them. She cursed at the officers, scrawled obscenities on envelopes, and acted out in every little way that was just enough to get herself locked in but never enough to catch a new charge. It wasn't that she couldn't control herself, it was just that she didn't care; of the eight months she did in county, she was in isolation for well over half.

My first cellie was Theresa. She was from out of town, rarely showered, and got shipped out to somewhere else within a few days. I know the guards put in her place a woman named Deb, who was in for drunk driving and repeatedly, loudly, let everyone know she planned to down an entire keg the day she got out. I can't remember Theresa's last name or where she was from. We weren't housed together very long—that's how jail works.

You get shuffled around from cellblock to cellblock, or jail to jail, rearranged like a game of three-card monte designed to hide the overcrowding. Even in a small place like Tompkins County, there were often more women than there were cells. You'd get intensely close to someone for a few days, or weeks— then get separated, by the guards or the courts. You might get moved to another cellblock, and she might be sent to prison, or rehab, or released on bail never to be heard from again. The releases were exciting; we loved sneakily standing in the windows to watch people run out the front door in free-world clothes—

suddenly a completely different person than the woman we'd seen an hour earlier.

But the constant flux was disorienting, like living on quicksand. Years later, I read about a lifer in California who called prison The Zo, short for The Twilight Zone. It fits. Up is down, everything is gray, and the supposed rules make no sense. Sometimes they're actually impossible to follow, or simply not explained. The people fade in and out. No one can answer your questions, and if they do, they might just lie for no reason at all. An officer will take away the clock, and tell you it's noon when it's actually two. Words don't mean the same things, and every day is a repeat of the day before. You lose sense of time, and nothing makes sense.

But for all I did not understand, I did know this: everything familiar was fading away. Because they'd gone on vacation, I hadn't spoken to my parents since my arrest—and I didn't want to tell them anyway. Alex had disappeared—and my repeated collect calls went straight to voicemail. I had no idea where my dog was—and no idea how to find out. Christmas had presumably come and gone, although I couldn't actually remember any of it.

A Cornell University Police Department representative wearing a Looney Tunes tie had come to jail to notify me that I'd been banned from campus indefinitely. I'm pretty sure I laughed at him—I was in jail without bond. Surely I wasn't going to turn up on campus any time soon.

It wasn't like being a fish out of water; it was more like being a freshwater fish in a brackish, clouded pond. I'd spent enough time traveling through drug circles that, even though I didn't know most of them on the outside, the people here were my people. But no one behaved the same in jail, where we were all bound by a new and secret set of rules and mores. In this pond, all the light refracted differently, and everything was slightly toxic.

Chapter 5

I'm hiding behind a bush with a finger down my throat. I'm in my puke-spot. I can't very well throw up at home because the upstairs bathroom is right next to my parents' bedroom. So I take a conveniently timed five-block bike ride every evening after dinner, if I haven't managed to avoid eating entirely. I strap on my helmet and head down to the deserted brick warehouse at the end of the street, where the shoulder-height bushes along the building form a dank network of leafy coves. I crouch down to crawl in between them, and hunch over where no one can see me. I've puked here so many times that the whole building emanates a vomity aroma on rainy days. Other people can smell it when they walk by.

This is all a relatively new development, this whole puking-in-the-bushes thing. Even as I'm doing it I know it is extremely fucked up, but my relationship with food has never really been normal. After that first diet to lower my cholesterol when I was four, I went on to be the kind of kid who consumed everything with abandon, a swimmer in an endless sea of need and appetite. I was tiny, but always in motion—and always ready to eat. Although I knew that I was not overweight, I remember looking in the big mirror at dance class thinking it would be nice if I were thinner, like the smallest girl at the end of the barre. I was probably eight or nine at the time—she was six.

Since my health nut mom didn't keep much junk food in the house, I sneaked it on the side—a secret pack of Oreos from a friend, bake sale brownies at school. Food that wasn't so boring. Most of the home-cooked family dinners were some variety of chicken, and I didn't manage to score a Big Mac until sixth grade. It was a treat, procured from the drive-through (a thrilling adventure!) on the way back from the rink in Harrisburg. It ended up being the only fast food burger I've ever had because I went vegetarian two years later.

The first time I threw up seems like such a pivotal moment, and yet I do not remember it. But I can imagine. I would have been twelve at the time. I must've pulled back my light brown hair—it was long then—and haltingly forced my finger down my throat, retching and heaving a few times before I was successful. Afterward, I would have cautiously peeked out of the middle school bathroom stall, checking that the coast was clear before I scuttled across the tiled floor to the sink to wash the vomit from my hand. I probably took one of the little brace brushes and pushed out the tiny chunks of regurgitated food—or at least the visible ones. Then, I must have looked in the mirror at my watery eyes and red cheeks, and decided it was a good idea to do this whole routine again. And again, and again, and again.

I didn't dive in all at once; it started as an occasional thing, like a social smoker who only lights up at the bar. Except there was nothing social and no warm fuzzy feeling after, just a fleeting dizziness and an empty sense of victory. Bulimia is by nature a solitary task—which made it well-suited for a pre-teen with strict parents and few friends.

At the same time I dabbled in starvation, skipping meals here and there. But I still ate an array of foods that would become unthinkable in later years: cheese-topped pasta, sugary baked oatmeal, an occasional coconut donut after Saturday morning skating practice. Anorexia would have required a sustained commitment to self-harm that I didn't have, at least not yet. So I settled on sporadic forays into disordered eating, throwing up on occasion when I'd eaten too much—but otherwise not entirely obsessing. I thought about numbers, but I had not yet begun jotting the calories of everything I ate in the margins of my notebooks, not yet begun sneaking into my parents' room to use their scale multiple times per day. It was not, at that point, an addiction, and every time I threw up it felt like a choice, a flirtation with darkness or a little-used escape valve I could open just to prove that it existed. It was a secret that was all mine, some insider knowledge that no one else knew.

I don't know the exact day that things changed, when those occasional glimpses at self-destruction became a pit bull I could not control, or when my escape hatch became the thing I wanted to escape from. But it was definitely sometime in ninth grade.

Early in the school year—or maybe even the summer before—I started swapping out breakfast for coffee and lunch for a bottle of Crystal Light. Almost without realizing it, I created unwritten codes for myself: no meat, no pasta, no milk except as creamer, no cheese except grated Parmesan, no candy except sugar-free Jolly Ranchers, and no ice cream—unless I planned a stealthy trip to the bathroom afterward. I never called these things rules; I saw them at first as goals or guideposts. If I achieved them, I could be happy; if I strayed from them, I would be riddled with anxiety.

Even as I began eating less, I did not lose weight like I wanted; that can actually be surprisingly hard to do if you're an athlete engaged in muscle-building activities all day. Between skating and off-ice training I was working out anywhere from four to six hours a day. At fourteen, I could leg press more than some of the college hockey players, and somehow convinced my ten-year-old brother Andrew to let me hoist him over my head like the female pairs skater I wanted to be. As I zipped around the ice every day, I looked wistfully at the girls who seemed like they were skin and bones, while I was skin and bones and muscle—more Tonya Harding than Nancy Kerrigan in stature.

So I ate still less. That sounds so simple—but it is not. Normies who have never been down this road may assume that people with eating disorders simply are not hungry, or that they forget to eat. That is extremely, utterly fucking false. The less I ate, the more I thought about it. Sometimes I would chew up food and spit it out in the bathroom. Other times I would eat an entirely normal or very small amount of something—twenty jelly beans, or half a Reese's—and throw it up anyway. And yet other times I would eat for hours, vomiting my way through an idle afternoon like it was some sort of recreational activity.

If I had a free period at school, I'd buy cookies from the cafeteria and eat them—a dozen maybe—during study hall, along with some random chocolates I'd picked up from teachers' candy bowls throughout the day. If I didn't have extra lunch money, I'd buy one cookie and steal a few, shoving the extras into my oversized red winter coat. One time the lunch lady caught me when she saw the edge of an oatmeal raisin peeking out of my pocket.

"You!" she said in shock. "I wouldn't have expected it."

Perplexed, she added, "I'm disappointed in you."

That makes two of us, I thought. Then, I headed to the bathroom to undo the damage.

Nonetheless, it was that fall, against the backdrop of depression and an utter lack of nutrition, I got my double Axel. As if by magic, a few weeks later I also got my triples—almost all of them, in rapid succession. The snaky rink mothers were surprised. My coach was thrilled, and maybe baffled. I could land a triple Salchow, then suddenly a triple toe loop, a triple loop, a triple flip, and I was painstakingly close to a big and beautiful triple Lutz, the hardest jump most female skaters were doing at that point.

On the ice, I suddenly had everything I needed or wanted, everything I'd worked for. But it had all come so quickly that it simply did not feel real. Every time I landed and looked down at the clean edge, it felt like a fluke, a victory I did not deserve. And it scared me.

Plus, on top of the inexplicable windfall, there was this: I couldn't *feel* the jumps. I was landing them, but I knew they weren't in my muscle memory. And when it really counts—in competition—you have nothing but muscle memory. I could dream in double Lutzes and double Axels, but in my sleep I could not do a triple loop or flip. Usually I knew that I'd gotten a jump consistently when it showed up in my dreams, when I could feel the right rotations even in Dreamland. I hoped that time and repetition would fix this all, and that if I just worked harder and trained more assiduously I would grow into these jumps and earn my newfound victories.

Instead, I got the flu. It was the sickest I'd ever been before or since. At one point, after I announced to my dad that I was dying, he took me to the doctor—and I needed help walking to the car. For two weeks, I sweated through a fever in my sunflower-themed blue bedroom and vomited up green bile into a metal bowl as I listened to a Queen greatest hits CD played on repeat. It was a badly named album because some of the songs were, frankly, not hits at all. But as a dramatic teen, the track titled "I'm Going Slightly Mad" felt apt. I knew that I was beginning to fall apart, and it seemed like it was undoubtedly my fault that I was a sweating, pukey mess reduced to sugar-free ice pops and diet ginger ale. Admittedly, it was flu season, so I could have gotten sick anyway. But I was pretty sure that the fact I'd gotten *so sick* had something to do with my utter lack of self-care in the weeks and months leading up to it. It wasn't even like anyone else I knew had gotten sick that flu season.

When it was all over, I got on the scale and was thrilled to discover I'd lost almost fifteen pounds. When I finally got back on the ice, I was horrified to discover I'd lost my jumps. I could do the double loops, flips, and Lutzes I'd been doing for years, but the bigger jumps I'd worked so hard for had vanished, replaced by failed attempts that came up a quarter-turn short every time. After a few panicked days of despair, the double Axel came back and eventually—months later—the triple Salchow. But the rest never did.

In retrospect I guess that was the first thing I'd ever lost to an addiction.

Afterward, I leaned more heavily into the starvation; I thought I looked great, made of nothing but muscle, bone, and self-discipline. I was ninety-three pounds and remained exactly that for the next few years, a task that required significant effort and ongoing dysfunction. I treated coffee as a primary food group, putting instant coffee in my brewed coffee, drinking black cup after black cup until my hands shook. When I could not drink any more, I turned to carrots: carrots with mustard, carrots with vinegar, carrots with black pepper, carrots with ketchup. Digesting them, someone once told me, burned more calories than you got from eating them. I clung to that un-fact-checked claim and decided that I could eat them with no inhibitions and no consequences. Never finding satiety, I regularly devoured two or more pounds of carrots a day, until the creases in my palms, the skin around my knees, and the wrinkles next to my nose turned so orange people noticed, and commented.

I feigned bafflement as to the cause.

When forced to eat, I hid food in my pockets or slipped it onto other people's plates. I lied to avoid meals; even though

I was an atheist, I was thrilled when my parents demanded I attended the church's confirmation class every Sunday night. It was during dinner, the meal hardest to miss at home.

The rest of the time, when I couldn't skip family meals, I went for long, allegedly leisurely bike rides afterward—even in the dead of winter—so that I could stop at nearby park bathrooms to throw up. After I found the regular public puke-spot closed one time, I switched to just throwing up in the bushes, crawling in between the leaves and the brick of historic buildings.

But while I starved myself with half-portions on the weekdays—food I often threw up anyway—on the weekends I binged, striving to fill an insatiable hunger in my mind. The physical pangs I thrived on, but the overwhelming mental desire for more food I could only stave off for so long. Days in advance, I'd eagerly anticipate the moment I could give in to my compulsion, knowing I would hate myself every minute. At the appointed time, I'd ride to the closest convenience store and buy gallons of mint ice cream, sheets of butterscotch Tastykakes, mounds of Reese's, and bags of chips. If I didn't have money, I'd steal half. Then, I'd post up in the bushes to eat my shame where no one could see, throw up where no one could interrupt, and kick some dirt over the whole mess afterward. Sometimes I'd do it just once, but sometimes I'd stay at it for hours.

Every time when it was over, I would cry and swear that I would not do it again. But I always did. By the spring of ninth grade, it had become a thing I could not stop. When, a few years later, I made heroin my uncontrollable addiction of choice, it actually seemed like a relief. At least heroin didn't make me cry every time afterward. I never tried to stop or tell myself this time was the last—I just didn't care. In some ways, that reckless abandon is the exact opposite of an eating disorder.

I had no abandon, and no reckless. Every moment was accounted for, noted meticulously on a paper planner laying out my life in ridiculous fifteen-minute increments. Weekdays, I skated. Weekends, I coached group lessons and wrote articles for the local newspaper. Nights, I studied alone in my room into the wee hours. I didn't seem to need much sleep, or not as much as I needed straight A's. In the summers, I took extra classes so I could end up a year ahead in math and two in Spanish. In retrospect it's almost impressive I even found the time to nurture an eating disorder.

One time, my mom caught me throwing up stir-fry in the downstairs bathroom. She'd gone out to do errands and returned earlier than I'd expected. Usually the loud, sliding garage door was a warning sign that someone was home, but this time I must have been so engaged in making sure I'd vomited every last bit that I did not hear her coming. She must have parked her car, then walked in the side door from the garage, and, finally—after months of suspicion—noticed the sound of retching a few rooms away.

She waited till I was done.

"I heard you," she said, afterward. I probably tried to deny it, or maybe she gave me an easy out and did not pry. Two decades later, all I remember about the entire rest of the conversation was the deep sense of shame pulsing through my veins. That was in the middle of ninth grade, but even before that both of my parents must have already realized there was something amiss, given

the sustained weight loss and increasingly bizarre dietary requirements. Predictably, they insisted that I go see a therapist—the
same one I'd seen briefly in sixth grade, and the same one who
would later pick me up on the side of the highway.

Unlike in middle school, I was at least willing to converse
with her—but I was never honest. I dished on a variety of fights
I had with my mother, but not in enough detail to merit regular
family sessions. I would talk about depression, but not about
how I often wanted to die. I would talk about my eating disorder, but almost none of it would be the truth. Who wants to
admit you're throwing up behind an abandoned building every
day? Or shoplifting gallons of ice cream?

Aside from therapy, at my parents' insistence I also saw a
nutritionist, attended outpatient treatment, tried antidepressants, and went to the doctor for twice-weekly weigh-ins.
None of it helped. Or maybe it did—maybe I would have been
much worse without it. Sure, I was unraveling but I had not
completely come undone. After all, I still had skating, the glue
that held me together. I could not fathom that it was about to
dissolve.

Chapter 6

Even when they're quiet, jails have a distinct sound. Every whisper ricochets off the cinderblock walls and heavy steel doors into a muffled cacophony—the echoing soundtrack of your mistakes in stereo.

Time melts. Watches are banned. There is no clock. Sometimes there's a microwave that you can use to tell time, but sometimes the guards take that away—maybe because you've pissed them off, or maybe because other inmates want it. So instead, sound becomes your sundial. The buzz-clunk when the guards first pop the cellblock door means it's 7 A.M. The rolling lunch carts in the hallway mean it's noon. The crackle of the intercom announcing count means it's 3 P.M. Your day is metered out by the noises of incarceration, an inescapable score that restarts every day and plays on a seemingly endless loop.

This is the new soundtrack of your life:

7:00 A.M.—*"Razors! Razors!"* You wake up to COs at the cellblock door screaming what sounds like a suicide suggestion but is in fact the offer to receive a single-blade razor for shaving. Five male "trusties"— the universal jail name for inmates who do the jail food prep and custodial work in exchange for extra privileges—bring in your breakfast tray. It is the one reliably edible meal: cereal.

7:30 A.M.—*"Supplies!"* The guard assigned to your wing comes by with a cart loaded with jailhouse hygiene supplies: sketchy toothbrushes, doll-size bars of soap, and fine-tooth combs that tend to leave teeth behind in your hair. If you're like me—which right about now you're probably very glad you're not—you'll always take a comb, rip off the teeth, and insert one in the space where your lip ring used to be. Comb teeth are the standard method for keeping body piercings from closing up when you're in jail and real jewelry is banned. You'll get used to it.

8:30 A.M.—*"Cell inspection at this time. Inmates, prepare for cell inspection at this time."* When you hear this announcement crackle in through the cellblock loudspeaker, all contraband needs to be hidden in your jumpsuit. Guards are about to either lazily check with a passing glance that your cell is in compliance or aggressively rip through everything you own—you never know which. Either way, the morning inspection definitely does not include a strip search. So you learn to stash the basic supplies of life on your body. Commonly hidden items include butter from lunch, sugar packets from breakfast, various condiments, fruit, and black pens. All of these things can get you in trouble, as can another banned item: books in excess of the permitted ten per person. If you are like me, you will stash at least half a dozen books inside your jumpsuit every morning, then frantically pass the extras to any other willing conspirators. For some reason the COs never seem to comment on the curiously lumpy figures that emerge in time for cell inspection.

9:00 A.M.—"*Stay tuned to TNT for back-to-back episodes of* Charmed." You've probably just drifted back to sleep by now—sleeping is a full-time job in jail, so you'll undoubtedly be doing a lot of it—but you'll be startled awake when the CO turns on the power to the TV. It only gets about five channels, so you will quickly acquire an intimate familiarity with TNT's daytime line-up: *Charmed, Supernatural, Law and Order, Bones,* and *Cold Case,* in that order.

Noon—"*Trays, ladies!*" Lunch is your only warm meal every day, and it generally consists of some type of unidentifiable meat chunks in gravy, two pieces of white bread, overcooked vegetables, milk, and a piece of fruit.

1:00 P.M.—"*Five minutes till rec!*" Five days a week for up to an hour and a half, you have the option to go out to rec, though the exact time slot varies. The fenced-in yard is a blacktop square—about fifty feet

by thirty feet—with a basketball hoop, but no ball or
net. There's also no track or grass or weight pile like
on TV, and it's surrounded on three sides by men's
cellblocks. The only thing you can really do is walk in
a circle while horny guys—some of whom you probably know or have slept with, because this is a small
town—bang on the windows to get your attention,
the jailhouse version of a catcall. Still, it is the major
social occasion of the day because it's the only time
you get to talk in person with the five women who
live across the hall in B-Block. The rest of the time,
your only communication is hand signs and charades
through the cellblock windows.

5:00 P.M.—*"Jumpsuits up—trays, ladies!"* Dinner is always lukewarm canned soup, a cold sandwich, fruit or
dessert, and milk. Most of the day you'll walk around
in your orange T-shirt or white long john shirt, with
the pants of your jumpsuit on and the top hanging
around your waist, held in place by the elastic cinch
in the middle. It's a universal trick of jail comfort,
but the guards demand that you pull your jumpsuit
all the way up before you can take a tray—an arbitrary requirement for mealtime formality in a place
where this matters literally not at all.

7:00 P.M.—*"How many for AA?"* The limited and incon-
sistent program offerings for women tend to take
place in the evenings in the visiting room. On Sundays you have church, on Mondays you have AA, and
on Fridays there's your twelve-step-based recovery

group. There is also a parenting class that has been "getting off the ground" indefinitely.

10:30 P.M.—*"Five minutes to lock-in!"* Sometime around 10:30 or 10:45, you'll hear the announcement on the loudspeaker that it's time to lock in for the night. Then the COs come through and slide your cell doors shut.

And that's it. That's all your day in jail consists of. Obviously, this leaves a lot of free time in a small space, and figuring out exactly how to fill it will be one of your main tasks here.

For my part, I filled my days with reading, obsessive crosswording, and running, making slow, plodding laps back and forth across the cellblock. In warmer weather, I could have run outside—but the sight of the sun wasn't worth the ogling eyes around me. So instead I stayed in, using a yellow legal notepad as a ruler to guesstimate the length of the cellblock: forty feet. Every time certain guards walked by, I had to stop and walk. They said we weren't allowed to run.

Lots of people run for the scenery, or the fresh air, or the rush of endorphins, or the feeling of accomplishment. In jail, I had none of those things. There, running was simply putting one foot in front of the other, no frills. No wind, no sky, no landscapes. After almost a decade of drug use, I'm not sure there was much left in the way of endorphins, and the sense of accomplishment was minimal. I did not, after all, go anywhere.

Since I was not exactly a star athlete anymore, achieving my daily four-mile goal was a time-consuming undertaking that ate up most of my mornings. Afternoons, meanwhile, were for writing letters, and evenings were for journaling, recording in detail every nuance of my new life in a fishbowl.

I had been a journaler much of my life, and when I was younger I'd written in a hieroglyphic-like code designed to hide dark thoughts from snooping teachers or parents. But over the years of decay that code had become a way to discreetly keep a ledger of my illicit dealings instead of my inner thoughts. Like so much else, the actual act of journaling had fallen by the wayside.

When I picked it up again in jail it was because of Susan, the pagan lesbian who'd joked about my apparent newfound fame.

"It could be a book," she told me. "At the least, it's too weird not to write down."

I laughed, but clearly she'd pegged me as the most likely writer of the group—and she wasn't wrong. Just after Christmas I ordered a stack of yellow legal pads from the commissary and began to write obsessively. Overdoing it as always, I wrote so much it became a going joke on the block: Anything dramatic or even vaguely interesting we said was "another chapter for Keri's book." A girl I used to get high with on the outside jokingly proposed a tongue-in-cheek title: *IV League*. It was a thing that absolutely none of us ever thought would really be published. After all, we were just a bunch of fuck-ups waiting to turn the page on our own lives. Who would want to read our stories?

In jail, there are risks to journaling. Everything in your possession is constantly subject to confiscation; the paraphernalia of your life can always be used against you one way or another, as some sign of guilt or ill-intent. Just to be safe, I sent a few pages of what I wrote to people on the outside every few days, mailing out pieces of myself like a molting animal.

The skins I shed were angry, or grateful. Insightful, full of bold self-deception. I'd be full of hope one day and wishing for death the next. Convinced I had finally found God in one sentence, and ranting about cellblock drama two lines later. At the time, I detailed it all with delight and snark—it seemed safe to laugh at the jailhouse disputes that I took for nothing more than low-stakes spectacles. Looking back, I see they were not. Behind bars, the stakes are almost never low.

One of the first dramatic episodes I detailed was that of Brandy, the rule-breaker who spent so much time in solitary. It all started after she called an officer an asshole and lost her job assignment. He probably deserved it, but the guards retaliated against her name-calling by taking everything she had. After she lost her job as a trustie, they locked her in solitary, threw out her commissary food stash, cut off her phone privileges, made her go to rec alone, and took her long underwear—the extra layer of clothing we all needed to stay warm in the winter. They told the rest of the women not to call her family or use the microwave for her. They refused to give her grievance forms to file complaints. She had nothing left and no recourse—so she just stopped giving a fuck. She began routinely flouting the rules, doing things guaranteed to keep her in trouble. It wasn't a mental health crisis or break with reality. It was just a woman with nothing to lose.

For the rest of us, it was exhilarating to witness. She said and did all the things we all wanted to, telling off the meanest guards as we cackled quietly in our cells. One day she got under the blankets at 9 P.M.; the rules say you cannot do that until 10 P.M. But now, Brandy didn't give a shit—and she decided to boldly gaslight the guards when they called her out on it.

"It's nine! I can get under the fucking blankets at nine!"

The guard on duty that night—Blackburn—was a gray-haired elvish woman, a few inches shy of five feet. She looked like a storybook grandmother, but one who had mysteriously traded in her wand to work in corrections. She was usually taciturn, with no sense of humor and a nasally voice.

"It's ten," she said flatly.

"No it's not. It's fucking not!"

"It's ten."

"It's nine! It's always been fucking nine!"

"It's ten."

"I don't fucking care! And you're wrong!"

From the sidelines I was thrilled at the standoff, which went on for ten minutes before Blackburn confiscated the blankets altogether. Undaunted but fuming, Brandy jotted a letter to her boyfriend, venting her complaints. On the outside of the envelope, she scrawled: "The COs, esp. Blackburn, are fucking cum-guzzling gizabel bitches."

Then, she put a stamp on it, waved it around to show all of us, and handed it over for outgoing mail. Blackburn picked it up, read the envelope, and promptly flipped the fuck out, running up and down the hallway telling the other guards about this incendiary act, and demanding to know: "Do I have to mail this?!" She was so short that, from our cells, we could only see the graying top of her head as she buzzed angrily back and forth.

"Brandy," I whispered, "I think you mean Jezebel. Gizabel isn't a word. Jezebel is a biblical whore."

She was thrilled at the input: "Now I'll sound smarter when I cuss her out next time."

She grinned conspiratorially, and we all watched Blackburn continue to flip out in the hallway. In the dreary world of jail, this was high entertainment—and Brandy was willing to provide it almost every day, with delightfully colorful language. But I probably would not have laughed as much if I knew how this would end: For her string of nonviolent, petty disruptions, Brandy ended up spending more than half of her eight-month sentence in solitary confinement.

Eventually, they shipped her out to a jail one county over in Tioga, where rules in solitary were much harsher. There, she was locked in a cell with a door instead of bars. She could not play cards at the cell gate anymore. When she went to rec—alone—she would be shackled. During the day, she could not even sleep on the mattress, let alone under her blankets. She had no commissary or possessions. She could not use the phone, so when her boyfriend decided to break up with her and move to New York City, he did it in a letter. Meanwhile, she sat alone in a barren cell all day, every day for months. It had never occurred to me that that was even a possibility.

I didn't know it then, but the truth is this: Jail is its own kingdom. The basic rules of engagement do not apply here.

It was into this world that my lawyer, a white-haired Southern man with a handlebar mustache and a tan suit, showed up one day as if out of thin air. He used funny phrases like "meaner than a two-headed rattlesnake" and "bless your heart," and seemed like a figure I'd more expect to see in a stage rendition of *Inherit the Wind* than sitting across from me at the tiny table of the legal visitation room. He'd previously worked as a federal prosecutor, but at the tail end of his long career, he'd decided to begin doing appointed defense work to keep himself busy.

It seemed that there was nothing for me to like about him—and yet I did. He was smart and understood both my drug jokes and my Shakespeare references. But most of all there was this: He treated me like a person, not an object of pity or the walking bundle of fuck-ups that I so clearly was.

I have no recollection of requesting his presence. I assume I must have filled out paperwork to be appointed an attorney. But if that happened, it was somewhere in my post-arrest drug haze, so I was somewhat surprised when this caricature of an old-school attorney showed up at the jail, telling me he would handle my case. There was, he informed me, not much he could do. While extraordinarily high, I had readily confessed. We could try to get the interrogation thrown out because I'd been so clearly incoherent—but it wouldn't do much good: Regardless of what I'd said or not said, I'd definitely, positively, 100 percent had a large amount of drugs on me. "And possession is nine-tenths of the law," he intoned wryly.

There wasn't any real way around that fact.

Almost as surprising as the sudden appearance of my attorney were the updates that flowed in regarding my life on the outside—or my former life, as it were. For one, I found out that I now owned almost nothing; my apartment had been ransacked after my arrest. This is not uncommon; when your arrest is in the newspaper, all your drug friends—and enemies—know you're in jail, and if they're assholes, they'll come help themselves to your belongings.

They were assholes. And so, somewhere in the first few days after I got picked up, looters took my books, my dirty underwear, the sheets on my bed, my memories. My collection of skating medals had vanished, along with the hand-me-down winter coat from my mom, my favorite Diesel jeans—and my dog, Charlotte. Had someone taken her? Did Animal Control intervene? Or did she just run away in the chaos of looting? I still had no idea.

At first, I'd held out hope she could somehow be waiting exactly where I'd left her in my trashy basement apartment. Maybe, I thought, some kind housemate had heard her whining and decided to feed her. Maybe, I hoped, she would just stay put until Alex got back. Maybe, I hoped, she was okay.

Charlotte had come into my life three years earlier, just a few days after I'd jumped off a bridge in Ithaca in a very earnest suicide attempt during the summer of 2007. At the time, she was in rough shape—just like me. She was not quite two, and her first owners had gotten her a little over a year earlier, after she'd been found in a farmer's field, abandoned and making herself a bed in the corn. They'd taken her in, but they already had four other dogs who bullied her and stole her food.

By the time I got her, her ribs still stuck out and she jumped at everything. She was scared of her own bark, and as soon as I brought her in the house, she saw my housemate's cat and promptly peed all over the floor in abject terror.

Over the next few months, she got healthier even though

I did not. Struggling my way through college, I brought her along to everything from office hours to final exams to English lectures. Her life suffered the same dichotomy as my own: We went to class by day, but crack houses by night. She saw it all—raids, robberies, tears, drunken fights. She stole my friends' hamburgers, and their weed. She licked the blood off my track marks, and one time in an unexpected outburst of loyalty, she bit my friend's drugged-out brother who'd punched me in the face. I didn't think she had it in her.

She was one of the few things I'd done right in my addiction, something I'd kept alive even when I was trying to die. But now she, like so much else in my life, was gone. She'd been my failproof companion, and I'd lost her. That should have been the reality check I needed. But it wasn't—not yet. Coming back to the sharp corners of real life after a blurry decade of drug use is a process. No matter how much you want to start over, you are not magically a changed person as soon as you set foot in the jail and enter a world of buzz-clunk-beeps and clangs. The clack of cell keys does not teach you remorse. The clash of a steel door does not bring you redemption.

There is no soundtrack here for that. If you want one, you'll have to write it yourself.

Chapter 7

I'm lying on a roof, naked, in the midnight rain—and grinning ear to ear. The shingles feel so gritty, so real. Textures are just amazing, and sound is so crisp: I can hear a universe of chaos inside each droplet of water falling around me. It's the last weekend of Harvard Summer School, and I am seventeen and doing ecstasy on the outskirts of Boston, giggling as I roll around with a teenage raver boy in a black fishnet shirt. We are on top of his parents' house, and I am hazily hoping that we do not fall off.

My senior year of high school will start in a few weeks back in Lancaster, but I will not be there to see it through. I will stay for just three days of the semester, and then I will come back here to run wild in Beantown, decaying with a vengeance—rolling on roofs, getting high in back alleys, roaming the hungry streets of Chinatown at 4 A.M. Whatever I'm doing, it's not pairs, it's not even skating—but it makes me not feel the hole where my future was.

A few weeks after my second Nationals with Mark—the middle of my eleventh-grade year—he broke off our partnership. To me, it came as a complete surprise. Sure, we'd hoped to do better at Nationals; we'd gotten fifth at the same level two years in a row, even though we both skated well and no one fell. But one day in early 2001, I walked into the rink in Delaware as usual and my coach Tracey called me into a mysterious office tucked into a back corner of the arena. I'd only been back there once before, and as she bobbed down the hallway with pursed lips, her brisk business steps leading the way ahead of me, I knew that something was off. My heart raced, with dread or excitement—it was hard to tell which.

The conversation itself is a blur, but for the next few days it played out again and again, on repeat like a skating program— but one where I would fall on every single jump. First, Tracey would tell me, then she would have to tell my parents. Then we would have to tell all the ancillary coaches—the spin and dance instructors, the choreographer. Other skaters would ask, and their parents would ask. And then I would have to tell them: No, I don't really know why. I guess he just wanted to branch out. To give it a go with someone new. As I told the very short tale of my very public rejection again and again, it seemed that his ambition had become my Olympic-sized tragedy.

Admittedly, I don't know whether that was the full story; it left me with unanswered questions—questions that I was too scared to ask. I was afraid of what he might say; even I could see that I was a mess, and I was terrified of finding out all the other ways in which this was my fault. Tracey seemed just as baffled as I was; if she knew anything more, she did not let on. Neither, for that matter, did Mark. He was, after all, still training at the same rink, and I saw him every day. Sometimes we still skated together, like a separated couple sharing custody of our careers. In the awkward limbo of this overtime round for our partnership, we actually got better. Within a few months, we got our first side-by-side triples and started landing our throw double Axel every time.

Except it wasn't ours anymore. Because there was no us.

Every night for months, I spent hours crying myself to sleep in the corner of my bedroom, curled up on a pile of oversized stuffed animals tossed on the ice by fans after competitions. To me, it seemed, my life was over. It was as if I'd gotten divorced, and also fired from my job—and also every job forever.

It was not the same for him. As a male in skating, he could find a new partner right away. And he did, in a matter of months. (She was younger, and easily twenty pounds lighter, a fact that did not escape my notice.) As a female in skating, I knew my future was not as clear. Teen girls willing to be tossed around were a readily available commodity; there were hundreds of me vying for the same pool of teenage boys and twenty-somethings. I might find a new partner next week, or next month—or never. If it had been possible to cry one into existence, I seemed to be doing my best.

My parents—with good intentions—suggested I go to Harvard for summer school. I think they did not quite know what to do with an anorexic seventeen-year-old moping around the house and crying inconsolably. Maybe they sensed the train wreck ahead and thought they could reroute my life in a less troubling direction. At first glance, Harvard seemed like a good idea. Though summer school mimicked the grueling application process of regular college, it was far less difficult to get into. Plus, I'd always wanted to go there, like my dad had. And if I did, I could still skate: There was an elite training center within walking distance of the freshman dorms, those two-century-old brick buildings where high school students got their first taste of freedom every summer. But for me that freedom became the first time I did not have anyone to interfere with whatever self-destructive activities I could dream up. Instead of getting myself together, I fell further apart, propelled by more self-hatred than I knew I had.

Sometimes, I had nothing but Starbucks coffee for breakfast, lunch, and dinner; I visited the place so much I made friends with the happy-go-lucky grad student baristas, Ben and John. Other times, I binged with abandon at the university mess hall. I couldn't throw up in the sixteen-person dorm, so instead I wandered the student center, homing in on the most isolated bathroom stall with the same nose for trouble I would later use to seek out heroin. I experimented with buying ipecac syrup, guzzling it down, then puking uncontrollably until I couldn't stand. I got my belly button pierced. I started smoking. I befriended the goth kids skulking around Harvard Square, then stayed up all night exchanging messages with them on AOL Instant Messenger. At home, I couldn't even use the computer without permission; now, I could do it at 2 A.M. while leaning out the window for a cigarette. I could smoke pot with a hippie, have sex with a high-school dropout, experiment with snorting orange lines of Adderall off the dorm room desk, or—eventually— down a couple tabs of some Superman-stamped ecstasy with a teenage raver on his parents' wet roof. It was exhilarating, and edgy, and self-destructive. I could live out my disdain for myself but enjoy every moment.

Through it all, I kept going to the rink, but with less enthusiasm—and less regularity. There was still no pairs partner in sight. By August, I'd been sitting on the shelf for almost eight months and became increasingly certain I was reaching my expiration date. I could see my future disintegrating before my eyes with each bad decision. As the sun set on my last lucid summer, I decided: I would give in to the decay. I would be radioactive.

When I came home to Lancaster, three days after the school year started, I disappeared. Depending on who you ask, I either ran away from home or got kicked out. Things were, at best, strained between me and my parents—and had been for some time. They'd stubbornly set a 9 P.M. curfew, and on that particular night in late August 2001, I stubbornly insisted on going out for a walk at 9:30 P.M. I wanted a clandestine cigarette— but the idea of setting foot outside the front door at that hour blossomed into a screaming match. What happened next is still hazy with anger, but I remember that it ended with me giving my parents the finger on the front lawn before striding off down the street, far too headstrong to look back or reconsider.

In search of a pay phone, I headed to the nearest gas station— one I used to steal from before I threw up in the bushes. Just after crossing under the railroad bridge that marked the city limit, I ran into my next mistake: a skinny teenager, with shaved head and a cigarette. I asked: "Can I bum one?" He took in my tear-streaked face and said yes.

I'd known this kid for all of five minutes, when I asked: "Do you know anyone who can drive me to Boston?"

Somehow, he did.

"I'll take you over to Terri's," he said. "It's like two blocks away."

Terri was in her forties, unemployed, and possibly 250 pounds. She and her two daughters—eleven and fifteen—and their dog, Doobie, rented out an attic in a duplex that reeked of urine from the owner's incontinent, aging husband. In exchange for a ride to Boston, I offered Terri some of the money I had left over from a few years of coaching skating on the weekends; it couldn't have been more than $100. Technically, it was probably illegal to be driving me—an absconding minor—across state lines, but she seemed to see it as an adventure, maybe a dark version of Mr. Toad's Wild Ride involving a troubled kid and some drugs. Unlike a Disney World attraction, this ride moved at breakneck speed, a roller coaster forever plunging down.

The adventure almost ended abruptly when her beat-up car broke down on the New Jersey Turnpike. Undeterred, I announced that I would ask a random trucker for a ride the rest of the way. The mechanic we found at the nearest rest stop overheard my plan and was horrified—so he volunteered to drive me the remaining 270 miles himself, for $70. I popped some Adderall I'd brought back from Boston and talked his ear off the whole time, trying to convince him—and every other concerned adult that I encountered for the next few months—that I had a plan to get a job and finish school. It just so happened that those two particular things would be hard to do as an un-accompanied minor, and even harder as an unaccompanied minor who was constantly high. That it made no sense at all to be making these plans in this scenario apparently did not occur to me. Like a short-circuiting robot programmed to overachieve, I did not know how to plan differently, even as I began to self-destruct.

We drove through the night, and I showed up in Beantown on a hot morning in late August or early September, naively believing I could crash with a friend I'd met over the summer at the Pit, the cement amphitheater by the T stop where druggie teens lurked. But my friends were all homeless or had parents—parents who were understandably not about to house a stray teenager with a budding drug problem. This was a wrinkle I had not accounted for; everything to this point had gone so improbably well, I'd begun to think maybe this bizarre series of lucky coincidences was just what life was like outside the bubble.

It was not. I spent my first night in the MIT student center, where the security guards left me alone, probably mistaking me for the sort of sleep-deprived overachiever I had once been. In the nights that followed, I slept on couches, in alleys, and once, on the rooftop of the Harvard English Department. It was a warm night, but a lonely place. I can't even remember if there were sounds or raindrops or distant chatter from the nearby cafe; I am guessing there were not, but in any case, my own echoing emptiness would have drowned it out. I learned quickly that there's an intrinsically desolate feeling to being homeless. It was something I did not expect, and it cut far deeper than the simple, logistical difficulties and social stigmas of being dirty and unhoused. There's something specific about not having a place where you are welcome or safe when the sun goes down. For an underage girl fresh on the street, safe was not really an option—but after a few days, I found welcome: the Family under the parking garage.

The Family was a motley collection of a couple dozen young homeless goths and assorted street people dwelling beneath the first level of the curving parking garage across the street from the Alewife train station—the end of the line.

But not just anyone could stay with them. They had a hierarchy, and you had to get permission. At the top were the King and the Queen, a couple decked out in colonial-style vampire goth, complete with white faces and occasional canes and hats. Like part of a fever dream, they popped in and out only on occasion, appearing breathtakingly coiffed and costumed like creatures from another world. They made the rules, but I was never actually sure if they were homeless.

Below them there were the Princes and Princesses, and the lesser nobles. They did not dress up beyond the typical lost kid uniform of facial piercings and wide-leg raver pants. Some of them I knew by face, but many I never knew by name. And then there were the nonroyalty like me. Some of us had regular names, and some had street kid names: Chaos, Weasel, Fate. (Fate was a dick.) We nonroyals had to get approval to camp out or even set foot inside. And, unlike royals, we could get booted for relatively minor misbehavior or bringing in drama.

The space under the parking garage didn't have much in the way of amenities, and even basic protection was kind of a mixed bag. The royals wouldn't let in an angry woman who thought I owed her money—but they weren't interested in doing anything to stop other royals or their guests from feeling up women in their sleep. There were risks, but it was a place to lay my head, and there were some important perks. For one, we had an in-house piercer who carried his whole set of piercing tools with him and would accept drugs as payment.

For two, we had drugs.

But with no income, I had no means to afford them. At first, I kept up with some freelance writing for the official figure skating magazine, calling my editor from pay phones and turning in assignments typed up at odd hours from the Harvard student center computers. But my summer school password finally expired, and I knew I couldn't really get a job as a minor with minimal ID. I tried spanging—begging for "spare change" with a cardboard sign on the corner of the sidewalk—but I worried it would attract the attention of police, who might notice that I looked awfully young to be running around on my own. Briefly, I tried stealing: With a couple older comrades, I would swipe books from one store, exchange them for CDs at another, then sell the CDs as used at third stop for $5 a pop. Given the risk and the time commitment, it was hardly worth it.

So I started turning tricks. It was quite a leap—I'd only had sex with a guy once at that point, and only a few times with a woman. Both were still awkward and new. But that changed after some scruffy teenager at the Pit introduced me to Mary Jane, a skinny white female pimp with a crack problem. She was just a few years older than me, and we had an on-the-go interview, strolling down the Cambridge sidewalk as she looked me over, asked what I would and wouldn't do, and explained the rules of Boston's Chinatown circa 2002.

"Okay, so when we get out there," she said, half-dropping the *r*, "you can't walk on the sidewalk. Girls have to walk in the street, unless the po-po drives by, then they can pick you up for jaywalking because that's how they'll get you, so you have to get on the sidewalk, but if you walk on the sidewalk when there are other pimps there don't make eye contact because if you make eye contact then they can take you and see that parking lot over there they would probably rape you and then they make you theirs and you have to work for them."

Her words spilled out fast and intense, in a thick Boston accent always trimmed with a hint of anger. She could see I was not taking this seriously. But how could I? The outcomes seemed impossible, and the rules felt like a dark and absurd gym class—not high-risk, underage street prostitution. I assumed she was exaggerating to keep me in line, but now I know she probably wasn't.

We went out early that night to scope out the streets I would walk and learn the boundaries of my range, discussing how far I could go before I was too close to nice places in one direction or too close to competing pimps in another. My first trick was uneventful, or at least that is how I chose to remember it. If I was nervous, I buried it. If I was terrified or if he hurt me, I forgot. Looking back now, I do not remember having any emotions. I only remember the stars.

In the many nights I would spend for years to come having sex in strange alleys and rusty cars and shitty motels across the East Coast, I would always count the stars through every trick.

If I could not see the stars, I would count ceiling tiles or specks on the floor. If I could not do that, I would close my eyes and count twinkling points of light in my mind.

From inside some sad man's car in Chinatown, I suspect I could not see any stars that night. But I remember them anyway.

As I walked the track for my first time, I did not—as I might have envisioned—strut down the street in a leather miniskirt, with stilettos, red lipstick, and the confidence of a woman making bank on the value of her sexuality. Instead, I wore an ankle-length black skirt because it was all I had, as I stumbled uncertainly between parked cars, twisted, lost, and too young to be there.

There were other women out but not a lot. I was the smallest, and the whitest. It was a relatively quiet area—maybe because Mary Jane couldn't compete with the male pimps at a more crowded marketplace. Or maybe because she didn't think I could handle it. The men would drive up in their shitty Hondas and rusty Fords, and roll down their windows. I was supposed to ask if they were a cop, then make them touch my tit before actually talking money, a naive ritual that probably did not offer the legal protection we thought it did.

It was fifty dollars for head. A hundred for straight sex. Two hundred for anal.

But any kind of sex usually meant they wanted to go somewhere: a potentially unsafe home or a time-consuming motel stop. Plus, I was small and sex hurt so much. Blow jobs were a better bet. In the best-case scenario, he'd be small, quiet, and take less than five minutes.

In the worst-case scenario, he'd drive outside the range of the walkie-talkies we used to keep in touch in that pre–cell

phone era. Then he'd try slipping off the condom, take forever to get off, and then drop me off in the wrong place. That
alone could be dangerous: Once, it ended with me being chased
down the street by an angry pimp lobbing unprovoked threats.
"*I'll make you an international ho!*" I didn't know exactly what
he meant, but I could imagine. As I bolted toward a worried-
looking city worker who let me hitch a three-block ride on the
back of a garbage truck, I must have been scared; the memory
is so crisp, I can only think terror must have seared it into some
part of my brain. But it seemed so surreal, unreal, could-not-
have-just-happened that, by the time I hopped off the back of
the truck, it was nothing more than a funny anecdote for my
friends under the parking garage.

I usually walked away from the track with at least enough
money to visit the only heroin dealer I knew who would sell to
a seventeen-year-old: Derek with the pointy goatee. That first
line off of *Sons and Lovers* had come from him, though through
some older intermediary who already had a habit. As a general
rule, I tried to avoid sobriety for even a second, because I was
as intent on abusing myself as I was on escaping. So from the
moment I'd climbed out of that mechanic's pickup truck and
set foot back in Boston, I'd been hoovering up every drug I
could get my hands on: Pot. Speed. PCP. Pills. Crack. Coke.
But the goal was heroin. Not so much because I was craving
the drug as because I was craving the darkness. I couldn't get it
every night—I didn't always have money or didn't always finish
working in time. But when I could, I'd score and head back to
the Alewife train station, then scribble the day down in my

journal, a rapidly expanding collection of notepads and loose-leaf pages. Most of them have since fluttered away.

The rest are a lurid, swirling compendium of sex, drugs, and vomit, day in and day out. I am smoking crack out of a Diet Coke can. I am wandering aimlessly around Cambridge, picking scraps out of trash cans. I am throwing them up. I am getting detained by police. I am high and listening to a busker playing Bob Marley on a warm September evening at the Pit. I am having sex with a woman on a Cambridge rooftop. I am showering at a homeless shelter. I am cuddling with a stranger who took me in for the night. I am trying to figure out if anyone had sex with me in my sleep. And I am writing and writing. I am mixing tenses and voices. Sometimes it's a poem, sometimes it's a screenplay, as if I am the narrator and not the one living it. There are no dates or page numbers.

"The rest of the day is a blur."
"We went on to the dealer."
"My body went numb."
"My mouth hurt because he was so big."

It's all in pen, as if I had no second thoughts or possible corrections. It seems I only regretted that decision one time: on page ten, where I whited out three words. Apparently I was the sort of girl who brought Wite-Out with me to a homeless encampment.

I have since lost most of the pages, but some things you do not need to write down to remember. I have nothing about my nights with Mary Jane. I never made note of the day I finally woke up slightly dopesick and realized I'd caught a small habit. I have no records of the drug dealer who held me in his house at knifepoint and forced me to give him head. I never wrote down the first time I was raped—or any of the other times. They never felt rape-y enough. I thought that rape was a thing that happened violently in a back alley, to a completely innocent victim—and I was not that. A homeless guy on acid who simply ignored me when I said no until I kicked him in the stomach? That did not count, I told myself. We'd been making out first. A stoner who ignored me, crying as I said no? That didn't count, either. I didn't fight back. There were others. Somehow they always did not count. In my head, I knew this was wrong. Rape is rape. But in my heart I could not—and many days still cannot—believe this. It could have been worse, I thought.

Plus, maybe it didn't entirely feel real. It had all happened so quickly. I was an aspiring Olympian, then in the blink of a dopey eye, I was not. My entire unraveling, all of my various back-and-forths between Boston and Lancaster, happened over the course of five months, between August and December of 2001.

From my sporadic pay phone calls home during that time, my parents knew where I was generally—and one time when I was in town they came to Terri's and staged an intervention that went quite badly awry when I jumped out of the moving car and ran off half-naked, having lost my shirt and one shoe as I fled. But they didn't report me as missing or as a runaway, and when the police picked me up in Boston for shoplifting at one point, they did not attempt to arrange my return home. I indignantly told myself that was a sign they didn't care whether

I stayed or came back—but in retrospect I think they were just at a loss. What do you do when your child self-destructs so extravagantly in front of your eyes? Nothing in any parenting books could have really prepared them for this.

Sometimes, I went back to Lancaster for a few days or weeks, but not to see them. I came so close to home, picking up shifts at the diner chain a mile away and crashing nearby with Terri or the young, druggie, gay guy I'd met at work. Occasionally I'd run into someone from school and tell them bizarre lies about what happened and what I was doing—but any fable I could come up with might have been more believable than the truth at that point. There'd been a rumor going around that I'd moved to Switzerland to train for the Olympics. It was a glamorous outcome I'd never considered, and one that shot through me with a pang of loss when I heard it.

I didn't want to hear these things anymore, these echoes of a now-past life. And so, I always went back to Boston. If I'm going to decay, I thought, I'll do it far away on rainy roofs and in back alleys. Like a dog crawling under the porch to die.

Chapter 8

Not long after learning the first lessons of jailing, I learned something else about doing time: you'll always be scared. But the things that scare you in jail are not what you expect them to be. It's not getting shanked. It's not dropping the soap.

Instead, these are the things that keep you up all night: What does the fact that you ended up here say about you as a person? Does it mean you are bad? Or just bad at life?

Every night, when the lights go dim and the cell doors clang shut, I curl up into a ball and stare at the beige cinderblock wall, rocking myself to sleep as I play over and over in my head the things I regret. It's a low-budget silent film for my eyes only, and I can't walk out. The scenes flash by in no particular order: The time the guy I was dating had sex with my half-conscious friend and I didn't stop him. The store thefts, the friends we ripped off. The day my housemates violently robbed a guy—he was probably only a teenager—and I just watched from the sideline. The times I told my parents to go fuck themselves. All the promises I threw away. The people I sold drugs to. The lies I told. The fights. The sob stories.

I add all these things up, a dark calculus of wrongdoing. And I wonder about the other side of the equation. If I did all these things, did I deserve the rest of it?

One time when I was eighteen, a drug counselor told me that if I'd been raped more than once, at some point I was asking for it. That played to my worst fears, or maybe to my deepest desires for self-loathing. On good nights, I told myself she was wrong. But still I wondered—was there a grain of truth? When I did that first line of brown powder off the cover of my *Sons and Lovers* summer reading, was this part of the bargain? And if so, should I have known that? Or should I be mad—at Alex, at my parents, at the whole world? At the least, I could be mad at that lady who found my Tupperware container and gave it to the cops, right?

If the clangs and shouts around me were the songs of my incarceration, then these questions were the lyrics, verses of bitterness paired with a chorus of chagrin: *What the fuck is wrong with me? What the fuck is wrong with me? What the fuck is wrong with me?*

In the close quarters of a cellblock, these were still songs I sang alone. Our bitterness we traded back and forth—and we all had plenty to go around. But our doubts we more often kept to ourselves. Even among friends, anger is usually safer than shame when you're locked up. In the long run, though, it is far harder to look back on.

Today, when I think through all the versions of me that make up these pages, this is the one I hate the most. My thoughts were filled with such dark sadness, but my words were so often angry and bitter. Even though I was ready to take on the familiar self-flagellation of regret and shame, I was not actually ready to take responsibility. Instead I let myself bask in resentment. I could not say that I was seventeen and did not know better. I could not say that I was on drugs and unable to control myself. I had no excuse.

This part of the soundtrack is a song I would very much like to skip.

After a few long, jailed days of radio silence, I started getting my first letters from Alex, his harsh chicken scratch inked on unlined, white paper. He used shorthand like *u* and *r* with the sporadic capitalization of a giant text message telling me that he planned to stay sober with me, that he missed me more than he'd ever missed anything, and that he would be there when I got out:

> *I don't give a fuck 3 months or three years I will be right here waiting for u. I will never betray u or even think about it. U are my soul keri it took me a minute to realize it but u r the most important person in my life and I would never risk losing you again.*

My reply must have been no less dramatic; we were star-crossed lovers convinced of our undying devotion—despite the fact that we'd only actually known each other for about eight months at that point, when I abruptly switched from one volatile man to another in the course of one weekend. For all the years I did drugs I was almost never single. Feeding an addiction is easier as a two-person task, with a literal partner in crime. Those relationships—usually with men, usually older—were always tough and intense, frequently abusive, and filled with overwrought declarations of undying love, or hate. Alex was no exception, and the emotional riot of early sobriety combined with the fallout from my arrest only ratcheted up the dramatics and passion. And that passion, he said, was exactly why he hadn't answered collect calls those first few days, and also why he hadn't written sooner: He couldn't. He was so distraught he'd been in the hospital.

"I had to come to the mental ward to keep myself from killing myself," he wrote. He just wanted to die after hearing what had happened to me.

At the time, I believed him without question. It was as if the charm he glowed with in real life oozed off the paper and into my heart.

But there was actually a bit more to the story than those scribbles implied. Through letters, and later through phone calls, he explained what happened according to his version of events. The morning of my arrest, he said, he'd listened along as police detained me. I'd left my phone on speaker, in the hope that he could hear it all and know what happened to me. And he did—until the arresting officer snapped the phone shut. At that point, Alex said, he decided to head toward the scene. When he discovered that I'd already been hauled off in cuffs by the time he got there, he caused such a ruckus that the remaining officer pepper-sprayed him in the face and arrested him.

The details were not consistent after that. Maybe he'd

swallowed a bunch of pills and then been given an overdose-reversing drug at the police station, or maybe he'd been taken to the hospital because the police were afraid they'd hurt him during the arrest. Maybe he'd gotten charged with interfering with an arrest, or maybe he'd picked up a drug case. Maybe he'd been involuntarily committed, or maybe he'd decided to go to the hospital after police released him. Given the amount of drugs involved in our daily lives at that point, it wasn't exactly a surprise that he presented several versions of events. Regardless, they all ended in the same place: detoxing in the psych ward.

And that, he explained, was how Charlotte ended up alone in my apartment, from which she had since disappeared.

Years later, I tried to verify his story and couldn't. The police records I found offered no indication that he'd shown up at the scene, caused a ruckus, or been transported to the hospital. Though I spotted a single line saying the cops had charged him after they caught him climbing out of my apartment window mid-afternoon, it's not clear what they would have charged him with and there's no record of an arrest that day. But I didn't know all that then—and it really didn't matter. Either way, I needed him; he seemed like the only remaining bridge between me and the life I'd left behind. It was in one of his early letters that Alex suggested we should get married, scribbling it down in a hasty postscript with his usual chicken scratch: "P.S. Let's get married first fucking chance we get."

I thought it was wonderful and tragic, a romantic leap of faith. I wrote in my journal that saying yes might be "one of the most impulsive things I've ever done"—which was almost certainly not true, given my years of doing almost nothing but impulsive things. "I figure if I do really weird things in jail," I added, "it certainly can't make anyone think any worse of me, now can it?"

I was probably wrong about that, too. My lawyer, for one, was quick to let me know he did not approve; he thought the marriage proposal was Alex's attempt to keep me from testifying against him.

"Alex is just afraid you'll put him in jail," he said, grinning slightly under that handlebar mustache.

"No, he loves me," I insisted. "He knows I love him—he would never think that."

The words lolled out of his mouth casually, but I did not like what they implied: "How much of those drugs were actually yours?"

"All of them!"

The reality is that my level of ownership was probably a bit less than I admitted. It is true that I was unequivocally a drug dealer, and had been selling everything from shrooms to blow to dope for years before I ever met Alex. When we got together, I took care of the day-to-day running of the business. But it was his connection that fronted us the bulk powder by the ounce, a huge step up from the individual bags and bundles I'd gotten before. It was his connection that made possible the six-ounce stash I had on me when I finally crossed paths with the wrong cop.

I was loath to admit this. It was not because I was proud to be a drug dealer, though that was convenient in terms of credibility in jail. But it was more because I was embarrassed to be the pitiful girl who got arrested with her boyfriend's drugs. That's the sort of woman you feel sorry for, and wonder how she could be so stupid. I did not want people to think I was a fool, or a naive object of pity—even though a lot of people in our drug circles already suspected Alex had something to do with my arrest, especially since the officer who busted me was a family friend of his. I wasn't quite willing to believe that, but there was no benefit to blaming him anyway: I'd clearly had the drugs on me, and clearly had enough of them that I was going to be sitting in jail regardless. Getting him locked up too was not going to improve my life.

This was not how I framed it all to my parents. Our first conversation was in late December, a twenty-minute phone call on the jail's recorded line within just a couple weeks of my arrest. My lawyer had already told them, so by that point my parents had had a few days to come to terms with the situation. They must have been disappointed by my arrest, but if they were, I did not notice—or at least there's no indication of it in my journal entries. "They were surprised by the gravity of it but no they were not surprised by the fact and nature of the arrest," I wrote later. "They were surprisingly jovial about it all, in fact."

I'm not sure if that was a cover or if they were just relieved to finally have some clarity as to what was going on in my life. Until that moment they hadn't quite been sure whether I was doing drugs again or not; my dad thought I wasn't, while my mom was certain I was.

But in our early conversations post-arrest, my parents didn't dwell on that. There was too much else at stake, I suppose, to argue over what I'd lied about and when—or when I was going to stop. I felt some pressing need to explain myself, and since there was really no good explanation for so much of the shit

I'd done, I told them many lies. Instead of admitting that I'd been getting high nonstop for years, I told them I'd had periods of sobriety—long periods. I'd only recently relapsed, I said. And since I wanted them to approve of Alex, I claimed that he hadn't been into dope until I came along. I apparently expected them to believe I'd found this older, heavily tattooed former prisoner and led him down the primrose path into heroin addiction. I repeated this lie for several weeks, and they nodded along quietly without much comment.

Instead, in that first call, they updated me on my life, like dutiful messengers from another realm of existence. My mom told me I'd been put on a one-year leave of absence from Cornell because of courses I'd failed or failed to complete before I got arrested. That was not exactly a surprise, and even in my bitterness I realized it was fair. But somehow it didn't occur to me that was probably not the end of it.

The other big piece of news they delivered was word of Charlotte's whereabouts. My dog, the one thing in the world I was responsible for protecting, was living with another family. The property manager for my apartment had convinced a woman she knew to take her home, indefinitely. She was now in a ritzy home in the best part of town, enjoying a yard with some trees and a stream.

The woman, Florianna, worked at Cornell training biology teachers, and her husband, David, ran a nonprofit to save the Serengeti. They had two well-adjusted daughters, one in high school and one in college. They owned a minivan and a dog named Bailey, and they went on family walks together in the gorges and woods. They were clearly nice and law-abiding people, and could give Charlotte a life that I never had. But I was not grateful, or happy. Sure, I was relieved to finally know where she was, but now I was also terrified that she was with strangers—strangers who might love her better until she one day forgot about me. I did not want to lose her forever, and I was afraid that was exactly what this meant.

My journals from that time show that I was a constant mess of emotions: One minute I wanted to die and the next I was ranting about my over-the-top gratitude for sobriety and a second chance. Then I was bitter, then maniacally laughing about that time Alex hallucinated bears. But when I think back to that first phone call with my parents, the only feeling I remember is loss. The one universal emotion of incarceration.

In those early days after my arrest—and for the next two years, really—women in varying stages of distress drifted constantly in and out of my life: Christine, Stephanie, Stephanie again, Brandi, Brandy, Liz, the other Stephanie, Christy, Angela, Angel, Michelle, Bethany, Tiffany, the other Tiffany, and the other other Tiffany. The list went on and on. Some I cannot remember, and some I could never forget. Until I ended up there, I had no idea how much turnover there was in a jail. A steady stream of new people would come in just long enough to lose a job, miss a school pickup, fail a few classes, get evicted, get robbed, skip a car payment. Sometimes they'd only stay for a day before they made bail, or a week until the judge decided what to do about the latest probation violation. Nationally, the average jail stay is just a few weeks. For women who still had a life left to lose on the outside, the effects of even a short trip to jail could be disastrous. To some extent, the same was true for those of us on the inside.

That was a lesson I learned on New Year's Eve. It was the first holiday in jail that I was conscious enough to remember, and we tried to stay up and watch the ball drop, peering out at the TV through the cell bars until a guard switched off the station with seconds to go and dimmed the lights. But I did not go to sleep—not because I was somehow excited about the New Year, but because the big holiday signaled the potential for a slew of nighttime arrests. And our cellblock was almost full.

As Tawny the Cheshire Cat explained to me, a nearly full cellblock was a risk; when there were too many women to fit in all the cells, some would get "boarded out"—or temporarily transferred to other counties, sometimes an hour or more away. You'd have to leave behind all your possessions: Books. Letters. Shampoo. Food. Pictures of your family. You'd be separated from your friends. Your money and phone accounts would not follow you. You'd be too far for regular visitors. Subject to a whole new handbook of rules to learn, and to the whims of rural guards who resented you as the hippie-type from liberal Ithaca.

But worst of all, you'd have to go through medical isolation all over again—which meant being thrown in a cold, barren solitary cell for a few days or a couple weeks. In theory that was to make sure you didn't bring any diseases from your home jail, particularly tuberculosis. In reality we'd already been tested for TB when we got booked, so the indefinite isolation felt like nothing more than a chance to punish us just for being there. The whole process underscored the terrifying randomness of jail life: You could be minding your business, not breaking any rules—and suddenly, for no reason, have everything taken from you, be shipped away, and get thrown in a forgotten cell all alone. And unlike in the Tompkins County Jail, solitary in the surrounding counties meant true isolation; instead of the metal bars that allowed us to talk to each other during lock-in, the other jails had solid metal doors that cut you off from the world like the sole survivor of a shipwreck floating alone in a dark ocean. But that was a feeling I did not learn about until later. At that point, I only knew what the other women told me: Getting boarded out was bad, and you should dread it.

Whenever we spotted a new girl being led into the booking room across from D-Block, we pressed our faces up to the long windows facing the hallway and tried to figure out who it was and what her presence meant for us. Was it someone we knew? Would she make bail? Would they board her out? Or would they board out one of *us?* The guards would almost never answer our questions honestly, so we were left to speculate.

Over time as I came to understand the risks, I developed a routine. First I would panic and pack up all my stuff, every time assuming it would be me next. Then, I would try to distract myself with crossword puzzles, nervously gnawing on my mangled pen all the while. Eventually I would give up on that, defeated by an utter inability to concentrate over the growing whir of anxiety in my head. So I would go back in my cell and lie down. I'd pull in my knees and curl my whole body into my oversized orange sweatshirt, tucking my head like a turtle and rocking back and forth on the metal bunk as my stomach churned with the rising panic that nothing could take away.

I'd whisper prayers. Nothing complicated. Just please-God-please-God-please.

I did not believe in God. But in jail I wanted to so badly.

Sometimes the waiting lasted only a few minutes; sometimes it lasted several hours. Eventually, a sergeant would come in and call out names of people who needed to pack out. You'd have fifteen minutes or so to clear out your bunk—and then you would vanish, picked off by some supernatural monster from a low-budget horror flick.

But on that particular night, the anxiety was all for nothing; no one got boarded out. There was only one new girl, and her name was Samantha. She got put in the last cell on the row where I, for the first time, had the thrill of sauntering up to the cell bars and questioning the new person. Except Sam, it turned out, wasn't really that new. She was what the guards would derisively call a "frequent flier." She was twenty-two but had already forgotten more about jails than I'd ever known. Prisons had been baked into her life as long as she could remember, she explained.

"You know how the first big word people—like, kids—learn how to spell is a state?"

We determined she meant Mississippi.

"Wellll, the first long word I knew how to spell was correctional facility. C-O-R-R-E-C-T-I-O-N-A-L F-A-C-I-L-I-T-Y. For reals."

She delivered the line like it was a joke, but it was not. That was mainly because of her dad, who was well known in town for his record: Rick had done a lot of time—decades—for manslaughter and drugs, including his most recent arrest for selling pills out of an old folks' home. He'd missed her entire childhood, but Sam adored him and in some circles was known mostly for being his daughter.

When she was not in jail, Sam explained that she enjoyed drinking, taunting authority figures, and lighting things on fire—all things potentially at odds with her desire to be there for her kids more than her father had been for her. This time, she said, she was in for criminal mischief. As she told me her story that night from the other side of the cell bars, I took in her gap-toothed smirk and bleached-blond hair that was always, always, always pulled back into a painfully tight bun, as if to clear every flyaway from her field of vision so she could view her surroundings with the full skepticism they deserved. Her demeanor was tomboyish, serious, and perpetually unconvinced. When we first met, she told me: "You look familiar."

"Well, I guess I've been all over the news. I'm the Cornell student who got arrested with a buncha heroin."

"How much?"

"Like six ounces."

"Oh! I heard about that! Congratulations. For real."

She was not being sarcastic.

I did not know what to make of her; in our little cellblock world where snap judgments could be necessary survival tools, she defied easy categorization. We had so little in common: She didn't really do hard drugs, had dropped out of school, and had kids young. She'd certainly never figure skated and had no interest in running or crosswords. And there was this: She was in jail, but completely and utterly unfazed by it. Maybe she, too, was kept up at night with nagging questions and dark songs.

But about this one thing, she was calm. I couldn't put the desire into words yet, but I wanted that for myself. So badly.

But more than anything else, Sam loved anything that threw a wrench in the system that had so clearly fucked her over her entire life—and a Cornell kid getting arrested with a Tupperware container of heroin seemed to fit the bill.

Chapter 9

New York City, 2003

I'm sitting on the floor of a crowded penthouse in Lower Manhattan and some middle-aged guy I don't know is licking my feet. There are glistening floor-to-ceiling windows overlooking the sparkles of the night city, and unidentifiable stains on the bedroom carpet. I'm wearing red vinyl shorts, clear stilettos, a string bikini top, and a dog collar—and it's all the wrong look for this place.

It's a fetish party, and these men are submissives. They want to be the ones wearing the dog collar while they pay—$20 for ten minutes—to lick sweaty feet. They want to cum as women trample them in stilettos. They want to be belittled. They want someone to tell them what to do.

But I am eighteen, and I have no idea what to do.

Not just with the foot licker beneath me, but with life in general. There's still a hole where skating was, and I have no idea how to fill it. I'm still feeling around the edges, trying to figure out how it got there in the first place.

The months of decay in Boston and Lancaster ended abruptly just before Christmas 2001 when one of my former high school teachers came back to town to play a gig with his friends' blues band. He was a skinny redhead with thick glasses, and his name was Luke. I'd always adored him. I would say he was the young and cool teacher, but really he was only cool if you were a hard-core literary nerd who viewed a moonlighting poet as the epitome of hip. In the throes of my eating-disordered depression, he was also the only person I had been vaguely honest with about what was going on in my head. He felt safe—sardonic but kind. He was willing to care about me when I could not care about myself, but sprinkled our interactions with a dark wit that let me feel like I was keeping his concern at arm's length.

He'd left Lancaster for another job earlier that year, just after driving to Harrisburg in June to watch my last skating competition, after I was already alone and partnerless. When he came back to town in December and appeared abruptly late one night at the chain diner where I was working while couch surfing and living on the street, I did not tell him to mind his business. I did not lie and say everything was fine, as I might have done to so many other people. He was the one person I would listen to, and I ran to greet him in the diner lobby just after midnight, a backpack containing my entire life slung over one shoulder.

"What the fuck are you doing here?!" I demanded, after jumping up to hug him.

"Funny story," he said. "But do you really want me to tell you here in the middle of the diner?"

I agreed that I did not, so we left and spent most of the next seven hours talking on a stoop where I told him how bad I had let my life get. "That really doesn't sound healthy," he would interject from time to time in his usual understated way. I'd continue, and he'd jump in with an uncomfortable laugh, "That doesn't sound good either!"

But that is the version of events as he recalls it; I had downed an entire bottle of cough syrup during my shift, along with some uppers and a jar of nutmeg, because some internet forum told me if you ate enough nutmeg you could get high. Like so many others, that night was a blurry night—but it was the night I agreed to go to rehab. It had only been a few months of running wild, but the drifting, the homelessness, the itinerant bulimia, the fear, the underage sex work had all worn on me. I thought the drugs would help me forget about the future I lost, the one gilded in ice and bright spotlights. But they did not; even when I was high enough that I could not remember, somehow I did not forget.

So when Luke repeatedly suggested I get help, I did not offer much resistance. He dropped me off at my parents' house just after 7 A.M.—they'd been the ones who told him where I was in the first place. And the following day they drove me to an inpatient drug treatment center an hour away, up a small, forested mountain in the middle of Pennsylvania. There, along with a gaggle of other wayward teens, I found out about the world of institutionalized living. I learned to speak the language of recovery, and to talk about personal inventories and "coming to believe." I said the Serenity Prayer with the fervor of someone who needed saving, and went to the rehab church every Sunday, crying along during the parade of teary testimonials at the pulpit and promises from broken people aching to start over.

Institutional living actually meant more freedom than I'd had at home with my parents, and in some ways it was the closest to normal I'd ever been. My detox was pretty minimal since I hadn't really been a daily heroin user for all that long—and unlike what those high school drug classes lead you to believe, you do not really catch a physical habit the first time. Soon I made friends with the other girls: the seventeen-year-old who sold icy shards of meth in coffee cups when she worked as a barista, the problem drinker who claimed to be an heiress, the white girl from Philly who wore a "Hustler" bracelet everywhere she went. I got my hair cut short and spiky with a red streak, trying to perfect the slightly punk look my parents would have never allowed a year earlier. This was the new me: me without skating or drugs, living one day at a time. Entranced by the unbounded optimism of early sobriety, I bought into the hope and promise—but not quite enough, as it turned out.

After the ninety-day rehab, I was packed off to a remote halfway house in the countryside near Scranton where I spent my days working in a sheet-metal factory and nights sipping weak coffee in the nicotine-stained rooms of northern Pennsylvania AA meetings. In photos from my time there, I am always grinning, faking the happiness I wanted for myself. But the truth was I hated every minute of it. The daily counseling sessions were confrontational, and the only thing I remember from them besides the accusing voices was the counselor who told me I was at fault, that I'd been assaulted too many times to be the victim. Hers are words I still cannot forget. All the other women there were older, and most were court-mandated. We had little in common besides a penchant for making bad decisions, which I continued to do. I had a brief and regrettable fling with a married man. I pierced my own nose with a safety pin. I threw up until my cheeks grew puffy and my face looked like it belonged on someone twenty-five pounds heavier.

For all the missteps, I got at least one thing right: I managed to finish high school. Even though I'd missed the first semester running around on the street and the second semester trying to find myself in rehab, the academic Powers That Be agreed—after much negotiation with my parents—that I could still get my diploma. I had been so far ahead in academics that all I really had left to do to meet the graduation requirements was complete two classes: history and English. I finished them both as independent studies, then took the related AP exams in some stuffy classroom at a prep school in Scranton.

Almost immediately after I got out of the halfway house in August, I went to college, miraculously starting on time in the fall semester of 2002. Despite my dark times in Boston, I still delusionally wanted to go to an Ivy League school, which seemed to be such a mark of achievement in my family. But my parents—who were, crucially, financing it—insisted on a college with a sober living dorm, and Rutgers University was the closest.

The dorm in question was a roomy yellow house a good twenty-minute walk from the main campus. It looked like a modest frat house—but without any of the parties. It was co-ed, and we had a bigger age range than most college dorms, with at least a few guys in their late twenties. The dozen or so of us who lived there all went to AA meetings and had an assigned Rutgers drug counselor. I wanted to stay sober, or at least understood that I should want to. But I was still too volatile, and wanting a thing is not always enough.

I tried throwing myself into my schoolwork, studying constantly for calculus, epistemology, physics. I went to office hours and study groups, then posted up in the downstairs section of my favorite Lebanese-owned coffee shop on Easton Avenue, staying after midnight and chain-smoking over textbooks until the place closed. On the weekends, I coached at a local rink and volunteered to mentor exchange students, teaching them how to curse properly in English.

Almost desperately, I stayed busy. I got straight A's, but still I veered off track. Through my new sober friends, I met another girl in early recovery who seemed intent on veering off track, too. Like me, Katie had gotten into heroin young and cleaned up just in time for college. She was slim, with bright eyes and long sandy hair, and though she wasn't living in the sober dorm, she knew everyone there. It can't have been more than a couple months into my freshman year when she came up with a suggestion: We should be strippers. She'd seen a tiny classified ad in the student newspaper—which advertised everything from dishwashing to porn—and she'd already gotten the requisite clothes and shoes. It would be quick money, once a week.

I was game. More than anything, I did not want to be dependent on my parents for support, permission, or approval.

I wanted to hold the reins of my own life, despite my clear recent record of abysmal outcomes when I did so. My goals for independence were small and big, reasonable and unrealistic: I wanted to buy a cell phone. I wanted some tattoos. I wanted to buy bad coffee at midnight at shitty diners. I wanted a car, or at least a low-end motorcycle. Hell, I wanted to pay for school all by myself. Although I wouldn't qualify for financial aid given my parents' incomes, with a high enough paying job and a low enough state school tuition, I told myself this whole plan seemed vaguely possible. It was as if I'd found a daring life-hack: I wouldn't have to work forty hours a week to pay tuition, so I would still be able to balance work and school, and it was far edgier than clocking in and out of some student center gig.

Even at the shady spot Katie and I walked into—a dimly lit joint a few towns over, rumored to be run by the mob—I could pull in at least $200 a night. And, unlike when I had worked for Mary Jane, this was entirely legal. There were no cops or competing pimps or people threatening to sell me to a foreign country. It was just me, and I was in control. True, my friends in the sober house disapproved, as did the Rutgers drug counselor. But I moved out after the spring semester, now able to afford an apartment across from the cafe, as long as I split the rent with a roommate or two.

Over time, I expanded the horizons of my sex work: All-nude clubs. Fetish parties. Photo shoots. Videos. Escorting. Things just barely this side of legal. I told myself it was fun and empowering. And sometimes it was. But, eventually, it wasn't. Charging men for access to your sexuality is only empowering when they follow the rules, when they do not push the boundaries. When they do not remind you that, in the end, they are bigger, and older, and can call the shots. But ultimately that wasn't the biggest problem; the biggest problem was where it led. Or where I let it lead—back to darkness and decay.

And that was how, on a Saturday afternoon in mid-2003, I found myself tied up in the back room of a tidy brick row house in Philadelphia, a few feet away from The Dude. That was not really his name, but he looked just like Jeff Bridges's bearded, long-haired character from *The Big Lebowski*. He was taking pictures, stills he hoped to sell to a bondage website. The price per image was so slight—a dollar or two at best—that it was not really enough to justify the hassle or the expense of the two-hour train ride I'd taken to get there. But he was a laid-back, pot-smoking former social worker, and he made me feel safe in a way that was never a guarantee in this line of work. He would adjust the ties and chains and harnesses between shots, and we would chitchat about our lives, like friends over drinks. Or like I assumed they would have—I still wasn't drinking or getting high. It was probably during my second or third visit that he told me about a guy he knew who'd just gone to prison and left him with a shit-ton of coke to get rid of, but no customers to sell it to.

I had an idea: my roommate. He went by Teflon, and he was a science nerd who loved selling and doing drugs. He had freckles and a shock of red hair, and scattered across his body were tattooed formulas of things like speed and entropy and Heisenberg's uncertainty principle. He was brilliant, but impish and full of trouble: One time he broke his foot when he kicked a sign after doing a shot of adrenaline for fun. Another time he got chased home by a rival drug dealer he'd pissed off when he urinated in the guy's coke stash.

When I told him that we could drive to Philly for an ounce or two of coke, he was game. He just had to borrow a car and get ready. When he strolled in with a friend and a set of keys, he was dressed for business and toting a silver suitcase. I did not have to ask what was inside before he gleefully volunteered.

"Two bags of grass, seventy-five pellets of mescaline, five sheets of high-powered blotter acid, a salt shaker half-full of cocaine, a whole galaxy of multicolored upper, downers, screamers, laughers. Also, a quart of tequila, a quart of rum, a case of beer, a pint of raw ether, and two dozen amyls,'" he said, quoting the opening scene of *Fear and Loathing in Las Vegas*, when Hunter S. Thompson's flyswatter-wielding character introduces viewers to his briefcase drug stash in the middle of the desert.

"I had to substitute PCP for ether," Teflon added. "And I'm running out of cocaine, have sold some of the mescaline, and don't actually have amyls."

Not familiar with the drug culture staples, I missed the reference and stared at him blankly.

"See, the salt shaker is not half-full of cocaine, but once we get back, it will be."

He deeply enjoyed keeping his coke in a salt shaker and grinned at the thought. I don't know whether I smiled back, but I was buzzing, intoxicated by the underworld adventure that I could tell myself was for a worthy cause: financial independence. Plus, we weren't really hurting anyone, we thought; we were just a bunch of kids fucking around with some drugs. What could go wrong?

When we got back, Teflon immediately resold most of the ounce. Then, a slightly eccentric six-foot-tall Korean guy I knew from the coffee shop and his best friend—who looked just like Darius Rucker from Hootie and the Blowfish—said they wanted some coke, too, so I sold them the rest. Less than an hour after our trip, I'd gotten rid of the whole $800 ounce. Then Teflon wanted more, and Hootie's friend wanted more, and my other housemate wanted some.

Suddenly, I was a drug dealer.

I didn't see it that way at first, but once Teflon enthusiastically showed me the ropes, I realized I was good at it. The business part of it came naturally, like acing a math test but with illicit drugs instead of integrals. It helped that I was nonthreatening, and willing to take risks I shouldn't, to schmooze people I shouldn't, and endanger myself in ways I shouldn't. Now, it's hard to understand exactly what the fuck I was thinking, what lies I was telling myself to justify the conflicting lives I was leading. On the one hand, I was staying sober and had even started working a summer job at a genetics lab. On the other, I was working in a toxic world of shady New Jersey strip clubs and selling eight-balls of coke into the wee hours of the morning.

In our crappy apartment drug den, I mixed my lives together like a mad alchemist, decorating the walls with hand-drawn molecular diagrams of all the drugs I had for sale, the common prescriptions they might interact with, and the neurotransmitters involved. I was entranced by drug chemistry, and it became part of my sales schtick, pointing to my Sharpie-and-crayon sketches to demonstrate the difference between Adderall—pharmaceutical speed—and actual meth, and why those extra methyl groups made the drug stronger. It was as if I thought cloaking my illicit dealing in an academic veneer made it all okay. Plus, there was this: I just liked it. Looking back now, that feels like the worst part.

Not long after I started selling, I got arrested. Police stopped me, along with Katie and two dudes she knew after they'd all three come to pick me up from a shift at the strip club. I only had a small amount of drugs—a few grams of coke and weed—but when the cops searched my backpack, they found a treasure trove of stripper gear, which prompted some raised eyebrows and coy questions. My heart raced as I tried to gauge if I could flirt my way out of this, finally finding a practical application for the skills I picked up at my night job. One thing led to another, and by the end of the night, I was surfing porn with two cops on the stationhouse computer. Around dawn, they let me out ROR, free to walk away without paying bail. Eventually, a judge gave me probation, which I narrowly and miraculously completed despite the fact that I was continuing to commit crimes on a daily basis and had so little understanding of the legal system that I never really knew how close I was to more serious consequences. But if that light brush with the law could have been a warning, I ignored it.

Instead, I did meth. By that point—late 2003—I was coming up on two years clean, though I was very, very clearly a complete mess. It could have been any drug I tried, but meth was one I'd never fucked with before and when Zain from the cafe showed up at a friend's house with some high-quality glass and a pipe, I was interested. It was new, a checkbox on my list of self-destruction that I hadn't x'd out yet.

The pipe didn't look like anything I'd used to get high be-fore; it was a three-inch glass straw attached to a small glass sphere with a hole in it. It was fragile, and Zain kept it in his Burberry glasses case, pulling it out ceremoniously as he ex-plained how to use it and where to put the drugs. "You put the shard in here and melt it," he said, rapping out the words in quick cadence as he began to demonstrate. "You're not actually light-ing the meth itself on fire," he added. "You're inhaling the vapor like crack, not the smoke like pot." He sucked in sharply, as if to punctuate the sentence. Then, it was my turn. For the first few seconds, meth felt just like heroin, the same rush of euphoria taking over like a portal to another world. When that fleeting rapture faded, I was wide awake and productive instead of nod-ding out into a netherworld. It seemed like magic—but once I'd tried it, I realized I could no longer make any claims to sobriety. And if I couldn't say I was however-many months clean, then what was the point of abstaining from anything?

As a dealer, there were so many more substances at my dis-posal than before. Shrooms. Acid. Opium. Designer drugs. Pure psilocybin that Teflon ordered online from China. I would try them all, with one exception. I would not do heroin again. That would be my new line in the sand, and as long as I didn't do that, everything would be alright. I wouldn't really be giving in to the decay.

Chapter 10

On the first day of the New Year, we woke up to the sound of dogs, eager yips and barks out of place as they ricocheted down the hall and filled the cellblock air.

I narrowed my eyes, confused and suspicious of this noise from a past life floating by, an eerie artifact from the free world.

"What the fuck is that?"

No one had time to answer me before the door burst open and the shouting began: "Up against the wall! Ladies, up against the wall!"

There was a new sheriff in town—literally—and he wanted us all to know. It was nearly 9 A.M., so we'd finished breakfast and count and showers and most of the block had gone back to bed, making it the perfect time for a surprise raid to kick off day one of the new administration. A former small-time village police chief, the incoming sheriff had beat out his predecessor in the elections a few months earlier, a fact that I was absolutely unaware of at the time. Back then, it had no bearing on my life. I didn't even really know what a sheriff did.

Despite all my years of drug use, my privilege—as a white woman, as an Ivy League student—had helped shield me from these things. By twenty-six, I'd had so few brushes with the law that I didn't need to know that it was elected county sheriffs who usually ran jails, or that their personal preferences had the potential to shape and reshape daily life in the lockups they ran. A shift in administrations could mean a big change—or it could mean nothing.

In this case, eventually it meant changes in the food (no more vegetarian or lactose-free meals) and the medical care (no more Suboxone to help detoxing). But all that came later; on day one, it just meant raids on every cellblock. The sheriff and his jail chief strolled in behind the dogs, flashing smug grins while they looked on from the doorway as if they took joy in surprising us. Our hearts pounded, and we whispered our confusion to each other as we stood against the wall in various states of dress, unsure why this was happening or what it meant. Were we going to be shipped out? Locked in? Was someone getting new charges? Why were they throwing our things on the floor? The officer overseeing it all hollered at us to turn around and shut up, as if our words were contraband, too.

After pawing through everything we owned, they came up empty-handed and ran off as quickly as they'd come, leaving behind torn books and disheveled papers as a reminder of how little power we had in our lives. I don't think I fully realized that then: The first time, a ripped letter is just a ripped letter. The tenth time, it is a reminder that you do not have value in here, that you do not matter.

Later that day, my parents showed up for their first visit since my arrest. They'd driven the four hours from Lancaster to Ithaca in my dad's blue-gray minivan and arrived in town in time for the 2 P.M. slot. For me, seeing their faces from inside the jailhouse visiting room was both a welcome dash of familiarity and a novel source of humiliation. For them, it must have been disorienting as they submitted to pat searches and metal detectors just to see their daughter through the visiting room glass. But we did not talk about those things; there were no shouts, or tears, or apologies. We stuck to safer topics: my dog, my apartment, what to do with the vestiges of my life.

It was only an hour-long visit, but I could not wait for it to be over. It was not because I dreaded seeing them, or confronting the bitterness and regret that hung between us. That was all there, but my head was somewhere else: I was focused on Alex, dreaming of his dark hair and the bold colors of the fire and water tattoos on his forearms. My parents had spoken to him that day—probably for the first time ever—and said he was out of the hospital and waiting for me to call. I was elated, and as soon as the visit ended, I scrambled back to the block and dialed the number of the one person tethering me to my old life, the only one whose voice would not sag in disappointment when we spoke.

"Keri-Schmeri!" he singsonged into the phone. "I love you! You wouldn't fucking believe this shit."

Once again, he recounted the tale of the lost hours after my arrest, and his lost days in the hospital. He told me he planned to stay sober, and then we schemed a way for me to see him. The next visiting day was three long days away, and we didn't want to wait. So we decided to schedule a sad, secret tryst through the tinted jail glass. At 2 P.M. the next day, he would come by to pick up his ID and some of his other stuff I'd had on me when I got arrested. At the appointed hour, I would stand up on the bunk and peer out the window in the hope of catching a glimpse as he walked in. Maybe, for a minute, he'd be able to shout and wave from the sidewalk—but that would depend on which of the guards spotted him first.

Unlike in bigger or stricter jails, in Tompkins County we called a lot of officers by their first names. Sometimes they even made small talk with us when they were bored, sharing tantalizing details about their lives in the free world. I was fascinated with figuring out who these people with all the power *were*—and which ones would let us get away with tiny disobediences. There was Chuck, a notorious asshole who enjoyed confiscating books. Fred, who pretended not to see rule-breakers and talked a lot about farming. Judy, who would let dumb shit slide and openly hated her coworkers. Johnson, who was generally not observant and unironically said he was "livin' the dream" several times a day. If I talked to them enough, I hoped, maybe they would see me as a real person. The truth, which I only figured out much later, is that that is futile; guards are either willing to see inmates as people or they are not, and no amount of desperate small talk will change that, no matter how relaxed or how small the jail is.

There were only about forty guards in total, and at least five of them seemed like clones of the same tall, thirty-something white guy. It was one of them—Lee—who spotted Alex slinking off the sidewalk and ambling up to the brick jail wall, silently counting over seven windows until he found mine. Suddenly, Alex started shouting his adoration for me in Greek—*Se latrevo!*—and holding up a handwritten sign in English—I LOVE YOU! From inside, I banged on the window to let him know I was there, while Sam stood by the edge of the cell, playing lookout to make sure the sergeant didn't catch me standing on my bunk. I scrawled the words back on a yellow legal pad and pressed it up to the window, but Alex couldn't see it. Drawing close enough to the building that he was just a couple feet away from me, he kept shouting until he attracted attention—and I hastily ripped up my sign before the guards could come check my cell and take it as evidence of my disregard for the rules.

It all sounds so silly, but the risks were real. I could get locked in for days or written up. Alex could get banned from visits forever or arrested—which is almost what happened when Lee came marching out, red-faced and demanding he leave. Alex complied, but only after a heated exchange and the threat of a criminal charge.

"That guy is crazy," he griped later on the phone.

Predictably, I thought the whole dramatic rendezvous was romantic and further proof we were doing the right thing by getting married.

When I eventually told my parents about our plans, they quite reasonably thought it was a horrible idea and promptly said they'd cut me out of their will if I went through with it.

That only made me want it more.

It wasn't just about spite or drug-induced puppy love; there were practical reasons, too. Alex and I didn't know where I would end up—rehab, prison, or somewhere else altogether. But we knew that he was a felon, and we worried that his legal record could complicate getting approval for visits while I was still on the inside or for living together once I got out on parole. In either case, we thought getting married would help.

Doing something as basic as filling out official paperwork for a marriage can be absurdly complicated behind bars—but I was glad to obsess over it. Fighting a battle against red tape and bureaucracy felt easier than anything else I had going on in my life at that point, and was a welcome distraction. I papered the jail brass with written requests, and Alex pestered officials with phone calls—and eventually they approved a date and a time: the morning of Saturday, January 29, 2011. It felt like such a victory over both naysayers and red tape.

But the hardest part wasn't the paperwork. It was finding someone to perform the ceremony at the appointed time— and in the appointed place, the jail visiting room. All the local judges and several pastors refused. In the end the only person Alex could find—or the only one willing to perform a marriage ceremony in a county jail without meeting either of the concerned parties in advance—was allegedly a bishop from Syracuse still on felony probation for a sex crime. Or at least that was how Alex described him. I have no idea if Alex was being honest, about the bishop or anything else, and I completely missed the obvious red flag, as I had so many others.

First thing Saturday morning, my supposedly sober husband-to-be screeched into the jail parking lot, pulling his truck up diagonally across three spaces before strolling inside droopy-eyed.

The rushed 8 A.M. ceremony was set to take place across the shoulder-height visiting room glass, before the usual string of hurt girlfriends and disappointed mothers filtered in for the day. I wanted Sam to come, but the jail wouldn't allow it, so instead she brushed my hair and saw me off. The short guest list included only me, Alex, his father, his best friend, the probationer-pastor, and a jail captain, who got sentimental as he watched me pull out my handwritten vows.

"Oh, well, go on ahead and get over here," he said, tossing out both the jail decorum and the rules as he turned misty-eyed and motioned for me to climb over the glass.

Alex started sobbing as I read what I'd written, quoting heavily from a dozen different poets and—ridiculously—*The Maltese Falcon*. He gave me a plain 10K gold wedding band, the only ring permitted by the jail. Then, a short kiss before I hopped back over the glass to go get strip-searched and return to the cellblock, still giddy and gleeful.

That afternoon, while the other women were still at their visits, or sleeping away a cold Saturday afternoon, Sam and I prepped for a two-person game of jailhouse soccer, building a lumpy ball out of socks, checkers, toilet paper, and maxi pads. It wouldn't really roll, but we kicked it back and forth like it would as I breathlessly recounted the morning's ceremony for her and then fell silent.

"Sounds good, so what's wrong?" she asked, pushing the mess of toilet paper toward me with her foot.

"I think I'm reasonably certain that he was high."

"Shit, Ker, you would know. I mean, if anyone would know, you would know," she said.

"Who parks sideways like that? You saw how he parked."

She nodded, and I kicked the ball back, then continued: "He said he was tired, but he looked like he was nodding out."

It hurt to actually say it out loud. I felt guilty for doubting him, but I knew what high looked like. And I knew the lie he was selling—I'd repeated it so many times myself. It was almost insulting that he thought I wouldn't be able to tell.

I might have been angry—angry that he was using without me while I was stuck in jail, or that he was lying about it—but somehow I wasn't. I guess it wasn't terribly surprising, given the circumstances. Staying clean through chaos is hard, especially with no real support. I understood that. But what really stung was that he couldn't manage to stay sober on our wedding day, of all days. As far as I could tell, this was the first time he'd used again since my arrest. Why did he need to get high just to get married to me? What doubts or regrets was he harboring that were so big he couldn't do it sober?

In the end I told myself it didn't really matter: He still loved me. He'd even left plastic flowers wedged in the snow outside my cell window to prove it. And surely, this droopy-eyed nodding was only a one-time thing. He was probably just nervous and slipped up. And he probably only lied because he was embarrassed. He probably wouldn't do it again. And if it only happened once, I could overlook it and pretend to believe him. If it happened repeatedly, well, that would be a different matter.

Chapter 11

Ithaca, July 2007

It's the middle of July, but everything is frozen. I am hovering ninety-eight feet in the air. Time has stopped. I just jumped off a bridge, and I am about to die.

It wasn't one particular thing that brought me here this morning. It was a combination of things, years of things. Things that do not seem to be getting better. I moved to Ithaca six months ago, and I'm not making friends. My grandmother died, and I did not go to her funeral. I don't think I even feel guilty, though I know that I should. I have been fighting with my parents. I have failed all my classes. I hate the cold, the dark winter, and this tiny city in the middle of nowhere. My new boyfriend, Todd, is always angry, always yelling. After a shitty spring of smoking crack together, I am falling back into heroin.

We got in another 4 A.M. fight this morning, and he told me how useless I am, how much I do not matter. He sprays spittle like venom out of the corners of his mouth when he gets angry.

Go jump, he says. He probably doesn't really think I'll do it. I am and have always been quite stubborn, not prone to taking suggestions or advice. But in this case, he's only saying what I've already been thinking. And frankly, I could not agree more. I cannot ever undo all the things that I have done, the hopes I have squandered, the people I have hurt, the loved ones I have let down.

And I cannot seem to stop doing it.

Just like I cannot seem to stop doing drugs—but maybe I've never really tried that hard, either. Right around the time I smoked that first hit of meth back in New Jersey, I started dating Hootie. I was nineteen at the time, and he was fourteen years older than me, with a shaved head and a pointy goatee. He'd grown up in the New Jersey suburbs hanging out with eighties punk kids but had turned into a computer nerd who preferred Oxford shirts and khakis. He was my first long-term relationship, and we looked like an unlikely pair.

When we met at the Lebanese coffee shop during my freshman year at Rutgers, I was aggressively sleeping around with men, with women, with anyone who would have me. But he stopped me in my tracks. He'd just moved back from New York City and was living in a house on the edge of New Brunswick's Collegetown with his best friend, who was the heavier drug user of the two. For months they were the last stop on my drug delivery route. Every evening, I would swing by the hard-partying frat houses, meet up with the townie cokeheads, trek out to the apartments way down Hamilton, deliver to all the pothead students I knew along the way, and circle back to anyone who needed seconds. Then, I would show up at his house in the wee hours of the night, armed with a Pelican case full of drugs and ready to blow powdery white lines until the sun came up and I felt awful. Coke had all the energy of meth but none of the clarity, and the come-down was miserable. It was not my favorite drug—but I couldn't get enough of Hootie.

He knew all these normal-person things that I didn't. I'd spent my whole childhood in the bubble of an ice rink and could barely figure out how to turn on a TV. I'd never seen *Saturday Night Live*. I didn't understand his references to the Brat Pack or Ice Cube. I couldn't name a single neighborhood in New York City, and he'd lived there for years. He seemed to have an encyclopedic knowledge of pop culture, could program computers in several languages I'd never heard of, and always had clever-sounding hot takes on the latest congressional testimony on C-SPAN. He seemed so smart and worldly. I couldn't understand why he was interested in me, but I was entranced and addicted. He filled the hole in my life.

In a matter of months, we moved in together and pronounced ourselves engaged. I stopped the stripping and sundry sex work, more out of devotion to him than any specific request. Even though I was only sporadically talking to my own parents at that point, I met his mother, and we hit it off enough that I eventually got invited to the family reunion in Vegas. A prim Black woman in her sixties, Hootie's mom was a health nut who lived one town over—just close enough that she must have suspected something was wrong in our lives.

For three years, Hootie pitched in on my drug business as we hopscotched across New Brunswick from apartment to apartment, staying just long enough to raise suspicions from nosy neighbors and watchful landlords who wondered about the loud guests appearing at strange hours. "You work on Schedule D," Hootie quipped. "The *other* nine to five." We lived in so many different places, at one point I rented a second apartment to use as my "office." I could afford it; despite all the drug-soaked nights, I had managed to save enough money to pay my own rent and phone bill. I'd also bought a used motorcycle—procured by trading three eight-balls of coke—and stacked a few thousand dollars in the bank, still hoping that I could pay for college myself as well.

At first it seemed possible—but then, heroin happened. Again.

This time, it was so much worse. In Boston, I hadn't really done it long enough to catch a serious habit—so I'd never *truly* been dopesick, never felt the clammy chills and crawling skin that come with that particular brand of desperation.

I don't remember much about the first time I got high again—at least not the when or the how. I have a foggy memory of the who: a skinny, big-eyed girl with a clean needle, and a willingness to shoot me up. And the where: a dirty mattress in an empty apartment in the middle of New Brunswick. I think Hootie and I had probably gotten in some kind of fight, and I'd probably stormed out, deciding I was such a fuck-up that nothing mattered anyway. I don't know. But I do know this: Heroin was somehow, unbelievably, better than I remembered. It might have simply been that I was getting higher-quality drugs now. It might have been that I knew what to expect, what a good high would mean. It might have been that I missed the warmth spreading through my body limb by limb, pushing out the cold of reality like the heat of a campfire burning with the flames of oblivion. It might have been that I craved that moment when a solid nod sets in, and your mind begins to toggle between consciousness and waking dreams. Or it might have just been that part of me had been waiting for this for months, yearning to race faster into the self-destruction I seemed so sure I deserved.

At first, I thought I would hide it from Hootie. But he realized what was happening—and it didn't take long before he decided to join in. I did nothing to stop him. After all, his best friend had already been doing it for a few months, and I think I was just relieved to finally have a full partner in crime, someone I did not have to hide my sins from. Hootie started by snorting, then switched to shooting up like me. We got our drugs together, on trips to Elizabeth, deliveries from Newark, and train rides to Washington Heights.

I was working so hard at falling apart—but at the same time I was utterly in love and convinced that we would last forever. Hootie would just decay with me until we imploded like a supernova of wasted what-ifs and would-bes. Over the three years we spent together, our lives consistently deteriorated. I stopped going to school. He stopped holding down a job. We blew lines and shot up and spent down all the money I'd saved from the early days of dealing. Sold the motorcycle. Got high. Got evicted. Got high. Started fighting. Got high.

But there was one unexpected upside to that period: It was the first time I did not have an eating disorder. My past life as a skater was receding, as was the tightly controlled world I'd grown up in. Now, I had a sprawling social circle I'd never had before, and I was in love. And, of course, I was on drugs—enough of

them that finally I just didn't care about my weight. I remember
the moment I realized it, early in our relationship, and not long
after I'd started using again. It was a Friday night, late—and I
pulled a pint of Ben & Jerry's Peanut Butter Cup ice cream out
of the freezer and started eating it with a spoon, straight out of
the container. It felt strange, like I had just accidentally turned
off gravity. And even stranger: I did not feel guilty—or at least
not guilty enough to throw it up. I breathed a sigh of relief. I
couldn't remember the last time I'd kept down ice cream. Surely,
I told myself, this was a sign of growth and an indication I was
doing something right.

Then, in early 2006, Hootie broke up with me. I do not remember what reason he gave, but deep down I knew the truth:
He had finally come to his senses. He did not want to decay. He
did not want to be a heroin addict, he did not want to sell blow
all night, he did not want to live in perpetual fear of who or what
was at the door. He did not want to fill the hole in my life. He
had enough years on me to know this was all a bad idea, and that
it could not go on forever.

Still, for several months, we kept living together and using
together. I think maybe he felt sorry for me, or maybe he felt
like he didn't really have a normal life to return to anymore.
I was glad to maintain our living arrangement; I wasn't ready
to give up the ghost of him, of us. It was like Mark all over
again—but the loss was personal instead of professional. For
me, that was far easier, but I was still devastated. For a few years
there, I'd really believed Hootie was the one person who would
be there for me forever, the one constant throughout my chaos.

Within weeks, I started escorting again. Part of me hoped

Hootie would either beg me not to, or cry that I was hurting him—just like I felt he'd hurt me. Instead he said nothing when I slipped back into our bed after a long night in the wild. I was working for a fat, balding Italian guy in north Jersey, the same place I'd worked three years earlier, with the same depressed drivers and the same poor women. Every evening, a nondescript white guy named Joe would pick me up, and I'd hop in his beat-up car with whoever else was sharing my shift. On busy nights, we'd crisscross the entire state, from Jersey City to the Jersey Shore, stopping at suburbs and quiet beach towns I never visited for anything but paid sex.

We'd park at a Taco Bell or a White Castle and wait for calls to come in, both hoping that they would and that they wouldn't. In the front seat, Joe bitched about his sad life. On the radio, Akon purred in his mournful lilt about smacking asses and climbing into shadowy Lamborghini Gallardos, rhapsodizing about a classier version of our transactional existence.

Maybe go to my place and just kick it like Tae Bo, and possibly bend you over.

The pay was not great: We took home no more than $150 an hour—and it was often a very full hour. There were rollicking bachelor parties, adventurous couples looking for a third, and shy nerds who just wanted a woman that wouldn't say no. But that was only some of the calls. There were also the calls in fleabag motels with married men who cried the whole time. The calls with men who would demand head for an hour straight, unable to cum after all the coke they'd done—and threatening to call and complain if you didn't comply. The men who insisted on keeping you there, for eight or more hours, just staring in silence at your naked body without having sex and insisting they would not pay till they were good and ready to be done. The men so old they were incontinent and would soak the bed in urine, accidentally peeing on you and in you before asking for a blow job. The men who wanted you to put your hair in pigtails and pretend to be a child. The ones who wanted to pretend it was rape.

When I first started in the sex industry in Chinatown in 2001, I liked to tell myself I had the power because I was setting the rules, taking charge. I was taking the money from powerful men. But making other people pay to fund your acts of self-destruction is not taking charge, especially when it is not optional. And this time around it did not feel optional. When I'd escorted before, ostensibly it was just because I was trying to pay for things on my own—but if I had wanted to quit my stubborn quest for independence, I could. But now I had bills to pay, and a dope habit to feed. I was simply sick of being peed on, play-raped, asked to be a six-year-old, fucked till I was raw by strangers who were never satisfied. The things I'd hoped would be freeing were just crushing instead.

Of all people, it was Hootie's mom who showed me an out. We'd stayed friendly, and still saw each other on a pretty regular basis. One day, she was helping me move a broken computer—something I couldn't do alone without a car—and as I picked the clunky desktop out of her trunk, she asked: "Why don't you apply to school somewhere else? Start over." She had no idea how bad things had gotten, or what exactly I—or we—had done. She didn't know her son had followed me into heroin. Or if she did, she never said anything. Instead, she told me she'd help me however she could. On paper, I seemed like a strong transfer candidate—I'd gotten A's every semester I'd taken, and I was still young enough that it was easy to chalk up the various semesters I'd skipped to "finding myself" or some shit. The skating accomplishments were unique, my SAT scores were good, and between all the drug addiction I'd still eked out a few freelance writing and editing jobs during my time at Rutgers. There were no indications I was a drug dealer; even that first little arrest on the way back from the strip club didn't result in a lasting conviction, just a year or two of probation and a case dismissed.

"You could probably get into a good school," his mother said. "Maybe Middlebury or Tufts. Or maybe Cornell."

Yes, I thought. Cornell. Maybe she was right. Maybe this was my chance to try again, reinvent myself without drugs or skating. To pull something out of the wreckage, with a new life in a new city. Plus, Cornell was Ivy League. It was also where my mom had gone to school, and as much as I wanted to chart a different path, I knew that alumni connection would undoubtedly help. It could be the little leg up I needed to overcome my recent lack of accomplishments. To apply, all I needed was to take another SAT II—which I did, zonked on coke and heroin—then write an essay and fish up all the requisite letters and recommendations. Somehow, I pulled it off. The hardest part was coming up with the $65 application fee, because that was $65 I couldn't spend on heroin.

When a few months later I learned that I—miraculously—got in, my parents stepped up to pay. I would like to think they were proud, and maybe they were. But from their occasional visits, they must have known that things were not going well in my life, and I can imagine that they, like me, hoped a new school would be my chance to start fresh. Paying for it would ensure that I couldn't fuck up this chance before it began, or vanish into the foggy ether of upstate New York. Meanwhile, I still stubbornly wanted to pay for it myself and thought I could get enough loans and financial aid to do it alone, without needing to rely on them. That was delusional; even if it had been technically possible, I would not have been able to figure it out between the chaos of escorting, planning a move, and getting high—which I definitely needed to stop doing.

In a new city, far away from all my dealers, I wouldn't know where to get heroin. Or at least not at first, and not regularly enough to maintain. Although I wanted to start anew, I wasn't committed to the idea of staying sober forever. Yet I knew that—for logistical reasons, at least—I needed to make sure I didn't have a dope habit by the time I moved to Ithaca.

So I bought Suboxone to temper the withdrawals, and for two bleary weeks sat on a friend of a friend's couch in a nice North Jersey suburb and did not sleep. Twenty-four hours a day, I watched the only channel I could find that did not have any commercials: Turner Classic Movies. There were no bleating Serta sheep, no quacking Aflac ducks to bring me back to the present. There was no heroin, either.

Just after the start of 2007, I moved the two hundred miles north to Ithaca—a mid-year transfer in the dead of winter, with no friends and fresh off drugs. I was a few years older than my straightlaced classmates, but I moved into one of the

Gothic stone dorms at the bottom of Libe Slope, the grassy hill that separated the academic buildings from the rest of the town.

Briefly, I joined the Cornell figure skating team and found that I could still do most of my double jumps. But this wasn't my world anymore. I would never be an athlete in my prime, would never have triple jumps, could never spend forty-plus hours a week circling my frozen dreams. Instead, I was like a jealous lover; if skating could not be my everything, I did not want it at all. What I really wanted now was heroin. Not every day, I told myself—but just for an occasional release, a night with oblivion.

At first, I started taking weekend bus trips back to New Jersey, picking up bundles of dope and eight-balls of coke and getting so high I would spend the entire ride back in the Greyhound bathroom, puking my guts out. Some people might see projectile vomiting as a bad sign, but I knew better: It just meant that I'd done enough. It was on one of those trips back that I met a guy who knew a guy who sold drugs in town. The dealer's name was Todd, and he was a forty-something white guy with a limp. He was not cute or smart or even a decent person, but he looked funny if I ate enough mushrooms—which is exactly what we did the first time I met him, ostensibly just to pick up a few grams of weed. After I got the pot, I found out he had shrooms, and so I stayed at his house all night while we tripped and watched *Fear and Loathing in Las Vegas* on repeat.

Then, I just never left.

He knew where to get drugs, and we started selling together. And sleeping together. And dating. I wasn't even attracted to him. But by the end of the semester I was—once again—a drug dealer and daily user, of whatever powder, rock, or pill was in front of me. Crack was Todd's drug of choice, but once we started finding more accessible heroin, he gladly shot up with me. Since we didn't know a lot of dope dealers in Ithaca, and what we did find was overpriced and weak, we started making regular trips a couple hours south to Monticello, where he knew a guy on High Street who could get us good shit.

It was on a trip there that I overdosed for the first time, in a shitty motel room where we'd decided to post up for a few days and get high. I guess it was a good batch, and I didn't take into account my waning tolerance. One minute, I was walking across the room. Then I blinked. And I was naked and wet in the shower. In between, everything was black. I did not feel death coming. There was no underworld calling. Nothing dramatic. Just . . . nothing.

"Yo, I wasn't sure you was gonna make it," Todd said when I blinked back to life. We did not have NARCAN—the overdose-reversing drug wasn't readily available to street users at the time—so he'd handled it the old-school way, throwing me in a cold shower and shooting me up with salt in an effort to raise my blood pressure.

"Why am I in the shower?" I asked, confused.

"You OD'd dude! You fell out."

"No," I mumbled, "I just fell asleep for a minute."

"Keri, it was six hours."

I was incredulous—but the oblivion didn't scare me. Some people who do dope every day do not want to overdose. They want to escape reality, but not go to the actual underworld. I didn't care. My instincts for self-preservation had long been flimsy at best, and heroin and self-hate had dulled whatever was left. My brush with darkness did not at all deter me—but what did were the logistics of maintaining a heroin habit in a place as remote from the drug trade as Ithaca seemed in the spring of 2007. I just couldn't get enough dope to have the habit I wanted, and so I supplanted it with the drugs I could get— crack, powdered coke—even though they made me feel worse, edgy and angry every moment till they wore off.

By the time school let out, I'd already stopped attending. Despite all the drug use, this was actually a first. I had never outright skipped college classes before. I'd always dropped them in time, or simply taken the whole semester off if I knew I was too entrenched in drugs to pass. That was part of how I'd walked away from Rutgers with straight A's. And in my mind, those grades were key: As long as I was not failing my classes, I could always tell myself there was a chance it would be okay in the end. I was frequently not committed to living, and often wanted to just decay or implode. But I always told myself there was some escape valve as long as I still had the possibility of finishing school, of going back on the beaten path.

But when I failed my classes, that escape valve slammed shut.

Finally, I had nothing to lose. I moved out of the dorm and officially started living with Todd, who was subletting an attic apartment from a shrooms grower. The room was beautiful and airy but never quite cooled down. When I think of that place now, I only imagine crack and heat.

It was after a long night of both that I ended up on the side of the Stewart Avenue bridge over Cascadilla Creek, the span that connected my life in Collegetown to my life on campus. The drugs had worn off by that point, replaced by a hideous clarity. I'd gotten a ride there from another housemate's girl-friend who was on her way to work or something. She did not seem to care why I wanted a ride to "the tallest bridge near here." She did not ask questions. Maybe she thought my life was as worthless as I did.

I climbed out of the car and into the crisp morning air. After she pulled away, I threw one leg over the rail, still not entirely certain if I wanted to do this, not certain if this bridge was tall enough. But the rocks in the gorge below seemed so far away, sparkling under a thin film of water. The birds were out, the sun was up, and it seemed like a beautiful day to die.

In a lot of ways, this day was no worse than usual. But it was still bad, like so many of the other days that had come before it. And that was entirely my fault. I'd had so much in life, and I'd fucked it all up so thoroughly, so irrevocably. As I rolled through the outcomes in my head, I heard the sound of a police siren in the distance. It was coming my way, and I realized that some interfering do-gooder had called the cops. More than anything else, I absolutely did not want to deal with the police.

"Oh fuck no," I muttered into the wind.

And I jumped.

My life did not flash before me. I did not regret what I'd done, or worry about what would come next.

Instead, I admired the leaves. As I fell, I could see each blade and vein in sharp contrast, with a perfect vision I've never had. It was July, so I know the trees must have been green. But

I remember them as reds and oranges and yellows, the most vivid shades of a life I would never see again. It was an image so crisp, I was sure it would be my last.

And then I noticed: There was a breeze, but somehow the leaves were not moving.

Everything is frozen, I thought. Like I'm already dead.

Chapter 12

Tompkins County Jail, 2011

Do you know the two-letter word for a whirlwind in the Faroe Islands?

It's an "oe." That is true whether or not you're in jail. On the black-and-white grids of a crossword, an "ait" is always a small island. A rocky outcrop formed by weathering is always a "tor." Even when nothing else makes sense in life, a three-letter word for French goose is still an "oie."

Behind bars, getting my hands on the crossword was my favorite morning battle. There were three copies of the local newspaper delivered to the jail every day, paid for by excess funds from the wildly overpriced commissary. Those $1 ramens and $1.50 Reeses we grumbled about on our twice-weekly order days were what funded our shared copies of the *Ithaca Journal*, where we could find the news, the arrests, and—a little further back—the crossword.

But with eight cellblocks and four dorms to share the papers, there was no telling when I would get my hands on one. Sometimes, a pristine copy would plop onto the table next to breakfast. Sometimes, a torn-up mess with coffee stains and missing sections would show up after the 3 P.M. count. It all depended on the benevolence of whatever officer was working and their willingness to retrieve it from whatever dorm had tossed it aside for the day. Usually, papers passed from cellblock to cellblock with no more than a cursory glance. News of the outside world is just a reminder that there *is* an outside world, a place where life is continuing without you.

Before drugs and before prison, I had a distant history of crosswording, starting with obsessive puzzling binges in high school. When I was still skating, Tracey once pulled me aside for a heart-to-heart about how I needed to start eating—and stop coming to practice sleep-deprived from too much late-night crosswording. After midnight, once I'd finished my homework, I would sit on the green-carpeted floor of my bedroom, open up a book of *New York Times* crosswords, and grab a neon gel pen, a red felt tip, a mechanical pencil—whatever was handy. In jail we weren't allowed those things, so I did it all in blue ballpoint, making my corrections in ink.

It seemed that crosswords were the one thing I could get right when I'd so clearly fucked up everything else. I wasn't sure how to handle life without heroin, but I knew how to figure out the long answer on a Friday or catch the trick on a Thursday puzzle. In the clanging chaos of the cellblocks, here was a black-and-white world of numbers and letters that fit together perfectly, a place where I had all the answers.

The other kind of letters that ate up my days—my missives

Corrections in Ink I 133

to the free world—were a different matter. Letters meant relationships, and apologies, and they were harder to navigate. There were long, pouring-out-your-soul letters; short, I'm-lonely-please-write-me letters; drafted and redrafted letters making amends; and random, I'm-bored-how-are-you letters. Some were to people who were still in my life every day: Alex, my parents. Some were to people who'd once been close: Luke, Todd. Others were to people I hadn't spoken to in years, now-strangers who reached out when they heard of my arrest. My middle school piano teacher. My parents' pastor. Each new contact brought a new wave of shame—confirmation of yet *another* person who'd heard of my demise. But I always wrote back, oozing glee about how I was a changed woman, eager as a born-again ready to proselytize. I wrote hundreds of letters during my time behind bars, but one in particular stands out—not for its contents, but for what I was doing when I wrote it.

It was a slow afternoon a few months into my stay, and I was sitting at the metal table in the common room, scribbling away on a yellow legal pad when I looked up and realized the block was silent. The TV was muted and the cells were quiet, none of the usual clamor ricocheting off the metal bars. A few of the women were out for legal visits or at rec or medical appointments, but the rest were simply still. It took me a minute before I figured it out: everyone was high.

I already knew someone a couple cells down had been getting pills smuggled in; in the close quarters of a jail, it was impossible not to know such secrets. I'd seen her milling about glassy-eyed for days, and heard the whispered schemes wafting across the cellblock as interested parties conspired to get more.

A few weeks earlier, I might have been jealous. I might have wanted in. But now, I did not. For the first time in a long time, I was the only person in the room who was not on drugs—and it felt good. The realization popped into my head unexpectedly, materializing like an answer for nine down or ten across. A five-letter word for getting my shit together. Sober.

True, I'd already been saying for several weeks that I planned to stay off drugs after I got out. But everyone—or almost everyone—says that behind bars. Sky is blue, grass is green, and junkies in jail are gonna stay clean. Finally, though, I knew I meant it. As I watched women dozing and nodding around me, I could see the future playing out for them: They'd wake up tomorrow, feeling guilty about their one-night stands with Morpheus and promising themselves it would never happen again. Then they'd crawl out of their bunks to face another day of lying to their loved ones, of worrying about getting caught, of aching for more—and wishing all the while that they didn't. They were zooming, hands up in the air on a lurching roller coaster, a ride I'd just gotten off. And from where I stood on the ground, it looked rickety and unsafe, and I did not want to get back on.

But even though I was ready to get clean, my new husband was not. Sure, he said he was. He claimed he wanted to stay with me, and to stay off drugs, or at least off hard drugs. But ever since Alex had shown up droopy-eyed on our wedding day, I'd had my doubts. Sometimes during visits he mumbled stream-of-consciousness monologues about celebrity encounters. Other times he did not show up at all. He briefly lost our marriage certificate, then reported back with a colorful tale about dumpster-diving in his pajamas to find it. At one point, he came in so high even the guards noticed and threatened to ban him if it happened again. He denied it with an indignant burst of obscenities—just like he did a few weeks later when he arrived so faded that his eyes were closed most of the visit. After I called him on it, he brazenly claimed they were open even though I could see quite fucking clearly that they were not.

Finally, he showed up with what I was quite sure were fresh track marks, angry and red in the crook of his right arm. I demanded to know: "What's that?"

He looked down, apparently perplexed.

"On your arm," I added.

"Keri-Schmeri, it's so crazy honey!" He always crooned his deceptions in the slight singsong of his cutesy voice, the best voice for telling a lie.

"I actually got that from a pot plant! You see, I was helping my friend take care of his plants, and I fell into one! It cut me all up!"

Perhaps it goes without saying, but pot plants do not leave track marks. And these were unmistakable, all positioned on the best veins for shooting up. But because I'd spent weeks doing my stubborn best to alienate my parents by getting married, it seemed that Alex was the only weight tethering me to the outside world. I needed to believe him because without him I would float away into the void of the criminal justice system and disappear. But more importantly, I needed to believe him because I needed to believe that people could change—not for him, but for me. If I did not believe that he could change, how could I expect people to think that I could? Eventually, I told myself, he would come clean. He would get sober. I would get out, and we would have our happily ever after as two changed people. I believed this with the certainty of a wrong answer inked into a crossword, a truth that fits until suddenly it doesn't.

While I struggled to work out these clues, life moved on. The monotonous days turned into monotonous weeks—time was either moving quickly or not at all. I started taking GED classes, just to get out of the cellblock. I went to AA, and showed up for church in the jail visiting room. I ran my four miles every day, and spent as much time sleeping as I possibly could. I dreamed of Charlotte, and skating, and life in the real world beyond the walls. Women came and left, and I got new cellmates, found new friends and frenemies, and met new crosswording partners.

One turned out to be Lee, the generic white guy guard who'd yelled at Alex outside the jail that time. For weeks, I'd resented him for that encounter—even though he was clearly not the one behaving unreasonably. Then one day I went out for rec and spotted three intricately sculpted pyramids in the six-foot snowbank at the edge of the blacktop. One was an Aztec pyramid, with crisply cornered steps. Another was Giza, with three tiny pyramids in front just like the Egyptian archaeological site. The third was half-formed, a work-in-progress.

I was intrigued.

"Who did those? Is that a ziggurat?"

As Lee glanced sideways at the snow mounds next to him, his face flushed bright red—his most signature move.

"Uh, me. I, um, see, I got bored out here. And, see, that's an Aztec one and that's Egyptian, and I don't know, that might be a landing spot for extraterrestrials. I'm still figuring that out."

He laughed nervously and pushed up his glasses. There were only fifteen minutes left in rec, and we spent most of them discussing his snow castles and whether he could make the third one into Mount Rushmore or the sphinx. It was an unduly satisfying conversation, quirky but cogent—a rare exchange that could have happened in the free world.

Unlike a lot of his coworkers, Lee was a nerd at heart. Though he liked guns and blink-182, he also liked video games and crosswords. When he worked, he would linger in the cellblock, offering me possible seven-letter words to fill in the blanks and occasionally leaving to clandestinely Google a hint. Sometimes we would chitchat, and once he strayed from protocol to show me a picture of his new dog. I wouldn't say he treated me entirely like a normal person, but he at least treated me like a human—a feat so rare in jail that I treasured it.

Another of my crosswording partners was a woman named Jenny, a parole violator who was about a decade older than me. In the course of a single drug charge, she'd done probation, rehab, probation, more rehab, probation, prison, and finally parole. She was smart and sarcastic, and she knew all the tricks to doing time—what to let slide, and what to get loud about. She was, as we put it, someone who knew "how to jail." Every day when she got up—which wasn't till at least 3 P.M., to avoid the daytime chaos—we sat together and puzzled out four-letter words for aide, and hoosegow, and the capital of Norway, while I pumped her for answers to all of my questions about my next step in life: going to prison.

What is intake like? What do they have on commissary? Is there a gym? Can I get this cavity fixed in my molar? Do they give you free tampons? How soon is parole? She told me everything, in patient, painstaking detail so I could commit it all to memory. But the truth was that, even from jail, prison was a world that I could not quite imagine, and her tales from upstate sounded more like spooky stories around a campfire than real-world advice I could use.

"It's like a whole other language they speak up there, okay?" she said. "Like if they say somebody's out for your life, it means they're trying to get you put in Keep Lock."

I had to ask what that was.

"It's basically like one kind of solitary," she told me. Apparently there were multiple kinds—and ending up in any one of them could keep you from going home on time.

"See, don't tell people when you're getting out or they can try to take your date," she added. I did not know the phrase, but the meaning seemed clear: If people knew you were scheduled for release, they might try to get you in trouble out of spite so that you could not go home. I did not understand how they would do this and was not sure whether she was entirely serious. But tucked among her olio of unsettling tales, there was a snippet of hope. It was called shock camp.

Jenny had never been to shock, but upstate she'd run into enough women who'd flunked out of it to tell me the basics. Shock camp was—and still is—a military-style drug treatment program in prison. If you got sent there after intake, they would shave your head almost bald and you would spend the next six months doing push-ups, running laps, cleaning toilets, shoveling snow with a spoon, and getting yelled at by drill instructors. The only books you could have were self-help, and you could only call home once every other week. You had to eat your meals in three minutes or they'd make you dump the extra food in your pockets, fistfuls of wet mush marinating in your uniform. I did not understand how this counted as treatment and thought it sounded awful except for this: If you made it through, you got to go home early. You did not have to stay for the rest of your sentence.

"I mean, like, you could probably do it," she told me. "You run all the time anyway."

But the trick was getting in, she explained. Sometimes a judge might order it as part of your sentence—but usually not. Instead, you'd have to hope that when you showed up at prison on day one, they would decide you were a good candidate for their horrible program. You needed to have a nonviolent crime, no more than three years left on your sentence, and be considered medically capable—no broken limbs or debilitating illnesses. If you were on any mental health meds, supposedly you needed to go off them. I was skeptical of that claim, but I totally believed Jenny when she told me this: Even if you met all the criteria and begged to go, it was not a guarantee. Nothing was a guarantee behind bars. But this was a possibility, and the thing I needed to keep moving forward. Steeling myself for several years in prison seemed unimaginable. But steeling myself for six more months? That I could do.

And so I obsessed, fixating on the slim possibility of shock as I jogged my slow laps back and forth across the cellblock, telling myself I was training for the thing that would set me free. This was what I dreamed of now—not life on the outside, but my future behind bars. A little bit more every day, jail was becoming my world, like a long, late afternoon shadow slowly pushing back the light. When I got news from beyond the beige walls, it was seldom good.

At the end of March, I found out that Cornell officials wanted to do more than just ban me from campus: They were talking about an indefinite suspension, or an outright expulsion. When my parents broke the news during a Saturday afternoon visit I was, somehow, surprised. The details weren't clear yet, but my dad told me that if I agreed to a suspension, I'd probably be able to reapply in five years—though whether they'd really let me back in was an open question. If I didn't agree, the school would just kick me out altogether.

Out of everything I had lost, and everything I would lose, this was the one thing I could not handle—and I was baffled and bitter at the idea that the university would punish me for something that didn't even happen on campus. *I'm already going to prison,* I thought. *Isn't that enough?*

For the rest of the hour, I kept it together in front of the other inmates and families crowded around the visiting room table. But as soon as I made it into the quiet of the window-less strip-search room, I broke down, sobbing as I took off my clothes under the watchful gaze of a guard whose eyes filled with disgust and pity. Tears ran down my cheeks as I squatted and coughed. My eyes turned red, my face grew puffy. And I did not care. Something inside had burst, and I was inconsolable. Suddenly, it all seemed so real. Without drugs to shield me from reality, I felt the sharp corners of my grief—not just for my lost degree, but for everything.

For several days, I did almost nothing but cry.

On some level it was absurd. I'd been less distraught at my initial arrest, shed fewer tears over my disintegrating marriage, and been less consumed with worry over the likelihood of going to prison for a long time. But this particular failure felt like a sign, and unlike so much else, it was a sign in a language I understood. Throughout all my years of getting high, my ability to stay in school—or at least avoid outright expulsion—was my measuring stick. If I could pull off passing some classes, then my life wasn't really that bad. If I could manage to graduate, then I was not a total waste. But now I was.

"I've lost everything I've ever worked for in my life, and I'm technically not even human—I'm county property, soon to be state property," I wrote in my journal, my acerbic words only hinting at the darkness lurking below the surface. Since my arrest, I'd had bouts of light—of hope and remorse. Eventually they would take over. Eventually, I would realize everything could have been much worse. If I'd been in a more conservative county. If police knew about even half the shit I did. If I'd been caught a few years earlier, when the laws were harsher. If I already had a record and qualified for a longer sentence. If I'd been Black and automatically viewed as more suspicious. But in that moment I saw none of that as I floated in a sea of aggrieved entitlement. On the inside I was dark and detestable; on the outside I was a well of tears and self-pity, a six-letter word for fractured.

Broken.

Chapter 13

I am handcuffed to a chair and crying hysterically. It is 6 A.M., the dog is whining, the house is destroyed, and there is no more heroin.

Instead, there are police. Their radios cut through the cold winter air, and their cherry lights fill up the night sky, flashing red and blue like neon signs advertising the end of the world.

This is a raid.

It started a few hours ago, when a small army in tactical gear burst into our apartment on Linden Avenue, breaking the door with their battering ram and staining the walls with the black smoke of their flash-bang grenades.

My boyfriend, Todd, was already asleep in the bedroom; he'd done his last shot sometime before midnight. But I stayed up till the witching hours finishing my schoolwork before slamming the last four bags of dope in the whole house. I was just settling into my high when the air exploded around me. For a terrifying second, I thought I had somehow nodded straight into a war zone.

My ears still ringing, the cops cuffed me to a chair in the kitchen and took Todd out to wait in the car, where I could hear him cursing and carrying on. For the next several hours, the SWAT team pawed through everything we owned, dumping the entire contents of our apartment into a single mountain in the bedroom. They found empty baggies on the floor. Rolled up bills in the couch. A wad of cash on the counter. Scales and needles and prescriptions and spoons stashed in unexpected places. At one point, they scrolled through Todd's phone and found pictures of dope he'd brazenly documented from past drug runs.

"This," one of the cops said, showing me one of the pictures as I cried in the kitchen. "Do you know where this is? This is what we're looking for."

No shit, Sherlock.

I put my sobbing on pause for a minute to shake my head before falling back into jittery tears of dread. I could not shake the fear that had settled in my chest when they'd burst through the door with their guns and chaos. Now a different fear had moved in: For the first time, the possibility of spending years in prison actually felt real, at least for the moment.

But it was fleeting. Sometime after dawn, the men—and one woman—in black abruptly gave up and swooped out, leaving the apartment a wreck and taking with them nothing but the $1,100 from the counter. My terrors dissipated, like a nightmare in the sunlight.

Afterward, I was far less shaken than I should have been. Part of me had been expecting that police raid for some time and was almost surprised they hadn't closed in sooner. Looking back, I suspect that if I were Black, poor, or not a Cornell student, maybe they would have. And I must have already been on their radar. In the two years since I'd moved from New Jersey, I'd become a known entity in town, one of a few dozen shadowy figures in a druggie netherworld. During my first few months in Ithaca back in 2007, I'd flitted around the edges of that world looking for a way in. After I jumped off the bridge that summer, I found it.

The drop was a ninety-eight-foot fall, police later told me. But I landed feet first and slid along a flat rock, wet and slippery under a quarter inch of gorge water. I reached down and felt the moss below the surface, checking that it was real before I let the disappointment wash over me. *Goddammit. How did I fuck this up?* I paused for a minute and then—improbably—stood up. The red-haired cop at the top of the bridge behind me shouted that I should sit down and wait for help.

Without even turning around to look, I gave him the finger. *Fuck you. Fuck everything.*

As I trudged to the edge of the gorge, the world around me started to fade, and I sat down. After that, my memories are hazy. I know paramedics showed up, and there was an ambulance. Then a helicopter. And in the end, I spent a few days in a hospital in Elmira, emerging with nothing more than a few fractured vertebrae, some broken ribs, a clamshell back brace, and a cornucopia of new pills—a regular supply of uppers and downers I could trade for better drugs, or mix and match for a good time.

When I got back to our attic apartment in Ithaca after leaving the hospital, Todd made probably the only good suggestion of our entire relationship: He insisted I get a pet, hoping that an animal to care for would be enough to keep me from trying to kill myself again. I was reluctant. We didn't seem responsible enough to keep much of anything alive, so I feared this would end badly. But a few days later, during a trip to Walmart, I spotted a woman in line next to me with a bag of kitty litter. On a whim, I asked: "Do you have an extra cat to spare?"

She did not. But, she said, her friend had a dog that he planned to take to the pound if no one adopted her by the end of the weekend. Two days later, a pothead cabdriver named Frankie took us out to the country for the pickup. On the way, I dreamed of possible names, bad ideas like "I Don't Know" and "Guess." But the skittish pup we brought home already had a name: Charlotte.

She was a greyhound and black Lab mix with hints of white around her nose that made her look older than she really was. The first day I got her she tried to bolt, slipping out the door and hightailing it down the road in the direction she'd come from. Panicked, I ran after her in my back brace, half-dressed and screaming her name in terror. "Charlotte! Charlotte!" *I can't let this dog die in less than twenty-four hours,* I thought. *What kind of fuck-up does that?* But she heard the hollering, stopped dead in the middle of State Street, and turned around to look at me as if she had suddenly just realized I was her human.

After that, we were inseparable—though our first few months together were spent largely in my bed, waiting for my back to heal. Because I'd failed two classes during my abysmal first semester, Cornell put me on academic probation and forced me to take the school year off, ostensibly to get my shit together.

But it's not like jumping off a bridge gave me some clarity or knocked any sense into me; I was still the same broken person, just now with a back brace and a prescription for morphine. People who knew what had happened—which, through the grapevine and one local news brief, was almost everyone— would tell me how lucky I was, asking, "Aren't you so *glad* you lived?" I never knew how to answer them. Sometimes I openly scoffed, sometimes I agreed and changed the topic. Just because my survival seemed miraculous did not mean that I had to appreciate it. And while I was not still actively trying to kill myself, I was not exactly trying to live, either. I was just drifting, like debris floating down a gorge stream.

Accordingly, I fucked around my entire year off. I watched pirated TV shows and bootleg movies. Some of them were newer: *The Wire, The Office.* Some of them were old, the sorts of flicks I'd seen on Turner Classic Movies while detoxing in New Jersey: *A Clockwork Orange, Rear Window, Notorious.* I did bong hits, and crack hits, and white lines, and brown shots. I assiduously wormed my way into the Ithaca drug scene, lingering late at hippie apartments inhabited by people with names like Dirty and Moon, who reeked of patchouli oil and oniony heroin sweat. I got aggressively high, again and again. And, for once, I didn't feel guilty about it. My injuries gave the nagging voice inside me an obvious out: Of *course* I wasn't in school or working. I couldn't be. My back was broken.

By the time my bones healed, I had fully reestablished a heroin habit, now buttressed by a rainbow collection of pills and the occasional hit of crack. But to get back into Cornell, I needed to show the university that I'd done something with my year off. So I started taking easy-A community college classes and working at a basement bar in Collegetown. It wasn't much, but combined with a heartfelt personal essay and some undeserved recommendation letters, it was enough to get me back in.

When I returned to school in the fall of 2008, the stage seemed set for disaster. But, improbably, I got straight A's. I joined the student newspaper, spending my nights proofreading features and going to student assembly meetings—then snorting lines in the bathroom as I struggled to meet print deadline. I pulled meth-fueled all-nighters to write papers on Shakespeare, gave presentations about Alfred Hitchcock's films while on smack, took nineteenth-century English literature exams while dopesick. The work I did was solid, but I offered increasingly bizarre excuses and descriptions of actual crises to explain my absences and perpetual lateness: *My angry boyfriend threw soda at my computer!* (True.) *I was in the hospital!* (False.) *I didn't know I was pregnant and had an unexpected and painful miscarriage!* (True.) *I couldn't find my dog!* (False.)

Always, it seemed, I slid along by the skin of my teeth. I have to believe that people knew, or at least had an idea, that something was off when I turned up to office hours or student newspaper meetings with a scabby face, greasy hair, and the occasional black eye. But this was an Ivy League school, and even when my professors or fellow students suspected a problem, they couldn't have guessed how dark things had gotten. Years later, I went back and started asking people about it. One kid said nobody knew I was on smack. Another said everybody did. They said I seemed troubled but still nice. Altered, but shockingly articulate. Intense, but defeated.

When I think back on those times now, it feels as if I am wading into a black lake, Woolf-like and weighted down by stones of shame. It is not one specific thing that formed this lake—but each bad act is another drop of water adding to the darkness. Some drops are small: Disappearing to shoot up in the bathroom while my parents visited. *Drop.* Coming to class so high I scared the other kids. *Drop.*

But some drops are bigger: Standing by idly while Todd robbed a guy, punching him till he handed over the drugs in his shoe. *Drop. Drop.* Running away scared when he and some three-hundred-pound biker held one of my best friends hostage for three hours, all over $60. *Drop drop drop.*

And some are not drops at all but buckets: Walking in on my boyfriend having sex with my friend as she slipped in and out of consciousness. *Splash.*

We were promiscuous, in an unofficially open relationship, so the fact that he was having sex with someone else was not unusual. The fact that she seemed unconscious was. Afterward, she said it was not rape. She said she was high and confused. She had been in a dreamland, lounging on a warm beach, interrupted periodically by jolts of reality—and she couldn't remember if she'd said no. I don't know if she really believed that. But I knew that I blamed myself for letting it happen. For not taking better care of her. For not coming home sooner. For not breaking up with him afterward or even really calling him out on it. But in my mind, I couldn't: I wanted to keep getting high, and I needed my partner in crime for that. It's not that I couldn't get drugs on my own, it's just that I knew feeding an addiction worked better as a two-person operation. I did not want to go solo, no matter who got hurt.

Even if I did not notice the water rising around me, there were plenty of red flags waving in full view, and I ignored them, too—all these run-of-the-mill risks of addiction. There was the time we got robbed at gun-point. And the time we got robbed at bat-point. The time I almost lost my arm because it got so infected from shooting up. The stand-off with police when someone called with a noise complaint, and Todd refused to come out until they gave up and went away. Through it all, our lives grew steadily more desperate. Our habits grew bigger and bigger. Scheming to get high took up more and more of our lives, and we were broke more and more often.

We moved so much during our time together that we were basically migratory—I can count at least ten apartments in the three years we were together. Sometimes we just took short sublets, sometimes the landlords ordered us to leave, and sometimes we just could not pay rent. We were rarely outright homeless, though; during the semesters that I was in school, my parents took care of rent and tuition. They couldn't decide for sure whether I was sober, like I claimed, or whether I was actually getting high and they were unwittingly enabling me. Looking back, I don't think it mattered whether that was enabling—I think it saved my life. School was my last, tenuous connection to any belief in my own future. Without it, I would not have found much reason to live. They never said it, but I think they realized that—just like they probably realized that paying for my apartment was the only way they'd have any idea where I was living or what I was doing.

Even when Todd and I were too broke to eat, every one of our trashy apartments had a flat-screen TV, usually fenced from Walmart and paid for with crack cocaine. We watched *True Blood* and *The Office* and *Community*, all the hit shows of the late aughts. Their theme songs were the soundtrack of our drugging, our nodding out, our counting down the seconds until the connection arrived with more. But in all the hours we wasted in front of a stolen screen, there is one thing I know we did not see: We did not watch the Olympics in 2010, the year that Mark made it.

I don't remember how I felt at the time, my immediate first reaction to finding out that he qualified. I think I must have been jealous—although maybe that's actually not quite the right word. There were also hints of loss and glitters of pride. Had I been more sober, I might have felt some self-recrimination or regret, especially in the quiet moments, at midnight or 3 A.M. when I was inexplicably awake and the cops were not crashing through the front door. But I was almost never sober. I was high, and broken, and my life was in such shambles that even regret seemed above me. Still, it was impossible not to dwell on the bittersweet thought: It could have been me. If I'd had one or two more jumps, been a little bit thinner, worked a little bit harder, been a little bit less of a head case.

Instead, it was Amanda, a beautiful Filipina woman just five months younger than me, with graceful extensions and a life that was not falling apart at the seams. For the free skate—the event that mattered—she and Mark wore blue and skated to Rachmaninoff. The world watched as they opened with a split triple twist and side-by-side triple toes. Then there was a throw triple Lutz, and a big, beautiful throw triple loop. She fell out of the side-by-side double Axels, but it was still a solid skate. They got 171 points, and one commentator noted that "no one" had enjoyed the Olympic experience more.

Breathing heavy, they took their bows from center ice and came in tenth overall.

Ten months and four days later, I got arrested.

Chapter 14

The little things matter when you are in jail. In part, that's because the big things don't exist. There are no concerns about getting fired or being evicted or making it to your grandmother's funeral. None of that's happening. So many of the tough moments in life, the decisions you have to navigate—you suddenly can't.

Sure, there are some things—big things—to consider: You can decide to stay sober, or not. You can take a plea deal, or go to trial. But most of the time, in the wan day-to-day of cellblock life, nothing important happens. So instead, you focus on the small stuff.

Sometimes that means heated fights over the TV. Sometimes it means repeatedly filing grievances about complaints you know no one will ever address, like why there is always hair in the food. And sometimes it means paying obsessive attention to beauty rites from when you were still home and free: makeup, eyebrows, hair. Stripped of our agency in life, we found these rituals were one of the few outlets of self-expression we had left, rare vestiges of identity that extended beyond our neon-orange uniforms and criminal charges.

But each bold stroke of makeup was also something else: a painted symbol of rebellion. A fuck-you to the system. That's because in county jail, makeup wasn't allowed. We couldn't buy it on the commissary like in prisons and our families couldn't bring it in to us—so we made it ourselves.

Every cellblock had sets of colored pencils, some swiped from the GED room but most purchased from the commissary and left behind by past occupants. In the women's blocks, every set was missing certain colors: brown, black, blue, sometimes purple. All the prime makeup-making shades were hiding in someone's cell, secreted away for personal use.

On visiting days, or sometimes just to dress up for the fuck of it, we'd heat up water in the microwave, getting it as close to boiling as we could. Then we'd stand in front of the metal faux mirrors in our cells and daintily dip the tips of the pencils in the hot water and drag them across our eyelids so hard it hurt. But the outcome was more dependent on the brand of pencil than the skill of the person holding it. Even in the best-case scenario, the result looked like face paint done by an eleven-year-old. Less desirable outcomes resembled clown makeup, caked on and out of control.

Jailhouse mascara wasn't much better, though the process required a little more preparation:

Step one: Break apart a black pen and pour the ink into
    a bowl.

Step two: Mix in toothpaste.

Step three: Somehow spread this minty fresh mess onto
    your eyelashes.

Step four: Remember this is not waterproof, and what-
    ever you do, do not cry all day.

We had other tricks: making blush out of FireBall candies, threading eyebrows with strings from our uniforms, mixing lip gloss out of Crystal Light and Vaseline, giving painstaking haircuts with the jail's one set of toenail clippers. I watched, but usually did not join in. To me, dressing up just felt like a reminder of how little there was to dress up for.

Plus, my primary obsession was not in the present; it was in the future, where I'd hung all my hopes on the possibility of shock camp. For that, I told myself, I needed to prepare. While that meant running, it also meant steeling myself for weeks without phones or visits, and getting used to the idea of a flinty-faced prison guard shaving my head nearly bald. To deal with the former, I spent hours and hours pre-writing letters to all the people I cared about, then folding them into stamped envelopes and handing them over to Sam to mail whenever I got whisked off to the Big House.

To deal with the latter, I decided to dread my hair. It was not because I thought it was cool or because it would look good. In fact, I was pretty sure I might fuck it up and have to lop it all off. But if I did, at least the loss would be on my terms.

Unfortunately, I did not know the first thing about dreadlocks, which I mistakenly thought would be low-maintenance. I also did not know the first thing about cultural appropriation, which was not even something in my vocabulary. I'd like to think that I would have understood if someone explained how a hairstyle could be yet another example of white people stealing things from Black and brown people. But public debates about rappers wearing Native headdresses or white singers wearing cornrows to look edgy or cool were still a few years off, and I was ignorant and self-absorbed. To me, it seemed like an easy hippie hairstyle that would let me feel like I was in control.

I was so wrong.

In the free world, one of the ways white people form dreadlocks in straight hair is by sectioning it off, then twisting, ripping, and sometimes crocheting each baby dread until it locks up. It's a process that can take hours—with the help of some tools and maybe some beeswax. I didn't have any of those in jail; all I had was time, and half a dozen women bored enough to help.

Figuring out by trial and error how to dread my slippery hair became a group activity for a handful of interested parties who found it preferable to sleeping all day. We tried rubbing my hair with socks, braiding it, backcombing it, letting it get dirty. We soaked it with every hair product available on the commissary, from gel to Blue Magic hair grease. We tried deodorant flakes, smuggled-in beeswax, and melted crayons. Eventually, a "helpful" guard suggested I try strawberry jelly, which she claimed she'd seen one of the men use.

Unfortunately it was not as effective as she led me to believe. But in the end—after dozens of hours of twisting and greasing—some combination of products and procedures worked. It seemed, for a bit, like we had accomplished something together, a messy act of defiance. Yet despite her love of defiance, there was one person who did not help: Sam. She was boarded out to another county the whole time and didn't see the result until she walked back in the cellblock one day, lugging the plastic bins of her belongings. As soon as she saw me, she lamented, "Ker! What happened to your head!? It looks horrible!"

She was not wrong. But I didn't care. It was one part a tiny proof that I could reimagine myself, one part my usual masochist tendencies toward destruction, and two parts a fuck-you to the system. But when you are in jail, all the fuck-yous in the world don't change the fact that you cannot win and you have no power.

On Friday, April 29, the female cellblocks were—again—at capacity. We knew that if anyone new showed up, people were going to get boarded. And sure enough, late that night a new girl arrived in booking. My bunkie at the time, a tattooed military vet named Stephanie Brouwer, was nervous. But this was the one time I thought for certain I would be safe because I had an upcoming court date: I was scheduled for sentencing the first week of May. If they shipped me an hour and a half away now, they'd just have to come pick me up again in a few days. Surely, I thought, this time I could breathe easy. For once I did not panic.

Just after we locked in for the night, a guard popped open the thick cellblock door with a heavy thunk and shouted:

"Blakinger! Brouwer! Pack up!" My hands shook as I threw everything I owned into blue plastic bins to leave behind in Tompkins County. We did not know where we were headed, only that we would be starting over as strangers, with nothing. After whispering goodbyes through the cell bars, we left our friends, and a guard led us to the holding cell to wait next to the vomit-caked shower stall that had greeted me on my first day.

We didn't get into the Chenango County Jail until 2:30 A.M., in part because the guards got lost on the way, while we bounced around in the back of the van, shackled in the dark. No one could see us when we finally gave in and cried—or when our tears and lack of sleep turned into delirious excitement.

"Steph, they have fucking soda on the commissary there," I remembered suddenly. "You know, like Jenny said—actual bubbly, caffeinated soda!"

Our sniffles dissolved into hysterical laughter.

"And it's two floors," she hissed back. "There are stairs! Not on the commissary, duh. I'm so excited to walk up fucking stairs!"

Punch-drunk on panic, we breathlessly recounted everything we'd heard: Two-piece uniforms instead of jumpsuits. Clean showers. TVs with all the channels. Three warm meals a day. Real coffee. Salt. Pencils. White paper. As we talked, I could hear the desperation lapping around the edges of her excitement—but I couldn't see it. It was pitch black in the back of the van, the only friendly face I knew replaced by a disembodied voice in the dark.

By the time we made it through booking, it was after dawn. We stumbled into our new cells bleary-eyed, still wet from delousing, and—I thought—ready to weather a few days in isolation as we waited for clearance from medical so we could mingle with everyone else. In the free world, I'd liked spending time alone, so solitary confinement didn't sound that bad. But solitary is not so much being alone as it is being buried alive. It only took me a few seconds to figure that out.

As soon as the door clunked shut behind me, the weight of seclusion hit me like a wall of dark seawater, knocking me off my feet and leaving me gasping for breath. I broke into sobs. The cell seemed so much smaller than the cells in Tompkins County. The window was a narrow rectangle near the ceiling that I couldn't see out of. The walls were a maddening shade of bright, neon white. And, unlike at my home jail, there were no bars at the front of this cell; it was a thick door with a tiny slit for a window, just like I'd heard about from other women who'd been boarded out before. One cell over, Steph tried to talk to me by hollering into the toilet, but I couldn't make out the words. The voices drifting up from the dayroom were muffled and nonsensical, like someone had slipped an opaque filter over reality.

The women's housing area—called a "pod"—was much bigger than in Tompkins County and probably could have held five times as many people. About a third of the bunks were in an open dorm, with rows of dangerously narrow stacked beds and a shared toilet out in the open. The other two-thirds—where they put me and Steph—were arranged into two tiers of one-person cells with a walkway on the upper floor, like a shitty motel.

From where I was on the second story, I could not see or hear the TV in the common area below. There was no clock, and no way to keep track of time. I only remember leaving once, to talk to a nurse downstairs with the meds cart. It was a two-minute conversation, and I told her my lips were chapped and bleeding from the dry air. I wanted to know if I could have one of the single-use petroleum jelly packets I saw sitting on her cart. She glanced up with a scowl and rolled her eyes, not bothering to answer. If I wanted such luxuries, I'd have to wait a week for commissary to come in.

For now, all I had was a plastic cup, a pencil, two sheets of blank paper, a rulebook, a toothbrush, toothpaste, a Bible, and orange jail-issue clothes that weren't nearly thick enough for the freezing Chenango cells. I didn't have crosswords to solve, or books to read, or space to run.

With no sense of time or place, I quietly lost my mind to a degree that still terrifies me. I had never known my grip on reality could become so tenuous, so abruptly. But it did, and I spent the next few days in a half-awake fugue state, unmoored and incorporeal—like the brain in a vat we used to talk about in philosophy class at Rutgers. I drifted between waking and sleeping, hardly able to do either and hardly able to tell the difference. I banged my head against the wall for a distraction and made myself throw up just to pass the hours. I tried to journal on my two pieces of paper but struggled to finish a thought. I tried to read but could not comprehend the words. I was numb and detached, losing time as I watched my life from the outside. One day—who knows which one—I dumped the milk from lunch on my head, just to see if I could still feel. How had this happened so quickly? Was this a complete break from reality? Was I insane now? Or had I always been? I'd never so badly wanted to separate my mind from my body. I schemed to figure out if I could, calculating whether it was possible to crack my head open and bleed to death with a carefully orchestrated fall or shove a noose through the air vent near the ceiling. Would that be enough to kill me? Or was I already dead?

In life, so much of who we are is defined by the choices we make, how we see the world, and how we relate to the people around us. Solitary takes away all that. We may call it SHU or segregation or medical observation, but whatever words we use are a shorthand for the truth, a coded way of saying: You are nothing, and now you have nothing. Your world is only a tangle of dreams and reality drifting through the sterile air of a nine-by-six coffin.

On the fourth day, Tompkins County finally sent over proof we'd already been tested for tuberculosis, and we were cleared for general population. Apparently, that was the only thing they'd been waiting on: a set of forms that took ten seconds to email or maybe a minute to fax.

"Goddammit," Steph hissed. "Why the fuck couldn't they have done that like an hour after we got here?"

We were still new enough to be surprised when things did not seem logical. And as we got out to explore, we found that was pretty much everything. There was an outdoor rec area with a basketball, but we weren't allowed to run. There was unlimited access to toilet paper, but you had to put in the request the night before. Every pod had its own newspaper, but you weren't allowed to do the puzzles. The food was great by jail

standards, but dinner came at 4:30 P.M. and you couldn't save
anything to snack on later. There was a TV with cable, but you
weren't allowed to change the channel. Breaking any of these
rules—even something so small as saving an orange after lunch
or sneaking an extra sweatshirt—could get you locked in, back
in solitary. That was their answer to everything, it seemed.

The structure of the pod made it simple. With all those
one-person cells, it was easy to just lock someone in and leave
them there. It didn't require relocating a bunkie or figuring
out whether there was enough space. One woman—the last
cell on the right—spent her entire time locked in because she
was mentally ill and kept acting out. Sometimes she screamed
or stood at her door and silently glowered. Other times she
stripped all her clothes off, shouted obscenities at the guards, or
smeared shit all over the walls. These were the sorts of things
I thought you would only see on TV or in a movie—but they
were *really* happening, right in front of me. And as far as I could
tell, she did not seem to receive any therapy or treatment beyond the pills that came around on the meds cart.

A few doors down from her was a woman who was locked
in for 120 days, the first 30 of which she wasn't even allowed a
sheet or a blanket or a cup. If she wanted to drink, she had to
cup her hands around the faucet. She couldn't have deodorant,
but they'd give her a toothbrush and toothpaste for a few minutes after each meal. She was only allowed to have a pencil and
two pieces of paper from 5 to 6:45 A.M., but couldn't have any
books or reading material. Any mail she received, they would
take away after five minutes. When she went out to her hour of

rec alone, she had to be shackled and handcuffed the entire time, just to shuffle around a concrete slab while she sang to herself.

Even though I watched these things happen in front of me, I could not quite believe my eyes and wanted to investigate further. She wasn't allowed to talk to anyone, but if I sat at the table nearest her first-floor cell and pretended to be reading, we could sneak in short snippets of conversation before the guards noticed. *Why are you in there? How long has it been? Are you okay?*

By her account, she'd gotten caught smuggling in Oxy-Contin, a few pills passed mouth-to-mouth during a quick kiss at the beginning of a visit. It only aroused suspicion, she said, because the person she kissed happened to be her cousin. Since then, she'd been in lock for about a month, as if isolation was going to cure her desire for drugs. It all seemed so absurd, but what shocked me the most was that she appeared to be handling it just fine. Despite the quiet chaos of solitary, she was coherent and sometimes even cheerful—living like she knew some secret to the universe that I could not learn.

For that, I faulted myself. The truth, though, is that there is no right way to respond to torture. Experts who study solitary confinement link it to anxiety, memory problems, sleep issues, anger, and disordered thinking. Some people experience "isolation panic," like the dark wave that swept me off my feet. Some people handle it just fine, and others deteriorate slowly. To me, it felt like unraveling—but looking back it also feels like a turning point, a moment at which I began to see how broken the system could be, and how much it could break a person.

When I finally got boarded back alone just a few days after I left, it felt like I'd been gone for weeks. The peeling paint and the muted tones of D-Block were all the same, but I was not. By the time I straggled into my cell it was past midnight, so no one was awake to see the tears in my eyes as I kissed the cell bars and whispered: "I'm home."

I winced at the words as soon as they slipped out, clinging to my lips like a smear of day-old lipstick.

Chapter 15

Tompkins County Jail, May 2011

Behind bars, sleep is sacred. Whether it is eight minutes or eight hours, each brush with slumber is a thrilling chance at escape. It is a moment to anticipate all day: When you close your eyes, maybe you will not be in jail. Maybe you will be on the ice, spinning before a cheering crowd in a packed arena. Maybe you will be at a desk, frantically writing the last paper you need to graduate. Maybe you will be in a warm bed, cuddling with a soft dog on a cold night. Maybe you will be at a beach or a bar.

Maybe you will be free.

But once you've been in long enough, jail seeps into your dreams, and you discover that you are incarcerated even when you're unconscious. By the end of my first spring behind bars, I did not dream of the outside world anymore. In fact, I did not dream of anything. Sometime after my stay in Chenango and my jolt of solitary, I stopped having dreams. When I closed my eyes, all I saw was darkness. When I opened them, all I saw was the dingy gray of jail, refracted through a kaleidoscope of fear and obsession.

Now, when I look through the yellow notepads of my jailhouse journal, I can almost see that constant dread glinting from between the lines like jagged glass. It is only today—ten years later—that I can spot the sudden shift from casually detailing every petty spat and minor oddity to spending page after page obsessing about just two things: my fear of solitary confinement and my fear of losing my marriage.

Another thing it might have made sense for me to fear—and the reason they'd brought me back from Chenango in the first place—was my sentencing. In my head, sentencing hearings were dramatic events featuring sharply dressed detectives scowling from the aisles, reporters furiously scribbling notes in the front row, and doomed defendants wailing at their disappointing fates. In reality, sentencing hearings are almost an afterthought, like checking the answers on a crossword puzzle you have already solved. Most people go into court knowing the outcome, since they've already agreed to it in some sort of plea bargain. The court date is just for the judge to approve it officially. Walking in, I knew I was probably getting two and a half years in prison followed by two years of supervised release—but I still expected signing away almost five years of my life to be more dramatic than it actually was. Apparently the guards did, too.

On the way to court, the transport officer warned me there might be media trying to catch a glimpse of the "queenpin" or even an angry rival drug dealer seeking some type of vengeance.

But there was none of that. There were only a few strangers absorbed in their own drama—and Alex, high as a kite and too paranoid to even come into the courtroom.

Pacing outside, he wasn't there to hear the prosecutor boast about how big the bust was. He wasn't there to wince as the judge told me that he did not need to recount the "tragedy" of my life because I was probably already doing that on a daily basis. I had hoped the friendly faced jurist would recommend me for shock camp, but he did not. That surely would have been devastating were I not so fixated on the empty space behind me—the bench where Alex was not sitting, flashing his cock-eyed grin of moral support. We were married, but I felt so alone.

The hearing was quick and all a foregone conclusion except for one thing: My lawyer didn't know whether the judge would agree to a rare request from the DEA, who wanted me to stay in jail a few months longer instead of going straight to prison. Normally, once you get sentenced to state time, you're shipped off within a week or two—as soon as the prison system sends over the transit order. But a few weeks earlier, a pair of federal narcotics agents had paid me a visit and asked if I could help them. My lawyer said I should hear them out.

So one afternoon, over burnt coffee in the sheriff's office deputy lounge, two scruffy undercovers had asked if I could snare them a big fish: They wanted me to set up Alex's dealer, the man who'd supplied us with all the drugs I'd been carrying around the day of my arrest. Criminal ethics aside, this was logistically problematic, seeing as I was in jail and in no position to be pulling off large-scale dope deals with a savvy kingpin in the free world. So instead, the feds suggested I get Alex to do it.

This was, of course, not going to fucking happen. I couldn't get Alex to consistently show up for visits sober, let alone sacrifice his longtime connection for me. And even if he somehow did, the pay-off wouldn't have been worth the risk. The DEA's plan was that I would be sentenced as expected, and then if Alex cooperated with them I'd get hauled back into court and magically *resentenced* to one year instead of two and a half—a minor miracle that would have been completely impossible to explain to my peers, like some sort of Immaculate Resentencing.

On top of all that, there was the ethical issue: Was I willing to let someone else pay for my mistake? Ultimately, it did not matter. No part of this plan was workable, and I knew I could never give the feds what they were after—which was exactly why I agreed to it. Even though I couldn't deliver, just agreeing was enough to get me something I secretly wanted: to burn more time in jail before heading off to prison. And so, on my sentencing day, the judge quietly signed a sealed order that would end up keeping me in Tompkins County for a few more months. If I didn't help the feds before that order expired, I would go to state prison as planned. If I did, I would be resentenced.

Most people in jail would rather be in state prison, where there are more things to do and more people to see and more ways to forget you are not free. There are jobs and vocational classes and longer visits. The medical care is a little better, the commissary selection is bigger, and the rec yard has real grass. But I didn't care about all that. I had books and crosswords here and could run laps around the cellblock. Sure, a gym might be better, but after my recent awful experience at another facility, I did not want to discover what fresh hell prison might hold. Plus, I had people here that I would miss: There were the volunteers who came in for weekly self-help programs and the friendly GED teacher who let me sit in class. There were the occasional visits from friends in town—and, of course, from Alex. Steph had been released, but I still had Sam, and Lee.

The nerdy guard was one of the few people I saw every day who was somehow not enveloped in the miasma of jailhouse drama. He moved through our tiny world, but was not of it. And unlike everyone else in my life at that point, he never knew me as a drug addict, or at least not really. He once said he remembered seeing me in the gorges years before I got locked up—but it was only in passing, and I didn't remember him. It was a fresh slate, for both of us.

Over the six months I'd been in jail, our conversations had strayed from ziggurats and crosswords into stories about our lives beyond the walls. I told him about skating, and Charlotte, and late nights at the student newspaper. He told me about his brothers, and his neurotic puppy, and hiking in the Catskills. Sometimes, he offered words of comfort—like when he reassured me that my dog would remember me when I got out. He felt less like a guard and more like a counselor, or maybe even a friend. I almost forgot that he was the same person who might search my cell in a shakedown or toss me in solitary if I talked back.

By the end of May, he was the person I turned to when I suddenly needed to get in to see the doctor. For no apparent reason, I'd developed a smelly gum infection and my whole mouth tasted rotten. It was not a life-threatening emergency, but it hurt and the solution seemed simple: All I needed was an antibiotic—if I could just get anyone from medical to respond. The first half-dozen requests I filed got me nowhere, and my attempts to make a saline mouth rinse by harvesting salt specks from commissary crackers were not overly effective. So I asked Lee for suggestions: Should I file a grievance? Have my lawyer call some higher-ups? No, he said, he'd just nudge the nurse to make sure I was on the list, and bring me some real salt while he was at it.

When I finally got escorted to the jail's medical department—a tiny closet of a room down the hallway, where a physician visited once a week—the doctor prescribed me penicillin, then got up to shut the door for a more serious conversation.

"We got in results from some blood work we did for you," he said. "You have hepatitis C."

Somehow, I was shocked. It was as if I'd expected the universe to give me a gold star and a free pass for *sometimes* being safe. When I was getting high I'd let myself believe it was enough that I'd generally used protection during sex and avoided sharing needles. I chose to ignore the fact that there were some pretty significant exceptions to that general practice. For one, I always shared rigs with my boyfriends, including both Todd and Alex—who'd also shared needles with each other. Now, I had no idea whether they had it, too, and no idea whether I should be mad at one of them for giving it to me or mad at myself for giving it to them. I didn't even have a good sense of whether I should really be worried in the first place, or if the diagnosis just sounded more dire than it was. If I hadn't been so overwhelmed, I might have asked more questions.

"I don't even know what to say," I wrote in my journal after

I got back to the cellblock. "I really suck at life." It wasn't so much a pity party as an observation that felt deeply true by that point.

When I nervously gave Alex the news during the next visit, he did not seem to give a shit.

"Oh, I kind of figured you probably had that," he said, repeatedly pointing out that I was lucky to have a boyfriend who loved me so much he wasn't even mad. I was instantly suspicious. Did he know that he already had it? Or was he diverting my attention from something else entirely? So many possibilities ran through my head, none of them good.

Though he'd finally begun admitting that he'd relapsed, sometimes he still said it was only pot or anti-anxiety pills—neither of which accounted for the track marks. Those explanations also didn't account for the time I heard him snorting lines during a phone call. They didn't account for the missed visits, the droopy eyes, or the ridiculous way he doubled down when he told me he'd gone to a self-help meeting at a rehab—on a weekend night when we both knew the place was closed. That time, he was so passionate about his claim that I started second-guessing myself and actually asked an inmate advocacy group to call and check the facility's schedule. Sure enough, they were not open at 8 P.M. on Sundays. When I asked him about it during a visit, he lashed out in anger.

"Fuck this!" he spewed, before stomping out mid-visit, leaving me alone with the questioning stares of the other visitors. Later that day, when I called to smooth things over, he told me that it was my fault if he killed himself and that I never stopped to think how miserable this all made him. We shouted and fought and I hung up hating him—and me. How did I become the desperate woman furtively fact-checking my husband, pitifully trying to convince myself he might be telling the truth?

My face flushed with embarrassment as the past few months now came into crisp focus. I thought back to the days right after my arrest, when he disappeared and abandoned Charlotte. Then there was the time I showed up for visit to find him making eyes at his ex, who happened to be sitting one seat over. The time I watched him exchange phone numbers with a girl in the jail parking lot, only to deny it afterward. There was the time he told a mutual friend that he was planning to move and didn't want me to know. The time I found out he'd been telling everyone our relationship was in trouble because I wouldn't stop writing other men.

"There's something off with us," he told me one afternoon in early June, sputtering uncertainly into the phone.

"Well, I'm in jail," I said with a wry laugh. "That seems off enough to me."

"No, that's not it," he interrupted. "You don't seem like you love me anymore."

I tried to hold my voice steady as I finally stopped dancing around my accusations: "Well, it's just difficult to communicate with you when you're so out of it that even the fucking COs notice. And frankly I just don't believe you when you say you're not using."

I finished speaking and closed my eyes, as if willful blindness would shield me from his response.

"You know what? Fuck it," he spat, his words coming out angry and fast, like torpedoes. "Yes, I was high yesterday. I was real fucking high. It's just been so hard to stay sober and this is a really fucking bad time for you to be doing this to me."

I took a deep breath and asked if he was at least planning to get sober—but he said it wouldn't matter anyway because he could tell he'd already lost me. When the call cut off after the allotted time, I waited a few hours to call back.

"I don't think you love me anymore," he moaned into the phone. "But I still love you more than ever, Keri-Schmeri."

Even through the scratchy jailhouse connection, I could hear the heroin in his voice, that deep narcotic droop edging around his words. They sounded like love but felt like manipulation. I did not know whether it was him or the drugs that were pulling the strings, but either way, I was done. I had wanted to believe in us so badly, to give him all the second chances I hoped people would give me. But no matter what he had or hadn't done, and no matter how much we did or didn't love each other, in the end it all came down to this: He was not willing to stay clean, and I was not willing to lose any more of my life to drugs. Nothing else mattered.

A few weeks later, I broke up with him in a phone call. He took it in stride, offering a nonchalant, "Well, I guess we're done then," before hanging up without any goodbyes. As soon as the receiver hit the cradle, I started bawling. It should have felt like liberation, but instead it just felt like defeat. A few days later, he showed up once more at a visit, high and claiming he would contest it whenever I filed for divorce. He drooled over the girl next to him and left after ten minutes.

I never saw him again.

Alone at the metal dayroom table in D-Block, I sat down

with a butter packet I'd swiped from a breakfast tray on pancake day and set about prying off my ring. It was a simple ten-karat wedding band, a rare piece of jewelry permitted under the jail's rules. The fit was almost painfully tight—but I didn't have to try hard. As soon as I started tugging, it broke in two. Not satisfied, I smashed it to pieces, then stuffed it in an envelope and mailed it to him with a bitter two-page note.

"You have clearly chosen drugs over me and you have clearly done so repeatedly," I wrote. "You have always said we could get through anything if we were honest with one another and you have been anything but. I will have six months clean tomorrow; you will have six months of lying to me about almost everything under the sun."

Looking back, it all feels like a fever dream, inexplicable and intense. In the moment, we'd made so much sense together—but it turned out that was only true in the twisted world of dream logic. Eyes closed, I had mindlessly soaked up the vibrance and passion before jolting awake with my heart racing, alone and in the dark.

Chapter 16

Sometimes, the memory hits so hard it almost hurts. Not just in your head, but in your heart—a literal pain of loss. Maybe you're standing in the rec yard or running laps around the cellblock when, in a flash, you remember the smell of fresh coffee. The taste of a cigarette. The musty aroma of wet dog. The explosive color of sunrise over the gorges. Suddenly, you hunch over panting, exhausted from the overwhelming sense of grief for the life that was.

I am a lifelong neurotic list-maker. After I got arrested, I kept a daily to-do list in a homemade planner, documenting everything I needed to get done even when it seemed there was nothing worth doing. Run in circles. Read one hundred pages. Call my lawyer. Write that teacher from fifteen years ago. I ticked them all off, again and again. So when I was looking to exorcise grief, I did it by making a list—as if writing things down would make me miss them less, or remember them more.

Some of these things were expansive and fundamental: trees, vegetables, color—blues and purples—a spectrum of life I could no longer see.

But some were smaller and more specific: highlighters, mint ice cream, my favorite punk rock playlist. It's hard to explain how much these things matter—because often they don't, not individually, not in the moment. It's when you multiply them by days and weeks that they begin to hurt. Sometimes, when I let myself wallow in that list, I would think that I did not have much more to lose. But I was wrong. There is always something.

After dinner one night in July, a small army of guards stormed into the cellblock and pulled a girl named Becca out of her cell, leading her away with no explanation. Then, they locked the rest of us in and stormed back out. As soon as the door thudded shut behind them, the air lit up with panic: *Did they catch her? Who told them? Did somebody rat?* We frantically speculated about what would happen—but we already knew what started it. For nearly three months, Becca's boyfriend had been sneaking in Suboxone during his twice-weekly jail visits, passing off the little orange pills mid-kiss. It was the same medication the jail nurse had given me back in December to help with detox, and it wasn't supposed to make you high. But some people swore if you didn't have a habit—maybe because you'd been sober for a few months in jail—you could catch a buzz. Plus, it was cheaper than high-powered opiates, and in the early 2010s it still came in pill form, making it perfect for a mouth-to-mouth pass-off.

That, we assumed, was why they'd rushed the block. We were only surprised they hadn't done it sooner. After all, it wasn't just Becca who'd been walking around with glassy eyes; she'd been sharing her stash, so some days half the block was half-buzzed. Since I wasn't, I assumed this bust would not involve me beyond whatever initial strip search or shakedown was about to come. Sure enough, just a few minutes after Becca left, a small platoon of COs streamed in, shouting, "Up against the wall, ladies! Up against the wall!"

They popped open the cell gates and tore through our belongings, ripping off the sheets, rifling through our dirty clothes, and tossing our letters and books all over the floor. It was angry, almost feral, with none of the smug superiority of a usual shakedown. And instead of making us wait there till they finished, the guards led us away mid-search, scowling and staring straight ahead as they pointed us down the hallway in tense silence. We passed by Becca, sitting alone in a small interrogation room with her stringy brown hair tucked behind her ears and her long legs pulled up close to her chest. She was skinny, with a loud laugh that usually drifted out of the cellblock and into the hallway— but right now, her blue eyes were dark and serious. The guards led the rest of us to that one holding cell with the vomit-caked shower and left us there, six people in a room with one toilet. There was no TV, no clock, no privacy, and not even enough room to pace. There was nothing to do but trade anxieties in hushed tones.

The women who'd been getting high worried about drug tests, the possibility of solitary, or even criminal charges. And as the night wore on, those of us who'd done nothing wrong started to worry, too. *Something's up. What the fuck is taking so long?* Finally, the guards came back and pulled us out one-by-one to strip-search us. We squatted and coughed and went back to our cells without any small talk. Once the gates clanged shut, Sam and I breathed sighs of relief and surveyed the chaos of our small jail lives strewn across the floor. We'd barely started cleaning up our shared cell when a guard burst back in the block with an announcement. "We found opiate residue in your cell," he said, peering at me. "On the windowsill."

Already exhausted, I had no response except stunned silence. The other cells fell quiet as the women strained to listen—no one was expecting this twist. We all knew who'd been getting drugs, and we all knew it wasn't me. I might have suspected Sam, but I think I was almost too surprised for suspicion. Plus, she was sputtering and outraged when the guards left her in the cell and pulled me out for questioning, pointing me to the same seat where they'd grilled Becca a few minutes earlier. There, in a room so cramped it barely fit two people, a seething sergeant hissed and hollered.

"You brought drugs into my jail!" he shouted, words jabbing at the air like an accusing finger. His face contorted in anger beneath the blond military buzz cut left over from his last tour overseas. "How did you get them in here?! I know you're involved in this!"

Leaning across the table, he stood to glower down at me: the enemy.

"I had nothing to do with this!" I pleaded. "Drug test me! You'll see! Drug test me!"

Even as he lobbed threats of solitary confinement, indefinite punishments, and new criminal charges, in the back of my mind I still had faith that somehow the truth would prevail.

Eventually, I thought, they would just drug test me and they would see: This time I was innocent. I was finally doing the right thing, and I was so confident that it would show. After failing to get the answers he wanted, the sergeant stormed out to interrogate Sam, then Becca again, then her cellmate, Ashleigh. Finally, they sent us all back to our cells and ordered the four of us to pack up and move to a different cellblock.

"They're fucking stupid," Sam said with a laugh as she threw her things in a trash bag. "They know I had Valium, not opiates."

My eyes widened.

"Wait. Did you tell them?"

"Yeah, of course, man. I mean, whatever they think they found wasn't mine. But I was the only one with drugs and I'm not gonna let you take the heat for that."

My mind raced, trying to figure out what the fuck was going on. For days, Sam had been running around saying she had drugs—but since she'd never produced any pills and never seemed high, no one believed her. We thought she was trying to be cool or just making shit up to pass the time, like the jailhouse version of creating an imaginary friend. And even now, even after the guards had found drugs in our cell, I *still* didn't believe her. But I thought that if she'd *confessed*, then surely it would count as proof I was innocent.

The guards did not agree, and directed me to keep packing. It was late into the night by the time we dragged our bins and bags across the hall, to a smaller block where it would be easier to keep an eye on us. Before letting us go to sleep for the night, they pawed through our stuff again and haphazardly began taking things. They threw out all the food we'd bought on commissary: instant coffee, granola bars, candy, drink mixes. They took all of Sam's stamps and her one pair of sneakers. They took half of my books and letters. And then, they locked in just one person—Becca—and left, slamming the door behind them.

"You guys, what the fuck?"

"Yeah, what the fuck?"

"I don't fucking know, man."

Clustered at the gate of Becca's cell, we tried to piece the night together but couldn't even untangle what had set them off in the first place: Did they hear Sam saying she was high or did they notice Becca's glazed eyes? Did they really find drugs, or was the sergeant making it up? Had a guard planted them, or was it just a false positive on a shoddy drug test? The only thing we all agreed on was that there was no way they'd found any opiate residue in that cell.

Our confusion hung thick in the air, swirling around with anger, suspicion, and streaks of fear. Ashleigh was livid, especially since they hadn't found anything in the cell she shared with Becca. Becca—who'd confessed to getting high herself—seemed suspicious of Sam's confession. Sam was pissed, at least in part because I was still being punished after she'd taken the blame. I was terrified about the possibility of solitary and disoriented by how quickly the earth had shifted beneath us. It had been such a boring, regular evening—until we got screamed at for hours, threatened with new charges, separated from our friends, and had almost everything we owned thrown out or taken, all over drugs that weren't really there.

The next few days were a blur. We were all strip-searched

repeatedly, sometimes six or seven times a day. They woke us up at night, locked us in booking rooms till 1 A.M., threatened us with things like cavity searches and more felonies, screamed in our faces during interrogations. (Sam—to our deep delight—eventually started screaming back, cursing out the sergeant so loudly we could hear her from down the hallway.) One time they locked us out of our cells and left us to sleep on the dirty laundry bags, then isolated Becca and demanded she go to the bathroom so they could check her shit for drugs. They tore everything apart so many times a day that we just gave up and stopped cleaning the messes they left behind, stopped being shocked when they found new things to confiscate almost every time. Worn out, we no longer bothered to pick up whatever they left scattered on the floor, no longer put back the sheets torn off our plastic mattresses during raids, and no longer put on underwear when we got dressed—we figured it would just come off in a strip search anyway.

Aside from all that, I feared a different loss: the loss of Lee's trust. As soon as the dust had settled in our new cellblock after the chaos of that first night, I'd begun wondering what he would think when he found out. For months, I'd been so vocal about my commitment to change, zealously expounding on my plans for a sober life on a near-daily basis. I must have sounded so painfully earnest. But I thought for sure that everyone could see that it wasn't just talk—I really meant it. It was such a small jail that the guards all knew that I'd filed for divorce, and why. They saw me going to the weekly self-help meetings and reading books about recovery. Now, their dirty looks and disdainful tsks screamed a stinging truth: to them, we were all just hopeless addicts, dirty, feral, and not to be trusted. No matter what everyone else thought, I still hoped that Lee would be different. I hoped he would see my sincerity. The idea that I was a changed woman felt so foundational that I did not understand how anyone could doubt it.

But when Lee showed up to work for his next shift, I couldn't read his face. For several hours, he avoided me altogether, once even averting his eyes and shaking his head when he strode past. My heart sank. Did he doubt me, too? Or had he just been ordered to stay away? Eventually, he walked in the cellblock and I hissed, "You know I had nothing to do with that, right?" His response was opaque, noncommittal: "Well, everyone makes mistakes." I couldn't figure out whether he meant that he'd erred in assuming my guilt—or whether he meant that I'd erred and he forgave me. With all the chaos around us, I knew I would not get a chance to ask unless things calmed quickly—but they did not.

On the fourth day of strip searches and questions, one of the higher-ups—Major Parker[1]—accused me of hiding drugs in my dreadlocks. Then, she led me to the nurse's station and ordered the nurse to search my hair. When that proved messy and difficult, they just decided to cut it all off, hacking away with a pair of blue Crayola scissors as I struggled to hold back tears. I was too shocked to protest as much as I should have: I could not wrap my head around the idea that I was being punished for something someone else had confessed to, especially when there was a test that would prove it.

---

1. A bitch.

"Why can't you just drug test me?" My voice quavered. "Wouldn't that prove I'm not involved? Sam said I wasn't involved. Wouldn't a drug test prove that?"

The major sighed dramatically and rolled her eyes, as if my request were simply a further indication of my guilt. Until that moment, I would have thought she could not—or as a woman, would not—do that. Until that moment, I still did not fully grasp how a jail could become its own kingdom, ruled by a petty monarch. Until that moment, I did not understand: They can do whatever they want to you and they do not really need proof or justification. Who are you going to tell? It seemed like the people in charge all thought we had gotten one over on them, and they were willing to break all the rules to get back at us.

Afterward, I returned to the block dazed, my head down to avoid meeting eyes with the shocked stares around me. I held in tears until I got back to my cell—but as soon as I looked in the mirror, I started to cry. I was shorn and shamed. The haircut looked almost purposely humiliating, like one of Peter Pan's Lost Boys had gone at my head with a seashell. One side was about four inches long, while the back was barely half an inch. Scattered all across my head were long rattails alternating with nearly bald spots. Too defeated to complain, I curled up on my bunk and hid my whole head inside an oversized orange sweatshirt as I struggled to come to terms with this feeling, this loss. Being in jail is a constant lesson in humility, humiliation, and powerlessness—but this was something else. It was more like being erased.

After that, they stopped with the interrogations—but the

searches somehow seemed to intensify. A few days later, they boarded all four of us out to Chenango. The major actually drove us there herself, something I'd never seen her do before. When she dropped us off, she told our new jailers that Sam and Becca were in solitary but I was not, since I had not been caught with any drugs and they had confessed. Then, she drove back to Tompkins County and promptly faxed over paperwork saying I was to go in solitary, too. I was drained, but also angry at the mealymouthed deceit, and terrified at what it could mean: Had they found some new "evidence" back in Tompkins County? The only clue I got was not exactly helpful: a single, vague paper telling me I was in solitary confinement and declaring, "You will be provided with a written statement setting forth the reason(s) for such confinement within twenty-four hours." It was ludicrous, and not even true; I never got a statement, or any explanation.

For the next three days, I pleaded with the guards for information, or at least permission to use the phone. I paced, I ran in place, I prayed. I waited for the insanity to set in—but I think my anger sustained me, or maybe my exhaustion. Even though I lost track of time, this time I did not lose the will to live.

And then, as suddenly as it all started, it was over. They boarded me back. Took me out of solitary. Boarded the other women back. Stopped the constant strip searches. Returned the things they'd confiscated. Looking back a decade later, it all feels unreal, like a story you tell about someone else. Not just because it happened, but because of the stark contrast with what came after: a reprieve.

For long stretches during the month of August, it was just me and Becca in the small cellblock—they'd put Sam across the hall, looking to keep us apart just in case. To my relief, somewhere in the course of our whole ordeal Becca had finally decided she wanted to stay sober. And now without the drugs or the constant searches, we became friends and built a small world for ourselves, a fishbowl so insular we could almost forget where we were. We talked, we laughed, we sang. "*Tra-la-la-la-la, Mr. Jones and meee!*" we howled, giddy with boredom and unspoken relief that we'd made it through worse. "*Lovin' is what I got, so remember that,*" we crooned. In those moments, I could be grateful, relieved at a here and now that I could survive.

Sometimes other people would rotate in or out of the block—there was the yogahead, the lady who nearly gave birth in the cell, the teen who shouted all night, the woman who accused us of stealing her hair. But we were the constants. If they were the verses, we were the chorus in songs of relief and gratitude on the playlist of our lives.

We dreamed about our futures, and recovered from our pasts. I signed my final divorce papers, and Becca prepared for her imminent release. We talked about sobriety, the lives we'd left behind, and the lives that lay ahead. She trimmed my hair with toenail clippers, one painstaking snip at a time. I hand-wrote fake tweets about jail life, and we giggled as I read them aloud to her before snail mailing them to friends in the free world. And she laughed along—but did not make fun—when another girl said I looked like Harry Potter afterward. She looked the other way when I flirted with Lee, and smiled knowingly when we spotted a tiny purple wildflower mysteriously left on my bunk one day. It was contraband, a forbidden gift waiting for me when I came back from the concrete rec yard. But even more: It was proof that life goes on. Long-lost color, in a world of beiges and grays.

Chapter 17

Tompkins County Jail, October 2011

When I heard the metal cell gate clank open at 6 A.M. one Monday in early October, I knew it was the last time I would hear that sound. There is only one reason guards open the gates before morning count: prison transport. I'd been expecting it for weeks, ever since the stay order from the feds had expired and I'd failed to give them what they wanted. I'd done my best to prepare for this day, drafting goodbye letters to my parents and friends, mailing home my books, and neatly writing all the important names and addresses on the inner margins of a blue softcover Bible—the only thing I could bring with me other than legal papers.

Afraid that the medical staff there would be as callous as they were in Chenango, I slathered Chapstick behind my ear so I'd have my own tiny supply for the next few days. Then I threw my last few belongings into a clear trash bag and hugged Becca goodbye. I ate my last lonely jail breakfast—Crispix—in the grimy holding cell where I'd first nodded out eleven months earlier. I was shaking so hard I had to balance the bowl on a concrete ledge to avoid spilling milk everywhere. I wanted to cry, but I didn't because I knew the COs would laugh at me. I'd heard them laughing before about who had or hadn't cried on the way to prison.

Lee got assigned to one of the two transport spots for my two-and-a-half-hour drive to Albion, the closest women's prison in the state. I'd spend one night there—at the twelve-hundred-person lockup near the Canadian border—and then get shipped a few hours south to Bedford Hills, the maximum-security unit forty miles outside New York City where new women get tested, poked, prodded, and classified before they're sent off to a permanent placement.

From the back of the patrol car, the drive north to Albion was nerve-wracking, a balancing act of fear and loss. In front of me, Lee sat behind the wheel, and his every darting glance in the mirror seemed imbued with a special significance—as if a raised eyebrow or steady stare could convey everything I hoped he wanted to say. *You'll be okay. I'll miss you. Visit soon.*

About halfway through, we pulled off at a rest stop because I had to go to the bathroom. A year earlier, I would have been mortified to be paraded around in public in an orange jumpsuit, shackles, and handcuffs, and with two uniformed escorts. But that morning, I didn't have time for pride or shame. I knew it was the last time I would see the free world at close range for a while, and I drank in every detail. The colorful array of candy at the rest stop convenience store. The smell of fast food and burnt coffee from the food court. The wide-eyed ten-year-old girl in a pink

T-shirt and jeans, gripping her father's hand in fear as she passed me and stared. And most of all, Lee. I tried to take a mental snapshot, watching him as he leaned his weight on one hip while waiting in line to buy a Reese's four-pack.

When we got back to the car, he turned around and passed me two of the peanut butter cups. The other guard rolled her eyes but said nothing. I smiled, realizing it was the first time we'd split a meal—like the saddest first date ever. As I stared out the window, the miles of rural farmscape ticked by so fast, and suddenly we were turning onto the potholed pavement of a long, rural driveway.

We were there.

From the main entrance, the first thing I remember of the prison itself was a lot of razor wire and an aging brick building. It seemed ominous and imposing—but I guess any building seems that way if it's surrounded by enough jagged metal. The outside grounds were neat and institutional, but when we got closer we could see beyond the fences to the crisscrossing walkways, grass quads, and century-old brick buildings that might've been more at home on an Ivy League campus than at a women's prison.

Yet if the outdoors looked vaguely academic, the interior spaces were anything but. Lee and the other guard deposited me in a nearly barren waiting room with beat-up wooden benches. Then, they signed some papers and left. Lee cast one last look over his shoulder as he walked out.

It all felt so real now.

There were maybe ten other new women waiting to go

through intake that day, and for the next four hours we were stripped, searched, examined, and questioned. Like specimens, we were weighed and measured, then asked about our tattoos and birthmarks and religious affiliations. The elderly woman next to me sobbed the whole way through the cold delousing shower, where we stood two feet apart from each other, stark naked and watched by guards. Afterward, we got our bags of forest-green prison clothes and our inmate ID numbers. Mine was 11G0845, the 845th female intake of 2011. Back in county jail, we hadn't had ID numbers; they'd actually called us by our names. There, I had always felt like an inmate, but at least a human. Prison was different. There were so many of us, we were all just numbers.

When we finished the intake assembly line, they sent us to another bench-lined room to wait and watch a shitty prison-made suicide prevention video on repeat. A white girl from Chautauqua County plopped down next to me and started talking incessantly.

"I am sooo glad to be out of that damn county! That place was terrible! Do you know they really made us wear black and white stripes like a fucking cartoon?"

Burbling like a brook and inexplicably happy, she introduced herself as Christina. She was just a few months older than me and also a former heroin addict, though she explained that her convictions were actually conspiracy and grand larceny, crimes she'd committed in the course of her drug use. Flashing a gap-toothed smile, she announced with certainty, "I'm gonna be home in six months!" Suddenly solemn, she looked down at her wavy, waist-length brown hair and explained, "I'm going to go to shock, and they're going to cut it all off." She pantomimed a dramatic cutting motion. "Snip!"

Around four in the afternoon, guards escorted all of us newbies to our housing unit for the night. Separated from the rest of the prisoners, we had one wing of a small colonial-looking brick building all to ourselves. There were wood floors and institutional beds in rooms laid out along a hallway—just like a college dorm. Except here there was security grating over the windows, and guards who locked us in and left.

That first night in prison, I barely slept. Most of us stayed up talking and playing cards. There was no clock, no radio, and no TV. We just had each other, and our endless games of spades. At one point, we smelled fresh cigarette smoke wafting in from the green-clad women on the nearby walkways, and we clustered around the windows to peer through the grating at the future versions of ourselves. They looked like hardened women doing their time, inexplicably calm and unflappable like they'd learned some secret Zen. As we watched them, we dreamed out loud about which prison we'd end up in, like little anxious witches staring down the darkest version of Harry Potter's Sorting Hat. Some women wanted what was closest to home, others wanted to be at the easiest units or the ones where they had friends—or at least no enemies. We swapped intel about the prison lore we'd heard and traded stories about the counties we'd come from and the people we'd left behind. But that was it. That was our night. No one got beat up, no one got raped, nothing terrible happened. It was just a bunch of women talking and bonding and sharing our fears.

The next morning, the guards got us up at 4 A.M. and escorted us to a dirty room in a brick building on the other side of the facility. We spent hours waiting for the Bedford bus to arrive. With nothing to do, I curled up in a corner of the floor and slept on the dirty cement. At one point, I overheard a couple of guards chatting about a woman in the Special Housing Unit. We usually called it SHU or "The Place"—our coded language for solitary confinement. They didn't say why she was there or for how long. But by their account, she'd taken a shit on a tray and pushed the whole smelly mess out the food slot into the hallway. In response, the guards had turned off the water to her cell. One of the officers standing there talking about it started wondering aloud what she was going to drink: "Wouldn't she get dehydrated?"

"She can drink out of the toilet," the other said. "If it's good enough for my dog, it's good enough for her."

My head snapped up in shock, and that is when I realized: Behind bars, there are no rules. Sure, there is a rulebook and there are things you cannot do. But when it matters, no one is watching. I should have figured this out in jail—and after they cut off my hair I learned they could do whatever they wanted there. But that jail was so small that all the petty injustices seemed anecdotal, a series of errant actions not representative of the bigger picture. Prison *was* the bigger picture. There were hundreds of women and hundreds of guards, and all the same problems, but on a larger scale. All the futility, the small cruelties, the refusal to see us as fully human—it was not a flaw in the system. It *was* the system.

The bus ride itself was every bit as awful as you think a

192 | Keri Blakinger

prison bus ride might be. We were cuffed so tight our fingers tingled, the security amped up with stiff black boxes clamped over the wrist chains so our hands were stuck six inches apart. Then, they linked the cuffs to the belly chains around our waists. For the whole six-hour ride, you couldn't reach up high enough to scratch your own nose, or brush stray hair from your eyes. But the worst part was that one leg was shackled to the woman next to you, so if that woman had to go to the bathroom—in the glass-enclosed toilet at the back, a foot from the armed guard—you had no choice but to help, and to hope that she did not have her period. With our hands stuck at our waists, none of us could pull down our pants or wipe alone.

After six exhausting hours, we pulled into Bedford Hills. Most prisons are in the middle of nowhere, but the women's max was improbably located in a bougie hamlet of the same name, part of a suburban town speckled with celebrity mansions belonging to everyone from George Soros to Blake Lively to Martha Stewart. A few miles and a whole world away, we climbed off the prison bus and clanked inside to reception. On the top floor of an aging administrative building, the reception dorm was an open room with forty or so bunk beds crammed together with no room to walk around. If you roamed the narrow aisles, you'd get yelled at by the guard perched at her raised desk by the door. "Out of place! You're out of place! Do you want a ticket or a private room? 109.10!!"

If there is a soundtrack to New York prisons, that might be it—the constant threat of a write-up for violating rule number 109.10. Usually, they shouted it in a sort of shorthand, hollering the number and nothing else: "109.10! 109.10!" At first, I was

baffled. It seemed so trivial to simply be in the wrong location within the right prison. But the result of a 109.10 violation
could be severe—anything from a verbal reprimand to solitary
confinement, consequences so arbitrary and disproportionate
they seemed to undermine the whole concept of consequences.
And plus, it was the sort of transgression that could be a complete accident. Late for work? Out of place. Sitting on a friend's
bunk? Out of place. The guards wielded 109.10 as a catch-all
to handle any person or situation they didn't like, to create an
infraction when nothing else fit. It was easy to do because the
rules about where you could be when were so regimented.

As part of our mandated schedule in reception, we woke up
every morning at 5:30 for count. Then meds, then showers, then
breakfast at 7:30 in the mess hall that reeked of sewage. We usually weren't allowed to talk during meals, so news and tips came
with a whispered urgency: *"Check your bowl—a cock-a-roach
crawled out of the cornflakes yesterday."* After we were escorted
back from the cafeteria—lined up in two straight lines, just like
in *Madeline*—there was another call for meds. Then it was back
to the dorm to sit on our bunks in silence until the 11:30 count.
Some days, there were places to go during that time—GED
testing, a psychiatric intake appointment, or maybe the one
gyno visit you'd get upon arrival. But when there was nothing
scheduled, we just did nothing. Talking, milling around, even
doing push-ups or sit-ups on your own bunk—it was all banned
in favor of sitting in silence, as if enough rules and warnings
and regulations would turn us from women into the warehoused
objects the system seemed to wish we were.

Sometimes in the late afternoon, we'd get access to a tiny

indoor rec area, with a TV, board games, three phones to call home—and the freedom to speak to each other, finally. It was the first time in the day we could talk without getting yelled at. After dinner, we'd get a few hours in the outdoor rec yard, with grass and dirt and more open space than most of us had seen in months. Some women paced or chatted or chain-smoked. Some nights, we played kickball just like something out of a shitty prison comedy. "If, as a child, I ever wished for my life to be 'just like the movies,' this is certainly not what I had in mind," I wrote in my journal. What I was beginning to realize— and what the movies don't show you—is how much of prison is waiting. How many hours of your bid are spent sitting on a bunk, or in an empty cell, or standing in a long meds line. Living, but really just waiting for time to pass.

I learned so much those first few days in prison, like a stranger acclimating to a foreign country. The currency here was Newports, and you should always have some on hand even if you didn't smoke. The clothes here were all made for men, but you'd get a disciplinary ticket if you altered them to fit. The most valuable commodity here was toilet paper—and since we only got five rolls a month, we collected magazines and newspapers to use as backup, like magpies conniving our way into basic hygiene. The most versatile tool was a maxi pad—the one free offering we always had in abundance and frequently used to make everything from earplugs to insoles to cleaning supplies. The most sacred thing here was your out date, which your enemies should never know or they might try to get you in trouble so you couldn't go home. Maybe they'd plant drugs in your cell, or maybe they'd punch you in the face so it looked like you'd been in a fight. In the language here, that was called "taking your date."

My date, I learned, was more than a year away. For months, I'd been pinning my hopes on shock: Six months and I could go home, I told myself. But it wasn't that simple; first I had to find out if I qualified. I was in the right age range, with the right kind of crime and right length of sentence. I met almost all the criteria—but I was on psych meds. Ever since my first stay in solitary, I'd been taking an antidepressant, a daily pill prescribed following a brief meeting with some kind of mental health worker I talked to for fifteen minutes in the tiny interview room of the county jail. The pills took some time to have much effect, but by the time I reached prison, it seemed I was a little calmer, a bit less obsessive, and my head wasn't such a dark place. In short, the drug seemed to be working—but it was also the thing that would disqualify me. Jenny had warned me back in county that this was the case. But it seemed so absurd and counterproductive that I didn't really believe it until I heard it officially from a bored-looking counselor who laid out the options: If you go off your meds, you will qualify for shock and go home in six months. If you stay on them, you will not.

Christina was taking an antipsychotic, so she was in the same boat. We'd only get all those months off our sentences if we stopped taking the medication that kept us from falling apart.

"I'll do anything to go to shock," Christina said, clenching her jaw.

"Aren't your meds kind of, you know, serious?" I asked. "Or at least pretty necessary?"

"Don't care. I'll do anything."

I scowled skeptically. This seemed like an unequivocally bad idea—for her, but also for me. By that point, I'd been locked up for almost a year, and my memories of the real world felt so far away, like a photocopy of a photocopy. Getting back there was the goal, but it felt less urgent. Plus, if I went off the antidepressant and qualified for shock, then I wouldn't be allowed to start any treatment for the hepatitis. I still hadn't been able to yet, but in general population there was a chance. And on top of that, I'd heard the stories—the same ones Jenny told me before, but now I'd heard them firsthand from people who'd lived them. With the running, and yelling, and physical punishments, shock sounded more like torture than treatment. And if a few extra months in prison meant avoiding a place that was even worse—both physically and in my own head—I could wait.

Without shock, I had sixteen months left. Sixteen months of counting down the days, of living life as a number—at least to the people in charge. To everyone else, I had a jail name, one of the personalized monikers we gave each other behind bars. There was a Blue, a One-Armed Red, a Peter Pan, a few Chinas, several Aces, a Butter, a Beans, and even a Pork Chop. There was a Bad Baby, at least two Misunderstoods, a couple Scrappys, and a Trouble. There was a Justin Bieber and a Tinkerbell. And there was me: Harry Potter.

In the free world, I don't think I really look like the wizarding wonder. But with my short hair, glasses, no makeup or piercings, and a collared prison uniform, the resemblance was— apparently—uncanny. Starting in my first week upstate, complete strangers would spot me on the walkway and shout, "Oh, my God, it's Harry Potter! Why is Harry Potter in prison?"

Anywhere else, I might have been offended. But behind bars, having a jail name felt like a confirmation of our humanity, a subversive demonstration that we could be something other than the numbers assigned to us by the state. These weren't names we'd ever used in the free world, and that kind of made sense: In prison, we were different people.

Chapter 18

Bedford Hills Correctional Facility, October 2011

When I was locked up, the gym was my happy place, the place where I could be most myself. On nice days, it was almost empty, when everyone went to the outside rec yards to see their friends from other dorms. That was the only way we could all spend time together without being "out of place." On cold days, the gym was busier, with women clustered around the card tables playing spades, drawing, gossiping, distracting ourselves from where we were.

At Bedford, the gym had a little weight room on the side, with aging dumbbells and beat-up barbells and worn, pastel yoga mats. The main gymnasium area sometimes smelled like the weed smoke mysteriously drifting in from the bathrooms next door, and it looked just like a high school gymnasium, complete with a small stage on one side and a basketball court in the middle. There was room to walk laps, and a universal machine and stationary bikes and a stair stepper.

I was still not in particularly good shape: slow-jogging across a tiny jail cellblock for nearly a year had not exactly made me into a star athlete again. But if I closed my eyes—for just a second, between strides—that didn't matter. Fleetingly, I could blink away the present, and the prison world would fade to black, replaced by the sound of my own strained breath and pounding heart. I could lean in to the mindless exertion, and when the gym air lapped at my face, I could imagine a slight chill to it. Like a frozen dream. Like skating.

If I concentrated hard enough, I could almost feel the ice beneath me. For a minute, I could be an earlier version of myself, the version I always want to believe is the truest, most real me: the version that did not know prison, or heroin.

The first time I went to the gym at Bedford was during my second week there. There were specific times of day when the guards would shout "Movement!" and you were allowed to go places, rushing out onto the blacktop walkways like it was the changeover between class periods in high school. During one of those movement calls, Christina and I ventured out to the gym together. We hadn't been able to buy real sneakers or sweatpants yet and were still sporting the signature gym attire for newbies: a forest-green collared shirt, green "shorts" that went well past the knee, and white canvas sneakers distinctly ill-suited for exercise. We got on the stair steppers and nervously chattered about the source of the pot smell before falling into silence.

There were a few tough-looking women flexing and showing off by the weights, and a cluster of old-timers gathered along one wall. A few people shuffled cards—or maybe gambled—as they sat at the tables along the other wall. Kelly Clarkson was playing quietly in the background.

"Here's the thing, we started out friends," she sang. *"It was cool, but it was all pretend."*

Then, with no warning, seemingly the entire gym broke out into song.

"Since you been gone, I can breathe for the first time," a choir of locked-up voices shouted. *"I'm so moving on! Yeah, yeah!"*

It was like a flash mob—or at least a flash chorus. In prison. Wide-eyed, Christina and I turned to each other, as if to confirm that we were both hearing and seeing the same thing. Staring, I murmured my shock.

"What the fuck . . . ?"

"Yeah, I don't know," she responded.

I was too new and too self-conscious to sing along. But I mouthed the words and smiled. It was as if some cosmic cog had slipped out of place, a celestial shift I would not have fully appreciated a year earlier. This was not just women singing, this was women learning how to steal joy in a place built to prevent it.

A couple weeks into my time at Bedford, I got my first visit—from Lee. Back in jail, he'd hinted that he might see me again soon, but I never really knew if he meant it until I went upstate and got my first letter, a scrawled note with little sketches of islands and beaches and palm trees tucked into the envelope. By the time he showed up in person, I'd already gotten him added to my official list of approved phone numbers, so we'd had a few calls and I knew to be expecting him. Through the grind of the intake assembly line, that anticipation seemed like it was the only thing that had kept me going. Of course, we had no idea where this would go or how it would work between us. But we started with a date in the prison visiting room.

Visits were in the same building as the gym and the library, in a big room with kid-friendly art at the back and about forty tables with taupe plastic chairs in the middle. There was a rule that I had to sit facing the guard in front—but there were no rules about where Lee could sit, so he nervously slid in next to me. There was no glass between us, and the on-duty guard didn't stop me when I put my head on his chest or leaned in for a kiss.

Our conversation was awkward and stunted, the first we'd had without clandestinely looking over our shoulders to see if anyone was watching. My heart was racing, and he shook visibly for the first two hours. If nothing else, we were well-matched in our anxiety. We talked about jail gossip and prison news and all the things we couldn't talk about before—what our future would be, whether we would tell our families, what the other prisoners would say when they realized he was a guard, whether he'd get in trouble at work. He'd scoured the sheriff's office rulebook and determined that it wasn't technically against the rules to visit me. After all, I wasn't in the jail's custody anymore. But we both knew that eventually, whenever the jail brass got wind of this, they'd have something to say—maybe it would be just a snarky comment, but maybe it would be, "You're fired." The unknown hung over our heads, like a pending court case.

In the meantime, we tried to play normal—as much as a guard and an inmate in a prison visiting room can. He'd brought a bag of quarters for the vending machines, which I wasn't allowed to touch, though I gaped at the array of choices. He bought packs of Reese's and chips to split, but I think he was too nervous to actually eat. After a couple weeks of prison food, I was too hungry not to.

It was one of few visits I had at Bedford, because a few weeks later I was back "on the draft," New York prison slang for being transferred. There were six possibilities for where female prisoners could end up: shock, Beacon, Bayview, Bedford, Taconic, or Albion. I already knew shock was out, and Beacon was off the table because it was a minimum-security camp and didn't allow people on psych meds. Bayview was the only prison in Manhattan, so it was usually New York City folk who ended up there. Bedford—which had the best reputation—was a max and usually reserved for people with a long time left on their sentences, the sort most likely to settle in and avoid trouble. Taconic, the smaller, medium-security facility across the street, was the only place I'd heard nothing about except that a hundred years earlier it was a reformatory for the "mentally defective." The biggest prison, and the one with the worst reputation for drama, was Albion. That was where I ended up. As the other women explained, people "jail hard up there."

It wasn't just the prisoners jailing hard; it was the staff, too. Albion had a reputation for making liberal use of solitary confinement and turning every little thing into an infraction of some kind. We nicknamed the place Ticketmaster because the guards wrote so many disciplinary tickets, for such absurd things: wearing pajamas during the day, loitering on the walkway, not standing during count. And, as a Black woman who'd been there before explained while we boarded the draft bus to head back, Albion was a particularly bad place to be if you were a woman of color. In the prisons near New York City, she said, there were more Black and Hispanic guards. But when you went as far north as Albion, it was a "buncha racist rednecks."

In New York—like in a lot of other states—the prisons were mostly put in rural communities, often as an attempted economic development program for struggling towns that once relied on factories and mills. The thought was that the state institutions would bring in stable jobs, help local businesses, and revive these dying outposts. That didn't always happen—but it did skew the demographics behind bars so that dozens of prisons sat in heavily white communities out in the country but held thousands of Black and brown people from the city. Of course, I didn't realize all this at the time. In part, that was because my privilege had shielded me. But in part it was because this is one of the ways the thing we call systemic racism works, by festering in the dark, churning out racially disparate outcomes in a realm so esoteric it can escape scrutiny. So although I understood in a passing way that the prison system sucked in people of color at a disproportionate rate, I didn't know that just its basic structure could make it harder for them to do time.

But the woman next me in the draft line got that—not the specifics, necessarily, but the generalities. And she also understood what it meant: If you put prisons in a place where it's harder for Black and brown people to do time, and they get written up more often, then they'll go to solitary more often, and it'll be harder to get out because they won't be able to make parole. A sprawling *New York Times* investigation laid these connections bare in

2016, with data analyses proving the disciplinary infractions and parole approvals, and deep reporting linking it to the makeup of the staff and the parole board members. At one upstate unit—the Clinton men's prison near the Canadian border—reporters found that only one of the 998 guards was Black, that Black prisoners were almost four times as likely to get sent to solitary, and that they spent on average thirty-five more days there than white prisoners. And since disciplinary records are a huge factor in parole decisions, Black inmates unsurprisingly made their first shot at parole less frequently. The woman next to me didn't have that data, but she knew what she'd seen, and when she cursed about the reality of things around us, she did it with such assurance that I knew to believe her.

When we climbed off the draft after another grueling six-hour ride to Albion, we were all sent to M1, the dorm for newbies. From the outside, the housing units all looked like boring brick buildings, short and wide like some kind of institutionalized version of an ice rink. From the inside, they looked like warehouses filled with cubicles, sixty or so to a dorm. Some cubes held one woman and some held two, and each was separated by a shoulder-height metal partition. There were no doors, just curtains that were largely pointless because passersby—including male guards doing their rounds—could still see over them. If you wanted any semblance of privacy, the best you could do was the bathroom, which had a row of stalls, but was also mostly unsupervised and entirely off camera. That meant it was the best place for smoking, getting high, having sex, or getting into a fight—the Wild West of the unit.

Those first few weeks we sat through a seemingly endless

procession of "intro to prison" classes, where seasoned prisoners and administrative higher-ups would come in one after the
other to teach us from a set curriculum about everything from
the grievance process to prison jobs to drug treatment programs. We did prison-themed word searches and inexplicably
watched videos on shaken baby syndrome—at a facility with
no nursery, no children, and not even any pregnant women. We
watched that ridiculous suicide prevention video a few more
times, and had an HIV awareness class in which the instructors
went off-syllabus and taught us how to best smuggle in heroin
and make dental dams out of trash bags. At one point, they
helped us understand the spread of disease by coordinating a
role-playing game in which half the class played the vaginas
and the other half played the HIV attacking them.

At the end of it all, we found out our long-term job assignments: I would spend my mornings in a vocational class to learn
horticulture, and then I would work as a rec aide in the gym. The
horticulture class was pointless, and the only thing I remember
learning was that you can't get high from purple passion plants.
It was a reminder the teacher occasionally muttered in annoyance, recalling a former prisoner who thought the plants' fuzzy
leaves looked promising and licked them all to death in pursuit
of a narcotic escape. Even though I wasn't optimistic about the
real-world usefulness of the required vocational training, I was
thrilled about my sixteen-cents-an-hour work assignment.

In theory, work as a rec aide meant handing out free weights
and jump ropes and basketballs and making sure no one stole
them. It was an extremely easy job that did not require multiple
people assigned to it. But since there were always at least three

rec aides, some of us could read, fuck around in the gym, play cards, or work out. It was a lot of the same equipment as at Bedford, plus a few more weight machines and bikes. And in front of a big glass window overlooking the facility grounds, there were treadmills. If I held my head up high, I could look over the other buildings and see only the greens of the free-world trees outside the fence. If I squinted, I could almost blur out the fence, too.

It was in the gym one day that I met my girlfriend. Even if you were married or had a partner in the real world, most women in New York prisons had a prison girlfriend. It was so common we had a phrase for it: "Gay for the stay, straight at the gate." Sometimes these relationships didn't involve much more than clandestinely holding hands, but usually it was more than that, with at least some flirting or kissing or maybe even outright sex—though all of those were risky, because if you got caught you'd go straight to The Place. That didn't stop most people, as I noticed pretty early on; there's an entire page in my journal dedicated to documenting all the weird spots I noticed people making out or having sex.

But it wasn't like hot, sweaty *Orange Is the New Black* sex in the empty library. It was two women with an electric razor on the grimy prison floor, it was eating pussy in the dirty rec yard porta potty, it was fashioning strap-ons out of toothbrush holders and Ace bandages. And in my case, it was making out in the gym closet, next to the weights and jump ropes.

When I turned around after getting off the treadmill one day in early November, I spotted a twenty-something

Latina woman sitting on a stationary bike, and struck up a conversation—not because I was trying to flirt, but because I saw that she was reading *The Portrait of Dorian Gray*.

"That's such a good book!" I announced, with no introduction. She smiled, and her face lit up.

"It's my first time reading it," she said. "I'm not very far along yet."

I told her about my favorite filmic version of it—the 1945 one in part black-and-white—and she told me her name was Dani. At twenty-six, she was a year younger than me, and she told me she was from the city, meaning New York. She'd been going to art school there at the time of her arrest. Now, she lived in the low-drama honors dorm and said she'd already been in prison for three years for kidnapping and torturing a man who raped her. By the time we met, she only had about a year left. She was smart, devious, dramatic, and absolutely gorgeous, with a cute smile, curly dark hair, and perfect makeup. Unlike in jail, that was something we were allowed to buy—but if you got too wild with your eyeliner they'd make you take it off, claiming it was some sort of gang sign.

I did not realize that Dani was flirting until that night, when I went back to the gym during my free time and she brought me a granola bar and some carrots, tucked into her clothing and smuggled past the ticket-writing guards. Within a few days she was my girlfriend. Having a girlfriend on the inside and a boyfriend on the outside was pretty common. And Lee and Dani knew about each other, but we all understood they belonged to different lives, in different worlds. In the world of Albion, Dani showed me the ropes, introduced me to her friends, crocheted me bracelets out of yarn, and wrote flirty notes for me to take back to my bunk. In prison terms, she was the femme.

As I learned in my first few weeks, there were two genders in New York women's prisons: femme and aggressor, or AG. The latter was slang I'd never heard before, but people said it was a New York City thing. The AGs were the men in women's prisons. Some cultivated a short fuzz of facial hair or shaved their heads. Others wore their pants baggy and eschewed makeup. I think one or two had actually been transgender before prison—but even though the AGs all used male pronouns behind bars, most identified as women when they weren't in their prison greens. I never really saw myself as an AG, but most people saw the short hair and assumed. When other women called me "he" or the guards or counselors called me Mr. Blakinger, I didn't correct them. There was no point; in prison, the free world doesn't translate.

Chapter 19

Albion Correctional Facility, Winter 2011

In prison, the forecast is always rainclouds and thunderstorms, ominous and gray like the cinderblock walls around you. No matter how dark things have gotten, the people who've been there longer can offer hair-raising tales of even darker possibilities that lie ahead. Those things don't always come to pass, but the worst seems to happen just often enough to justify a never-ending cascade of anxiety: If you are in jail, you can go to prison. If you are in prison, you can go to The Place. If you're in The Place, they can take away your water.

For me, the next fall in the cascade was when I got moved from the dorm for newbies into a more permanent housing assignment. The dorm name, L1, seemed banal enough—but the other women warned me: *That place is The Jungle—it's wild out there.*

They might have meant the other dorms generally, but I

assumed they meant L1 in particular. When I walked in, everything looked the same, a clone of the place I'd just come from. The layout was identical, and I even recognized a few faces from the gym and rec yard. The guard pointed me to a top bunk in a tidy cube across the dorm, and I tossed my bag of clothes into the empty locker before climbing up the metal ladder to read on the bed. Just before 4 p.m., a Black woman in her early forties with a neatly ironed uniform and slicked-back hair stormed into the cube and glared at me.

"I hope you're not one of those bitches who steals shit—do you steal?"

I told her I did not, and she stomped out, muttering under her breath about how *she* had to get a bunkie when there were other beds free. When she swept back in still glowering a few minutes later, I asked her name.

"You don't need to know that," she said. Since we would be living together in an area approximately the size of an elevator, it seemed to me that really I did need to know that—but I didn't press her. The name tag outside our cube showed her last name was Washington.

"What's this on my bed?" she snapped, bending over to look at some invisible dirt on the taut blanket. "You got dirt on my bed!"

Then, she raised her voice for everyone to hear: "That's dirt! You're dirty!"

For the next few days, this became our routine. She'd accuse me of not showering, then announce to the whole dorm that I didn't shower. She'd accuse me of moving a greeting card she'd left sitting on her locker, then announce to the whole dorm that

I touched her stuff. She'd accuse me of not rinsing my coffee cup, then announce I was leaving dirty dishes and attracting insects.

At night, she'd pound her fist on my bunk every time I moved in my sleep, muttering about how I needed to stop shaking the bunk like I "weighed three hundred pounds." If the edge of my blanket slipped down where she could see it, she'd bang on the metal frame until I moved it. She seemed intent on making every day as unpleasant as she could, and in only the pettiest ways. But in prison, petty was a problem—and problems led to The Place.

If you got in a fight, of course you'd go to SHU. But the same was true even if you got attacked and didn't fight back. Since good behavior offered no guarantees, it was better to be ready with a good cover story. This was one of the lessons prison taught us. Not long after I arrived on the unit, I watched a girl with a huge black eye tell a suspicious CO she'd gotten the shiner from slipping in the shower.

"The shower punched you in the eye?"

"Yep," she said, and kept walking. The CO shrugged and went along with the charade—probably because it meant less paperwork. But guards weren't always willing to look the other way. The day I moved onto the unit, the other women told me about April, a spacey twenty-something who they said had just been shipped off to solitary because she got punched in the face—by a woman named Beatrice, who'd allegedly cornered her in the bathroom and accused her of invading her dreams. When April walked out with a black eye, the guards said it was evidence of fighting and wrote her up.

Just existing in prison was a high-stakes game, and we all

learned that following the rules would not help you win. That's why I was torn about how to handle a bad bunkie. I didn't want to put up with her nighttime pounding and daytime shouting indefinitely, and just ignoring her wasn't guaranteed to keep me safe anyway.

Unsure of a solution but looking for some peace, I stomped off to the bathroom bleary-eyed at 2 A.M. one night. I was only hoping for a few minutes of uninterrupted sleep, maybe while perched on the toilet—but the bathroom was the place for fights, so the rest of the dorm assumed I was lying in wait for an off-camera attack. As I cried in the stall from sheer exhaustion, I was completely oblivious to the chatter outside. When I came back to my cubicle an hour later, the other women either shot me dirty looks or gushed in awe at my willingness to challenge someone with at least a hundred pounds on me to a fight in the middle of the night: "You're a *bad* bitch!"

I did not correct them—but I breathed a sigh of relief that Washington had not taken up the challenge and landed us both in SHU. Instead, she'd just pretended to be asleep as I climbed onto the top bunk. A few days later, I got moved to another cell, not because of the near-fight, but because I'd gone to a woman named Niesha for advice. A forty-something Black woman with dreads and a thousand-yard glare, Niesha had been in prison a long time. She sold drugs, so she knew everyone, and deeply believed that prisoners needed to band together against the navy-uniformed people in power, the guards.

"It's not supposed to be Black against white in here, it's supposed to be green against blue," she told me, her eyes flashing with anger. I wasn't convinced race had anything to do with the tension with Washington—I thought she just seemed miserable and intent on spreading her misery. But I wasn't about to question Niesha, and she offered something better than advice: She put in a word with the Powers That Be, and less than twenty-four hours later I was in a new cube on the other side of the dorm. She asked for nothing in exchange; her girlfriend said I was cool, and that was enough.

Over the next few weeks, I had a whole string of different bunkies. One, who looked like an aging blond elf, got sent to solitary in mysterious circumstances after catching a ticket for hoarding her own hair in an envelope. Another was a smart-ass AG who was selling drugs out of her locker and could get heroin, pills, or pot delivered to our cube. In fact, for an extra fee, it was even possible to get a hypodermic needle pilfered from the medical building. I was not tempted; drugs finally felt like a past life, an escape I did not miss. Unlike so many of my friends, I was not haunted by cravings or drug dreams, and I felt like I'd almost cheated my way out of addiction. Sometimes, I'm still not sure to what extent I got sober and to what extent I just found more socially acceptable obsessions like running and crosswording and writing. But even though I wasn't scheming to get high, I was constantly worried that I'd end up in SHU if my bunkie got caught and we both went down for it—so I took to walking around with Chapstick stuffed in my vagina so I'd have a supply on hand to avoid weeks of cracked, bleeding lips if they hauled me off to The Place.

Across the aisle from my new house was a woman named Tubbs. She was short and muscular, a New Yorker with a gravelly voice and quick, furtive movements. She claimed this was

214 | Keri Blakinger

her seventh state bid, and though she didn't look old enough for that to be possible, I believed her—mainly because she was so volatile. Some days she just stared at people, brooding and silent. Other days she yelled at everyone who walked by, berating them for transgressions she warned would bring down the wrath of the guards.

She was the prime suspect the night my friend Christy got roofied and robbed for three packs of Newports, but she might have been forgettable as a neighbor except for the fact that she kept darting into my cube and pantsing me like we were on an elementary school playground. Then, she started telling people that she planned to rape me. I thought it was probably an idle threat, but I'd heard the tales of a brutal rape over some unpaid debt a few months earlier when four women had held a girl down so a fifth could sodomize her with a broom handle. I didn't know if that story was true, but I started sleeping with a sharpened pencil in my hand just in case.

Even if it was The Jungle, L1 didn't seem any worse than some of the other units, where we heard similar tales of chaos. There was the inane fight over a Christmas card that ended with punches and blood all over the floor. The mystery as to who shit on Flip's bed when she failed to repay a debt. The intrigue over who Charity had ratted on when she overdosed on pills and got sent to SHU. The shock after one woman nearly bit another woman's finger off her hand during a heated dispute involving too much finger-wagging.

On the surface, these stories might all sound like evidence that prisons are full of terrible people who cannot be redeemed. But even as I sharpened my pencil at night, I knew that wasn't it. Prisons are mostly filled with people who are troubled, not terrible—and those who are didn't usually start that way. More than half of women in prison are survivors of physical or sexual violence and roughly three-quarters have mental health problems. A fifth of young prisoners—people under thirty—spent time in foster care. Most prisoners grew up poor, many are not literate, and studies show most did not graduate high school.

Most of the time, I didn't know these specifics in the lives of the women around me. In some key ways I didn't even know the specifics of my own life: I'd never know exactly what happened when I was nine and how I got hepatitis B. For me, that's always been a blank space with questions. But no matter the answers, I knew that in the big picture I was one of the lucky ones, coming from a place of privilege. I knew that so many of the women I lived with had been through everything I had and much more. I was only seeing the end result. I knew I was only seeing the right now when I watched Beatrice aggressively shout grocery lists or argue with an invisible pimp. Was he entirely made-up, or a vestige of her broken past? I couldn't tell. I knew about the girl who ate glass, the girl who had sex with her sisters, the girl who was so illiterate she could not dial a phone, the girl who grew up in group homes watching her friends get raped.

And then there were the Tubbs and Washingtons of the world, who were already distant and unknowable by the time I met them. I never learned about their pasts or their problems. But once I understood the broad strokes, in some ways the details didn't matter. The whole premise of prison began to seem absurd: Locking hundreds of traumatized and damaged women in together and threatening them constantly with additional punishments is not rehabilitation. It is not corrections. It is not public safety. It is systemic failure.

Since my arrest had been in late December, Thanksgiving of 2011 was my first Turkey Day behind bars. Thanksgiving was not the worst holiday to be in prison, but it may have been one of the saddest. The best holidays on the inside were usually the ones that had been the least exciting in the free world—things like Labor Day, Memorial Day, and Super Bowl Sunday. These were the times when it didn't feel as much like an entire season of celebration was continuing without us, when our absences at family gatherings were a little less noticeable.

A lot of people had families in prison—not biological relatives from the outside, but people behind bars they called mothers and sisters and uncles, entire structures mimicking the world we left behind. Aggressors took the masculine roles, adopting titles of brothers and fathers, and just like on the outside, your mother's brother would be your uncle. These were the people who'd have your back, the people you could break bread with and expect presents from on holidays and birthdays. I did not have that—I was too new, and not interested anyway—but on Thanksgiving I was still one of the lucky ones: I had a visitor. Lee skipped spending time with his own family and drove up to see me. All we had to celebrate with was candy from the visiting room vending machine, but we pretended it was a full feast. We took a paper clip and carved the word TURKEY into the back of the Snickers and wrote MASHED POTATOES on the Reese's.

Afterward, I went back to the dorm to read, crossing my fingers and hoping that we wouldn't be stuck with the asshole CO who liked punishing us for trivial or entirely imagined offenses by making us stand in the corners of the dorm for hours at a time like schoolhouse dunces.

But that day, we had a good officer. When he came in for his shift, he saw Washington and a few of her friends cooking together in the common room, hogging the hot plates so no one else could make food. And he issued an order: "It's Thanksgiving. If you're cooking, you're cooking for the whole damn unit."

So they did. The rest of us got together and donated commissary items. Supplies were limited, and spices weren't allowed—except what we got on the prison black market, smuggled out of the mess hall in strip-search gloves. When it was all done, they shouted, "Get your bowls! Get your bowls!" We lined up at the common room tables and gaped.

Despite the lack of tools and the hodgepodge of ingredients, the result was amazing: pasta salad, spiced cabbage, rice, yams, turkey, cranberry sauce, green beans, macaroni and cheese, and ten or fifteen different kinds of cakes and pies. Most of it was a little orange because Sazón is the number one spice in prison, but it tasted so good, and no one fought, no one stole, no one got sent to SHU.

After so many stormy days, it was a rare moment of shared humanity. Then everything went back to how it was. This was not a fresh start or turning over a new leaf. But when I look back on it, I still think that this is how change happens; one day at a time, people learn by stacking together individual moments that eventually add up to a different person. Those moments felt so scarce behind bars, but in my thoughts, they are vivid, highlighted in bold hues by a desperate mind that did not want to forget.

Chapter 20

When I went to jail, I no longer saw the sunrise. After years of staying up till dawn, suddenly I could not see the morning sky. But in prison, I could. Every day, the walk to meds started off heading east into the sun, where contraband colors lit up the crisp air above us, glinting off the razor wire. The jagged silver blades caught the light, but sometimes they also caught free-world trash dancing in the wind or low-flying birds that would squawk in the fence for days. They would struggle, no one would help them, and then they would die.

Nobody was more attuned to the dark symbolism of all that than a thirty-eight-year-old named Stacy. She was an average-height white girl with brown hair and an unremarkable appearance—except for her dancing, distracted eyes that looked past you for at least half of each conversation, like she was always dreaming of ways to fuck the system. Out in the world, she'd owned two Curves fitness studios, which were what landed her behind bars. The businesses started to fail, her checks started to bounce, and she ended up in the pages of the Middletown *Times Herald-Record*. "Curves is a dying concept, with all sorts of problems," she told the reporter who called. "I couldn't live like that, hoping for things to pick up." The company spokeswoman said she'd never heard of an owner getting arrested before. She'd probably also never heard of an ex-owner teaching Curves in a prison gym, but that is where Stacy and I met.

Before she got her job in the gym, Stacy had worked as the inmate grievance coordinator—a position she eventually lost as a result of one of her many trips to The Place. But from that gig, she'd learned all about the petty and egregious wrongs that went on behind the walls—and she'd racked up disciplinary tickets for trying to help. Aside from 109.10, one of the other cardinal rules of prison was that you couldn't help anyone with their legal case. The first time I heard that, I was shocked—it seemed like a brazen admission that prison officials were actively working to thwart justice if it involved incarcerated people. But it was right there in the rulebook: 180.17. If you got caught with someone else's paperwork on you, you were going to The Place. Stacy didn't care. "It's not right! That's not justice," she told me one night at the gym. "What's the average reading level in here—fifth grade maybe? Some people can't read in English at all!" Unlike most jailhouse lawyers, she worked for free, secreting away legal files in her pants, hiding them in books, stashing them between other papers. Sometimes she got caught anyway and ended up in The Place—but by the time we met, she was pretty sure she'd just come up with a brilliant scheme to avoid that.

She hatched her plan after her friend Laura had gotten a

ticket for going to another unit to shower because the shower in her own dorm was too dirty. That may seem like a minor offense, but in prison it was such a brazen violation that I remember gasping out loud when I first heard it. It was as if she'd been caught driving on the wrong side of the road, then told the police it was because she thought the pavement was fresher in the other lane.

Usually, going so far "out of place" would land you in SHU, but Laura was clearly not well. She had an obsessive germ phobia so intense that she got packed off to "obso" instead, our shorthand for the psychiatric observation unit. It was an even more restrictive form of solitary than SHU, with a guard always watching you and no clothes allowed except for the "suicide-proof" smocks that you couldn't tear to make a noose. Unlike The Place, trips to obso usually only lasted a few days. But it was dirty, and the conditions were maddening, and Stacy was worried. She wanted to go check on her friend—so she decided to fake a mental health crisis. Nothing so big it would get her sent to a different facility, but nothing so small it could be ignored.

She asked to see a mental health counselor and explained: There'd been a seagull stuck in the fence a week earlier. He'd been hanging there for days, his wings getting sliced every time he moved. The women tried to throw him bread crusts from the mess hall, but they wouldn't go far enough. One night, he wrenched himself free—only to end up hemmed in on a little paved strip between two fences, where he waddled back and forth, unable to fly. A torrential rainstorm hit the facility, and he drowned.

His suffering felt too close, Stacy said, and now she was

deeply depressed: "He's just like us: dying in the wire," she told the counselor through sobs and wails. She did her best to seem like someone who'd snapped. But instead of sending her to obso, the counselor celebrated it as a breakthrough and called her back again and again to "work through" her feelings. Finally, Stacy announced that she was all better—not because of the counseling but because Laura had gotten out of obso, so there was no need to keep up such a time-consuming ruse.

"I was just being dramatic," she told him. "I was faking it."

The counselor refused to believe her sudden change of heart and bafflingly called in a psychologist—perhaps in the hope of salvaging the "progress" he feared was slipping away. But with that unexpected escalation, Stacy saw an opportunity. A few months earlier, the state had passed a law banning the use of solitary confinement on severely mentally ill prisoners. If Stacy could snag that label, she'd be able to continue her legal work without fear of going to The Place.

So she smuggled a half-dozen greasy chicken bones out of the mess hall and stashed them in her locker.

"The next time I get a ticket and they come pack up my stuff for SHU, they'll find all these fucking chicken bones and they'll be like, 'What the fuck is this?' and I'll start crying and tell them it's my pet seagull that I rescued from the fence, and they should call him by his name."

His name was Henry.

"I can do all the legal work I want! They'll never be able to stop me," she added gleefully, pulling out a bone in the middle of the gym as she told me the whole story.

Sometimes, it turned out, she carried Henry around in her pockets.

"Is that . . . gonna work?" I asked, incredulous.

"I have no fucking idea," she snorted. "But I guess we'll find out! See, here's my next thing: You can't start any petitions because if two inmates ever sign the same piece of paper, they consider it inciting a riot. But I'm totally starting a petition for a pay increase. They keep raising commissary prices because the cost of things just goes up over time, but they haven't raised inmate pay since like the nineties."

Wide-eyed, I just listened in wonder. In prison, the stakes were so high, it was one thing to take a risk for yourself—hoarding contraband makeup or smuggling cinnamon from the kitchen—but it was another thing entirely to take a risk for some free-world concept like justice. So many people lost the will for it. I sure felt like I had. For a year, I'd been living my life in fear of solitary. I wouldn't do anything to attract attention lest the Powers That Be decide to retaliate. Even when the jail had cut off my hair, I hadn't filed any grievances, formal complaints, or lawsuits—mostly because of the unspoken threat of The Place. It loomed over everything, unpredictable and terrifying, like a sea monster rising up from the deep, ready to lash out with a slimy tentacle and drag us into the dark waters one by one. I wanted to hide in the cabin. But here was Stacy, standing on the deck, hands on her hips in defiance.

Even though I was not ready to join her, I knew that she was the person to go to when I needed a certain kind of advice on outwitting authorities—and by that point, I did. Shortly after my arrival at Albion, I'd embarked on the process of getting approved for hepatitis treatment. Back then, treatment meant a forty-eight-week-long regimen of weekly interferon shots, daily ribavirin pills, and a year of unpleasant side effects. Hepatitis is a slow-moving disease, so starting treatment wasn't urgent—but I wanted to get it out of the way while I was in prison and had no real responsibilities. While a year of nausea or dizziness or debilitating fatigue might interfere with my life on the outside, in prison I had no life for it to interfere with. To qualify for treatment, first I needed to get routine clearance from the prison psychiatrist. But when I showed up for a fifteen-minute appointment at his office in some back room of the mental health building, he did not seem inclined to offer his approval.

"One of the possible side effects is depression, and I see you've had a suicide attempt," he told me.

"Yes, but that was five years ago—and I'm sober and on antidepressants now."

Barely paying attention, he was not impressed.

"You'd be leaving me open to a lawsuit if you tried to hurt yourself," he said.

"But I'm in prison, around people all the time," I countered, still hopeful. "If I wait till I'm out then I won't be under any kind of supervision and it seems like I'd be at *higher* risk then. I would think that—"

"You know when I'll care what you think? When you finish your residency in psychiatry."

The sudden vitriol stunned me into silence. I opened my mouth, ready with some sly snark—then closed it again as I remembered: Doctors could write disciplinary tickets, too. I waited a beat, then continued where I'd left off. But I was flustered, and every few sentences, I would forget and let it slip: "I think."

And every time, he would remind me that he did not care what I thought, like a verbal game of whack-a-mole. We went back and forth for a whole hour and got nowhere. At one point, he said he'd approve my request in six months. Then he said I had to sign a release form allowing him access to all my prior mental health records, wherever they may be. Then he said, actually, the risks outweighed the rewards regardless. Then there was the thing he didn't say but that I suspected: He just didn't want to approve spending money on me, an inmate.

At the time, I didn't realize how common this was. Since then, prisoners from Texas to Colorado to North Carolina have sued their states for refusing hepatitis treatment. But in New York women's prisons back in 2011, hepatitis had so much stigma—more so than in the free world—that it was not a thing we spoke about freely. Communal living made communicable diseases far more dangerous, so if you had one you generally did not talk about it. One person I did tell was Dani—and she was livid at the shrink's callous attitude. I was mostly confused and defeated. It seemed like something I should get taken care of sooner rather than later, before there was liver damage instead of after. But clearly there was no one in medical I could trust to tell me how necessary treatment was or wasn't. At Dani's suggestion I turned to Stacy. But on this, even she was stuck.

"Here's the problem," she said. "You can't grieve that guy. He's part of OMH, the Office of Mental Health. Technically, that's not a part of DOCCS—it's a separate agency, so they're not subject to prison grievances."

"So, what do I do?"

"Hope he quits—or that you get transferred. I bet if you were at Bedford or Taconic, they'd sign off on it."

Even if it meant that I could get treatment, I did not hope for a transfer. It seemed hard enough figuring out life at *one* prison—I didn't want to start all over again, or risk ending up some place that turned out to be worse. With fifteen months left, I just wanted to make it out the other side. In a few short weeks, I'd be able to say: "I get out next year."

Those were such big words in prison.

Sometimes, that felt so close—but when I looked at the dirty dorm and the long faces around me, it felt so far. I still had no idea how to restart real life afterward, whether I'd be able to find a job, or where I would live. I had no money and no driver's license, so getting by alone in upstate New York seemed unrealistic. But Lee and I didn't know whether the state would let me stay with him while I was on parole, and we also didn't know whether his job had even found out about us yet. I desperately missed my dog, and despite some assurances, I didn't really know if I'd get her back, since my parents wouldn't let me talk to the family who kept her. I suspect my mom thought I was still too bitter and unstable. I think she was wrong—but I know that over the years, I'd given her plenty of reason to be cautious. So I didn't push too hard and instead settled for secondhand anecdotes.

"Florianna says Charlotte's going on lots of walks and learning to play tug-of-war with Bailey," my mom would tell me, trying to sound upbeat so I wouldn't flip out. "I guess they're dog friends now!" The stories sounded so different from the Charlotte I knew, a skittish dog so convinced she was a human that she refused to play with other dogs and rarely barked. It seemed that while I had been sitting around waiting for time to pass, Charlotte was building a new life without me.

Meanwhile, the traces of my old life were vanishing. My college friends had graduated, situations had changed, people had moved on. And almost exactly a year after my arrest, Alex got arrested, too—in a completely unrelated case. Just like me, the cops caught him with some heroin. But it wasn't nearly as much dope as I'd had, and his demise was not blared across the front page of the paper as mine had been. The only reason I found out about it was because of Lee, who found out about it when Alex got booked into the county jail.

My reflexive response was smirking satisfaction, but that was not the person I wanted to be anymore. When I searched for a better response, I realized it wasn't so much that I wanted to see him in prison—it was that I just didn't want to see him *at all.* I did not want to get out one day and find him lingering around town with his heroin and his lies. And the idea that this could be avoided filled me with a selfish sort of relief. But soon I realized instead of ensuring that he would stay out of my life, his arrest only brought him closer. It was not a situation I'd foreseen—even though it should have been entirely foreseeable.

Now, Lee would see him at work every single day for months and hear all the salacious stories he'd tell his jailhouse friends about me, the ex-wife he said cheated on him and gave him hepatitis. Some days he claimed I'd set him up even though I was already in prison, and once Lee overheard him spewing angrily about how "something" would happen to me when I got out. Even secondhand, his venom unnerved me. His presence, just outside my field of vision, perpetually felt like another old shoe waiting to drop.

Aside from all that, I was still trying to untangle whether I'd really be able to finish school. The university had, after months of back-and-forth, decided that I would be suspended three years to indefinitely—and it wasn't clear if they were really willing to entertain the idea of letting me back in, or if it was just an empty gesture posing as a second chance. But they had begun laying out the requirements, and the first one almost made me laugh: When it came time to reapply, the university wanted to know what I'd learned in prison.

For proof, they wanted copies of any certificates I'd earned. I thought through the classes I'd taken so far: The orientation class where we watched shaken baby videos. The HIV class where half of us played vaginas. The horticulture program where we found out we should not lick fuzzy plants. It seemed increasingly clear that anything we were learning was in spite of prison, not because of it. But for as much as I'd learned about gratitude and change, in that moment my reflexive first response was still shaded with bitterness and entitlement, a dark humor tinged with annoyance at the naive assumption that we were learning something here.

"Do they have certificates for learning how to sleep with a knitting needle for protection?" I wrote in my journal. "For learning how to make tampons out of pads so the specified number of pads you get per month lasts longer? Making a dental dam out of a corner of a trash bag? Do you think they even know that in this day and age in America, the people in charge can withhold water based on behavioral problems? The things that will help me I've learned from other inmates, not in drug abuse classes or orientation or HIV awareness classes. I'll have a year clean on the 20th and I won't get a certificate for that, but it's the only thing that I deserve one for. But then, I guess maybe nothing really important in life can be validated by a piece of paper."

The words were not wrong, though looking back I am not proud of the acerbity I can almost see dripping off the pages. But sifting through my journal a decade later, I also saw something else: After a year off drugs, those outbursts of anger were now the exception, not the rule. There were things, it seemed, that I was finally learning.

Most of the time, the core of prison life was somehow both utterly shocking and entirely predictable, a mélange of boredom and chaos, amplified by the anxious ticking of the clock. But counting down the days and hours had become an aim so singular that sometimes everything else faded away, like a dimming symphony falling silent. In those moments, I was beginning to find something deeply Zen about living life with no other goal but for time to pass. It was the one thing we were guaranteed to accomplish each day. And nothing else mattered.

Chapter 21

Albion Correctional Facility, Winter 2011

On a cold winter afternoon, I curled my legs up into my forest-green sweatshirt and sat on the freshly waxed floor of the day-room, right next to the phones. It was just before Christmas, and the line to call home was longer than normal. When the woman in front of me finished her teary conversation, I scooted over to dial Lee's number and waited patiently as the robotic female voice informed him that this was a call from prison.

Press 1 to accept the charges.

He did, and his words started tumbling out, skipping over the hello and how are you.

"I have some really great news for you, sweetheart," he said quietly, his voice quivering. "So, I look you up on the DOCCS website every few weeks just to check you're there. And you know how it always says your out date is February 2013?"

My heart stopped.

"Now it says September 28—of next year! 2012."

I stared at the phone slack-jawed, as if I could see the four months that had miraculously fallen from the sky and back into my life. In the real world, four months seems like nothing. But in prison, it's a whole season of loss, now miraculously erased. The website didn't offer any clues as to what happened, but I suspected maybe the Powers That Be had simply done the math wrong before and only now caught it. The number of days that disappeared was exactly one-seventh of my sentence—the difference between parole eligibility for a violent crime and a nonviolent one, perhaps a distinction some paper pusher in Albany had just noticed.

Teetering between skittish suspicion and wild, unbridled joy, we debated whether I should inquire further, then decided it was best not to draw any attention to this unbelievable good fortune. Like a magical desert oasis of lush palm trees and better times, we worried that it might disappear if we stared too hard. After I hung up the phone, I walked back to my bunk, glancing at the sad holiday decorations sitting on lockers and windowsills in the cubes along the way. The paper trees. The ornaments drawn in colored pencil. The Christmas cards made with eye shadow. And as I passed them, I realized: This was about to be my last Christmas behind bars.

As it turned out, though, there was still a whole other prison between me and freedom. In mid-December, I got a paper in the mail telling me that the central office in Albany had approved me for a drug treatment program, and then work release. For six months, I would spend three hours a day in group counseling and live with thirty women on the special dorm designated for CASAT, the Comprehensive Alcohol and Substance Abuse Treatment program. Since that program was only offered at Taconic, I'd first have to get transferred back downstate, to the one prison where I didn't know anyone. I wasn't thrilled about that—either the imminent draft ride or the new prison—but the possibility of work release terrified me.

Sure, in theory, it sounded great. If I could find a job near Lee, I could live with him during the week and come back to prison on the weekends. If not, I could at least get some factory gig near Albion and go to work during the day, then come back to prison every night until my real release date. I'd be able to wear real-world clothes and talk to people who wouldn't treat me like an inmate. But Dani warned me: "That shit's a setup."

The rules about what you could and couldn't do during work release were so strict and so arbitrary that you could end up in The Place for just about anything.

"There's a girl who went to SHU for wearing a different bra back into the facility than the one she wore out," Dani said, her pearly white smile disappearing as her face fell somber.

"But . . . why?"

"I think it had underwire or something. So this girl got kicked out of work release, went to The Place, and lost her date. But I heard about people who got booted for wearing back an extra pair of socks or an extra pair of earrings."

She offered more examples, but I already knew I wanted no part of this. On the one hand, it was such a tantalizing possibility—but on the other, it seemed like a high-stakes gamble, the exact sort of risk that sober me knew I should not take. It wasn't a choice, though. If I refused, I'd lose my date and go to lock. All I could do was prepare: Find people who'd been to

Taconic and could dish on the place. Give away all my contraband—my red pen, my secret third hoodie, my clandestinely
hemmed pants—so I wouldn't get in trouble when they packed
me out for the draft bus. Squeeze in as much time with Dani
as I could.

In prison, there's a saying that everything lasts only "until
draft do us part." Once I got moved, we knew it was all over—
not by our own choice but because prisoners were banned
from communicating with other prisoners. We wouldn't be
allowed to call or write each other, and if we got caught going
through someone else on the outside—having a friend or
parent pass along our forbidden missives—we'd go to SHU for
"third-party mail." All the bonds we'd formed to survive would
fray and then unravel, like the edges of the brown yarn bracelet
Dani made me before I left. It was the one piece of contraband
I took with me.

On the road to Taconic, all I heard was tears. We left early
on the morning of January 4, and I was shackled to a seventeen-
year-old named Diamond, who sobbed most of the way. She
didn't want to go to a new prison or do work release, either—
her whimpering cries sounded just like I felt. She was a light-
skinned Black girl from Harlem, and she looked so young, I
couldn't quite process it. It was naive of me, but until that moment, I never would have believed that kids too young to vote
or buy cigarettes could go to prison, let alone that New York
sent them there routinely. I only found out years later that the
Empire State was one of the last two that automatically prosecuted sixteen- and seventeen-year-olds as adults.

When she calmed down enough to talk, Diamond told me

she was here because she'd stolen some cell phones and credit cards, then fucked up her probation. Somehow, someone had decided adult prison was the best answer, as if showing a young Black girl how easily the system could throw her away would miraculously make her better. As we bumped along the highway, I tried to be comforting, telling her that it would probably be better where we were going, though I had absolutely no reason to believe that.

When we pulled up outside, the first thing we saw were the gravestones. They were the last traces of the few dozen people—men, women, and babies—who'd died in prison with no one to claim their bodies. Hidden from the main road by trees, their wasted lives felt like an ominous sign of what lay ahead. Some of us exchanged raised eyebrows, but after a long day in shackles we were too tired for any grim humor. It was well after dark by the time the guards walked us to our new unit, a two-story brick building near the middle of the prison grounds. There was an officer's desk just inside the front door and long L-shaped hallways extending in either direction. Down each hall were single cells, with windows to the outside that were big enough they actually needed curtains. The bottom half of the glass was frosted, but if I stood on my bunk, I could see over that and to the woods, the razor wire, and the creepy old prison buildings that looked just like the aging reformatories they were. By day, it looked like Hogwarts, and by dark, it looked like a horror set.

Because the prison was right across the street from Bedford, a lot of women nearing the end of long sentences had been transferred over from the max to finish their time. There were a handful whose ID numbers showed they'd been incarcerated since the 1980s, as long as I'd been alive. Those old-timers knew how to jail well, quietly getting what they wanted and keeping the peace. And with only three hundred-some prisoners on the compound, that wasn't hard. Even the air felt less chaotic here.

The CASAT unit was not like the rest of the prison; we were supposed to be held to a higher standard because it was a "program dorm." Our shoes had to be tucked under our bunks, the toes all touching the same line of tiles in the cell. Our clothes had to be hung up in a specific order, with everything facing the same direction. There was an hour each day of required meditation or journaling, which we had to do alone in silence. Even in the summer, we weren't allowed to use any plugged-in items—including radios or fans—until after 3:45 P.M. We couldn't sit on each other's bunks or even set foot in the door of another cell. You couldn't wear sneakers or sweatpants until the evening, and you had to be able to instantly produce your state-issued razor at any time. When one woman accidentally flushed hers, she got sent to solitary and nearly kicked out of the program. You never knew exactly what the consequence would be for breaking a rule—but we were repeatedly reminded that we were learning accountability and that being here was a rare privilege. After all, there was the possibility of half-freedom at the end. They did not let us forget that.

Our regular daytime officer, Russo, was a tall white guy with a round face, glinting eyes, and a permanent smirk, like a real-life Draco Malfoy. He was the only guard who called us by our first names, a seemingly kind gesture that he somehow made menacing—like a constant reminder that he could be as personal as he wanted, and we could not set boundaries. Sometimes, he'd wax poetic about using solitary confinement, and once he earnestly explained how much he wished the prison could use sensory deprivation instead of mere solitary. Just twenty-four hours without light, water, food, a toilet, or clothes would work wonders for minor disciplinary infractions, he thought. When he was on duty, Russo liked to put his keys in his pocket so you couldn't hear him coming as he strolled down the hallways to catch us breaking rules. But unlike most guards, he wouldn't write you a disciplinary ticket; he preferred doling out petty punishments on his own.

The first time he got that opportunity with me was two weeks after I arrived. It was during headcount, when we were all expected to stand in uniform at the window slit of our closed doors and wait until the guard strolled down the hallway to check that we were all present. That happened about a half dozen times a day, but the counts—which could last anywhere from five minutes to an hour—didn't always start on time. We only knew to be in place when we heard the officers shouting.

"On the count, ladies! Count time! On the count!"

But Russo was being sly the day that he caught me. He'd never actually called count before he began sneaking down the hall, so I was still sitting on my bunk when I should have been standing by my door. He rapped on the window slit.

"Blakinger! I will stand on the count! Write it a hundred times!"

He turned to leave and called back over his shoulder: "It's count time—you should have known, Keri!"

Skeptically, I asked the woman in the next cell if he meant

it, whether he really wanted me to write lines like an errant schoolboy.

"Oooooh, neighbor, he want you to do it," she said. "And once you do and you give him the paper, he gonna carry it around all day in his pocket and wave it at you. If you don't, you're goin' to The Place."

I shook my head and rummaged in my locker for a notepad. Sure, this was a light punishment; it wasn't solitary, it wasn't sensory deprivation, it wasn't even particularly onerous. It was purely a display of power, with a dash of humiliation. As I wondered what life lessons we were expected to get out of this sort of thing, I pulled out a pen. In a tiny act of defiance, I wrote the sentences in circles and swirls and upside down, making it impossible to count them all—or to tell that I was one short. When I walked down the hall to his desk to turn it in, I was still terrified that he would somehow notice. But he just smirked, flashing a sly grin I couldn't quite decipher.

A few hours later, he suggested that I stand naked for him at the next count. My heart sank into an icy chasm of fear, a familiar panic rising up from the depths of my past like a slimy monster in an ancient bog. I laughed like it was a joke, but I knew it was not. If I did it, he'd be able to hold it over my head; if I didn't, he'd be able to hold it against me. I decided to play dumb, as if I did not think he was serious—but if he decided to push the issue or bring it up again, I didn't know what to do. As he'd already made clear, he was the one in charge here. He had all the power.

Our regular evening officer, Jackson, was usually the nice guy. He was a short Black man who always smiled. Sometimes he loitered in the common area like he wanted to hang out, but a lot of the time he left us alone.

One evening, when a skinny white girl named Hailey came back from the mess hall, she found him already in her cell doing a search. That was pretty normal, since the guards did at least one random cell search on each shift. But this time, the normal five-minute search dragged on to ten, then twenty, then an hour. When it came time for Hailey to make her evening call home, Jackson told her she'd have to miss her phone slot and stay nearby while he kept searching. Lingering at the cell door, she paced and chewed her nails, certain something was wrong.

Over the next few hours, Jackson destroyed her cell—taking out all her food and books and clothes and leaving them strewn about. He checked in all the pockets, then turned to her pile of mail and read every single letter. By that point, Hailey was nearly in tears. She was terrified—whatever was going on, it seemed to be serious. And she knew that if she got in enough trouble on a program dorm, they'd send her to SHU and kick her out of CASAT. Then, she'd lose her date and have to spend a whole extra year in prison. Jackson completely ignored her rising panic, not even looking up to make eye contact until Hailey got the nerve to inquire: "Can you just tell me, *what*, what are you looking for? What's going on?"

"Got a tip that you got third-party mail," he said, his usual smile turned sideways into a grimace of admonishment. He went back to searching.

Hailey sat down at the door and started crying, quietly at first, and then descending into complete hysterics. For four hours, she panicked and sobbed while he tossed every corner of her tiny cell. He read her most personal letters, while she tried to come to terms with losing a whole other year of her life on a false tip. It was well after dark by the time he finished and turned to leave empty-handed.

"April Fool's!" he announced with a smile. "There was no tip."

Hailey's face froze in shock or maybe confusion. But when she realized the whole terrifying ordeal was really over, she laughed in giddy relief, breathing out heavy sighs before any of us stopped to think: *It wasn't even April. It was early March.* As Hailey started to clean her now-destroyed cell, Jackson meandered back to his desk, a gaggle of other women following behind to demand answers they would never get. We were mad then—but by the next morning, we'd all soak it in, accept it as the new normal, and move on. Then, we'd tell each other that prison isn't supposed to be fun. *It's not Camp Cupcake,* we'd say. Not the Hilton. This was how we coped and was probably why I now remember Taconic almost fondly as the best prison I was ever at. It was not any better than the rest; it was just the place where I'd finally learned to cope.

Most of us in the program had jobs for half of the day and drug treatment the other half. For me, that meant mornings working in the mess hall and afternoons sitting through group counseling. After lunch, me and a dozen or so other women would slow-walk into the common room, arrange the chairs in a circle, and get out notebooks, as if we were going to write down the magic secret to stop fucking up our lives.

But instead of learning magic secrets, we had heated debates about who'd scrawled "bitch" on the white board, how much

Diamond should be punished for exposing her midriff while dancing, whether Kourtney had really carved another girl's name on her leg, and why people kept screaming "suck my dick" down the hallway. Once, we spent twenty minutes confronting Coda about why she kept sticking her fingers up Gloria's nose. The meeting devolved into screaming and tears and nothing changed: Coda was still rude, and Gloria still hated her.

But those were the easy days. The sessions I dreaded were the ones when Mr. S showed up. Technically, Mr. S was the counselor assigned to another drug program in the same building, but he liked dropping in on CASAT just because he could. He was a skinny Italian guy from the Lower East Side, in his late fifties, perpetually tanned, always talking trash, and often standing outside the dorm chain smoking in his black leather jacket. His full name was Santos Sardegna, and he'd once been addicted to heroin himself. But now, with twelve years sober, he seemed cool and confident. You wanted him to like you, but he didn't seem to like anyone. He was a true believer in that tough-love style of counseling that feels more like abuse than therapy.

Sometimes, he'd call people crackheads or morons. Once, he made two women sing "The Itsy-Bitsy Spider" for forty-five minutes because they hadn't cleaned well enough. After watching him spend an entire session telling one woman how she must be dumber than she thought if she ended up in prison, I decided I would never talk to him. I hoped I could just keep to myself and he would not notice—but he did.

"You're just skating by here without doing anything, Potter," he sneered in my direction one day in group. It was the first thing he'd ever said to me, and my heart raced. Even after almost a decade in the drug world and a year locked up, the thought of squaring off against a petty bully still made my chest tight like it did when I was in fourth grade.

I stared ahead, silent.

"Yeah, you can't say anything because you know it, I know it, and everybody else knows it," he said, with a sour roll of his eyes. "Just go out and intellectualize your way right back here a few more times."

Still, I said nothing. For the next several months, I said nothing every time, whether he made fun of the way I walked or the fact that I wore glasses and "couldn't see what was right in front of me." I stayed silent when he made snide comments about my hair, which was still short and messy, because I'd cut it myself in the shower. He said he'd given up on me just like I'd given up on it. They mimicked playground insults, but with an added barb designed to make them sound vaguely relevant, bullying thinly veiled in the language of drug treatment.

In my heart I knew that he was wrong—or at least I hoped that he was. Over the course of the past year I'd tried so hard to become a better person. To be less resentful and more grateful, calmer and less volatile. Ready to make better decisions, to stop hurting people, to stay sober. And since I'd never spoken more than a couple words to him, he didn't know that. He didn't really have anything to go on—but he did have one thing I didn't: Twelve years without heroin. There wasn't anyone else in my life who could say that. He seemed so mean and miserable, but he was the only role model I had and I was scared to ignore him completely. Sure, it felt like I was on the right path—but I was still in prison, and until I could actually try out the new me in the real world, I'd never know. You can say you'll stay sober all you want when you're locked up, but what matters is what happens when you get out.

Chapter 22

Taconic Correctional Facility, February 2012

In the beginning, every horror story you hear in prison seems incredible—not just extraordinary, but impossible to believe. When a woman tells you about the officer who punched her in the face, you think there must be more to it. When old-timers warn you about the brutality of women raping each other, you wonder if they're hazing you. When you hear about the girl who caught a heroin habit in SHU, you think that cannot be true. But eventually, you learn. Eventually, you've heard the guards talk about withholding water, you've seen prisoners smearing feces on the walls, you've met women who've offered blow jobs for extra toilet paper. You've gotten used to the idea that objectively shocking shit happens—and almost nothing seems so shocking anymore. Almost.

One day when it was still too cold to be outside, I spotted two new girls sitting at a card table in the tiny, overcrowded Taconic gym. They were nervous-looking white women in their early twenties—but they caught my eye because of their shaved heads, the sure sign of a shock camp reject. In theory, if you finished the six-month program—the one I'd so badly wanted to get into—you'd go home early. But if you got injured or sick or kicked out, you'd go back to regular prison to finish the rest of your sentence, with a telltale military buzz cut, shining like a scarlet letter.

Some women saw that beacon and shook their heads in quiet sympathy, but others saw it and pursed their lips in disgust, turning around and muttering about the sort of woman who didn't love her family enough to just tough it out for six months. When I saw it, I slid into an empty seat at the card table, looking for answers. I wanted news about Christina, the chatty, long-haired girl from reception who'd gone off her meds to get into the program. *Did they know her? Was she still at shock?* And, most importantly: *Was she going to make it through?*

One woman—the younger of the two—said nothing, staring at the table while the other responded in whispers. Yes, she said. Christina was doing okay—unmedicated and impulsive, but still on track to graduate and go home. We kept talking, trying to figure out who else we knew in common: shock drop-outs I'd seen at Albion and new intakes they'd seen at Lakeview. Usually when I met women coming from shock they seemed vaguely sad, as if they were still mourning their lost chance to go home early. These women were sad, but this was different. They also seemed shaken, with a skittishness I mistook for the usual unease of being fresh meat at a new facility.

When I told them this wasn't a terrible place to end up, the older one said it didn't matter because they wouldn't be here long. They were both going home in sixty days, the same time as the rest of their platoon. I cocked my head to the side, thinking I'd misunderstood. I knew that if you got kicked out of shock—whether it was for a broken leg, or too many disciplinary tickets, or just because the drill instructors thought you weren't trying hard enough—you had to do the rest of your time. You didn't get to go home.

Before I could ask more, a smug woman eavesdropping at the next table jumped in.

"I was in shock before," she said, matter-of-factly. "The only reason that you could possibly still get out when the rest of your platoon graduates is if you got raped by a D.I. So unless that happened, someone's been lying to you."

She did not wait for a response before turning back to the card game in front of her, but her words lingered in the air. The women from shock exchanged a heavy look, and the younger one got up and left. Her friend waited till she was out of earshot to explain: It happened one day during GED class.

Everyone else was in school or outside enjoying a cherished cigarette break, but these two women didn't smoke and already had their high school degrees. So they stayed behind, and that was how they ended up alone with a guard who gave them no choice. He told them what to do and warned them they'd be kicked out of the program and lose their dates if they tattled.

So they kept quiet. They put their freedom first—ahead of their safety, ahead of their own bodies, ahead of everything. When she told me their story, Angela did not lay out all the graphic details, but I did not need to hear them to understand the contours of the scar this would leave.

All the other women in their platoon knew what happened, and some joked about them "taking one for the team"—though eventually it was one of those other women who reported it. But out of everything, this was what shook me the most: When the Lakeview higher-ups finally found out, they tossed Angela and her friend in solitary, supposedly for their own protection.

A few days later, they got shipped to Taconic, where they turned up at the barren card table with their hard truths and haunted looks. That night, as I sat alone in my cell after lock-in, I played it all back in my mind and pulled out my journal. After everything that I had seen and heard in prison, this—this combination of sexual assault and solitary confinement—was something I struggled to digest. Sure, in an abstract sense I understood that it was possible for such things to happen to someone, somewhere. But this was different: These were two women in front of me. I could reach out and touch them and feel their pain. And as I wrote, I realized: *I don't smoke. I have a diploma. If I had done shock, that could've been me.*

The thought hit me with a stinging clarity I would have missed a year earlier. Then, I would have seen it as another unfortunate thing that happened to another unfortunate person, but now I finally understood something incredibly basic about life: chance applies to you, too. If there is a chance something might occur, it actually fucking might. You might get arrested, you might go to prison, you might catch something from a dirty needle. This is a slice of reality you have to ignore when you are getting high or the steady stream of risk is just too much to ford. For more than a decade, I had ignored the rising waters eddying around me. But, sober, I could not. On the one hand, that meant I now seemed to register other people's pain more clearly, maybe because I understood how easily it could have happened to me. But on the other hand, that meant that I saw risk everywhere.

When I called Lee one evening after group, he answered the phone and his voice was quiet, speaking in the hushed tones he reserved for fear and joy. At first, I was worried it had to do with Alex—that he'd made some threat, or done something horrible that I hadn't dreamt up. *This is the other shoe dropping,* I thought. I braced myself.

"Here's what happened," Lee whispered, as if a lower volume would make it less real. "So the chief and the undersheriff pulled me aside at work and said they knew about us. They knew that there'd been letters and phone calls and that I visited you."

Somehow, I was surprised. We'd always known they would find out eventually, but it seemed like so long without consequences that I'd almost begun to wonder if the Powers That Be knew and simply didn't care.

"Who the fuck told them?"

"Well, it's weird, they must have got logs from the prison, but they don't normally check that shit. And somehow they only knew I visited you at Albion—they never found out I started seeing you back at Bedford."

That seemed like a clue: Whoever the tipster was, we thought it must be someone who'd seen us together in the Albion visiting room. He didn't know any of the guards, but there were a dozen or so other women from Tompkins County who might have recognized him. Any of them could have written the sheriff with a tip, mentioned it casually in a letter to a jailed friend, or even accidentally let word slip the one time a lieutenant came up to interview a few of us for an unrelated investigation. We'd never know exactly what happened, and we did not dwell on it because in the end the consequences were relatively minor: Lee lost some vacation time and got a write-up—but that was it. As it turned out, no matter how much the higher-ups at the jail pursed their lips in distaste, visiting a former inmate wasn't actually against the rules.

In some ways our whole relationship felt like a fuck-you to the Powers That Be, spitting in the faces of his miserable bosses and snatching a shot at happiness from the sticky claws of the system that engulfed us both. At Lee's next visit, we were jubilant, shocked we had escaped the biggest risk on our shared horizon. We poured out our relief over vending machine candy and endless board games. But we never talked about whether this—us, our relationship—was actually a good idea or whether we would really be able to move on and go from guard and prisoner to equal partners.

Instead, what we talked about in the visiting room was his camping trips, my prison drama, our shared jail gossip, and updates on whether he'd succeeded in teaching his adorable but incredibly stupid dog any tricks. Those visits were my only chance to see vestiges of the real world and build bridges to life on the outside. But they were never enough; no matter how much your friends and family come to see you, it is so hard to nurture a relationship over nothing but a beat-up card table and a partial set of Scrabble tiles.

Plus, every visit came with a price: There was the strip search before and after. The humbling act of squatting and coughing for a stranger several times a week was something I'd gotten used to back in county. But here there was a new twist: If you were on your period, you had to take out your bloody tampon and put it on the floor so the guard could be sure you were not smuggling anything back from your visit. This requirement—one that prison officials later denied ever existed—always baffled me. Did they think if we stuck drugs into our vaginas they would fall out unless we shoved a tampon in there, too, like some sort of contraband cap for our lady parts? Did they think we would put the drugs inside the tampon? Or were they just trying to make sure we did not mistakenly start to respect ourselves? When I think back on those visits ten years later, I wish that the sharpest emotion I remembered was happiness or relief or even the bittersweet pain of saying goodbye again and again to the people I loved. But it is not. The feeling I remember most is the shame at the end.

My only other visitors at Taconic were my parents, who made the three-hour drive from Lancaster every month or two, and sat across the table from me, doing their best to see through the inmate ID number emblazoned on my chest. For more than a decade, our relationship had been awash with tension and doubt—but since my arrest, the tides had shifted. Now, I told them everything: every prison horror story, every terrifying fight, every threat of The Place, every hope for the future. By that point, any veneer of normalcy I'd been nurturing had decayed so thoroughly that there were no more pretenses to keep up and nothing to hide. For the first time ever, I think they knew that I was not holding back.

And now, when they listened without flinching, it felt like maybe they had accepted: Whether or not I had measured up as the daughter they wanted, I was the daughter they had. They did their best to be there for me when I did not expect it or feel like I deserved it. They put money in my commissary and ordered the prison-approved clothes and food. They sent me books that I devoured—*A Clockwork Orange, The Color Purple, Orange Is the New Black.* They gave me updates from the free world, about my brother, about Mark, about people they'd run into around town. They told me how Charlotte was doing, and how she'd learned to steal blueberries straight off the bushes when David and Florianna took her to a blueberry patch outside of Ithaca. And when I scribbled secret observations in my journal, they were the ones I sent it to for safekeeping, away from the prying eyes of the prison guards.

That spring, one of the things I most wanted to keep from the guards, and the other prisoners, and the snarky barbs of Mr. S was my hepatitis treatment. Just a few weeks after I showed up at Taconic, the psychiatrist and doctor both cleared me to start the yearlong regimen of pills and shots. Unlike at Albion, there were no dismissive reminders that I did not have a medical degree—just a few more tests and a trip to the local hospital for a liver biopsy. It felt like such a victory, as if I'd won some kind of healthcare lottery.

The night after I got my first shot, I woke up around 3 A.M., nearly puked, and fell back asleep. The next day, my body ached—but that was it. Then a week later, I broke out in a rash. It started as two small, red patches on my hips and spread to my thighs, my feet, my stomach, my shoulders, my hands, and even the backs of my ears. Every inch of my body itched, and when I scratched myself till I drew blood, the wounds grew sour and infected. The doctor gave me Benadryl, then Zantac, Claritin, and steroid creams, but none of it made any difference. My hands turned red and wrinkly until it looked like I'd fallen victim to an evil wizard's curse. Soon, I grew anemic and pale, and started losing hair, then losing weight. My closest friends began telling people it was chemo; even on a unit full of women who'd carved whole lives around doing drugs, hepatitis still held too much stigma, and they wanted to protect me. But they could only do so much: If I simply wanted to know whether this was normal, there was no remedy for that.

When you're in prison, you can't go get a second opinion, scour the internet for more information, or call up some friend of a friend who's a nurse and can offer a quick hack or dash of reassurance. Figuring out the best course of action feels like complete guesswork—and you can only take the word of a doctor who works for the same system that didn't want to treat you in the first place. Sometimes, they shoot you a glance that says they think you're just a scheming inmate or an ungrateful drug addict who doesn't deserve this care. Sometimes, they just assume you're not smart enough to understand what's happening. At Taconic, when I asked too many questions, the doctor told me that I should consider finding religion: "Modern medicine can only do so much," she said. I couldn't decide if it was life advice from a devout believer or a warning that I was at death's door.

There was only one person I knew who had been through hep treatment before and might have insight, or at least some experience to compare mine to: Mr. S. I'd heard him mention it before, so I knew that he'd done the yearlong course of interferon and ribavirin at least once, that it had been rough, and that it hadn't worked. But four months into my time in CASAT, I'd still barely spoken to him. When I did talk in group, it was only on the days he wasn't there. On the days that he was, I kept my mouth shut while he told me my silence meant I wasn't doing the work, that I was bound to come back if I did not open up to him. I so badly wanted for him to be wrong, but my track record showed that so often I was the one who was wrong. For months, his predictions bothered me—until suddenly they didn't.

One day in May, after he started in once again about how I wasn't talking enough about my "issues" and my past enough and hadn't done anything to change, I told him that was not true.

"I do talk," I told him. "I've *been* talking in group. Just not to you."

Pushing the boundaries, I added: "I don't see what's so magical about talking to you in particular."

He registered a flash of surprise, then rolled his eyes. After group ended, he leaned over from his chair and lowered his voice.

"All your bullshit about not wanting to talk around me is just a cover," he said. "You're just too chickenshit to share in group."

I shook my head and held up a hand to stop him. "No. That's not it at all. It's just that I don't care what you think about 'my issues' because I don't want the kind of sobriety you have."

My heart pounded as I spoke—he could put me in SHU if he wanted, for any imagined reason he might make up. He could give me extra chores, or have me locked in, or write me up so I'd lose visiting or phone privileges. But I was done being gaslit into believing I needed abuse to become a better, healthier person. My gut said this was unnecessary—and finally I was willing to trust myself. He did not interrupt, and I continued.

"I sort of thought that if I didn't follow the advice of someone who had managed to stay sober for twelve years, I was taking a risk," I told him. "But you seem miserable, and I don't ever want to be like you."

When I finished, he again rolled his eyes, but did not fire back.

After group, I bolted back to my cell, my pulse still racing as I pulled out my radio, a pen, and a piece of blank paper. As I sat down by the locker I used as a desk, the familiar chords of a Gotye hit came on, and I hummed to the reedy voice rhapsodizing about somebody that he used to know, and a past that did not make sense.

I'll admit that I was glad it was over.

I started writing, pausing to add in a missed word, making my corrections in ink. When I finished, I put away the loose pages of my journal, sat down on the bunk, and let myself fall into the music, leaning into the notes as if I were gliding on ice.

I don't wanna live that way.

I sang along softly and smiled at the unfamiliar sense that I was doing the right thing. I'd trusted myself, because I was now a person who could be trusted. I closed my eyes to soak in the moment and this feeling—this thing that seemed like hope.

Chapter 23

Taconic Correctional Facility, June 2012

When the end is near, time slows to a trickle. Not the way it does on the ice at Nationals, when adrenaline moves faster than the ticking clock. Not the way it does at the top of a gorge, when the world is frozen. And not the way it does in The Place, when the hours blend together and disappear.

This is not reality fading away or closing in but simply refusing to move forward, with such stubbornness that it seems physically painful—like the struggle of a wild animal trapped in a tar pit and straining to break free.

In prison terms, this is getting short. That's the word for when your bid is almost over, and you are about to go home. By the start of summer, I was getting short. My twenty-eighth birthday that June was my last behind bars, and a few of us celebrated in the CASAT dayroom. My new girlfriend—Hailey, the woman who'd been the target of Jackson's cruel April Fool's "joke"—cooked dinner on the unit hot plates, then tried making ice cream with nothing but sugar, milk, ice, and Snickers from the commissary, all ground together in a contraband plastic bag for twenty minutes. It was an abject failure and we ate it anyway, then giggled over her gift: a foot-tall stuffed zombie made of paper sewn together with dental floss and filled with the fluffy insides of a disemboweled maxi pad. On the back were notes from my friends:

Thank you for being in my life.
Hope u have a better time next year.

On the front was the ghoulish grin of a creature ready to come back to life.

That same month, I got an official schedule change and found out that I would now spend my mornings in a pre-release program for the handful of us getting ready to go home. Some of my classmates had been locked up for more than a decade, and yet were expected to learn about success after prison from two weeks of role-playing and handouts. There was no internet access to teach us about finding jobs online, no cell phones to show us how to send professional emails, and no computer to type up résumés. At one point, the instructor had us write our own obituaries, as if this were the thing we would be more likely to need. Like the intro to prison classes back at Albion, it was not helpful—but this time around I was so thrilled to be there that I did not care.

As excited as I was about leaving, I was also worried about the approaching threat of work release. As soon as I finished my six months in CASAT, I'd still have to take part—even though I was scheduled to go home for good in September. Given how sick I felt from the seemingly unending hepatitis treatment, I wasn't even sure if I *could* work. As it turned out, the prison system wasn't sure that I could, either, because in mid-July I found out I'd been medically disqualified.

It was Mr. S who told me—but not with a sneer or a roll of the eye. Things between us were different now. After our stand-off in May, he'd begun sitting near me in group and making jokes under his breath—jokes that were *to* me, not about me. Then, we started having normal conversations; I'd ask him why he'd finally gotten sober late in life, or how he'd done it without the usual twelve-step program—and he'd answer, without the insults or snark. Eventually, he wanted to make me the unit coordinator, the prisoner in charge of making sure chores were done, conflicts were resolved, and everything was running smoothly. It was a time-consuming position of headaches and scolding, a responsibility usually foisted on women close to finishing the program.

"I don't think I can do that," I told him.

"You don't get a choice, Potter! I want you to be coordinator."

"No, I mean I physically can't. Like, I have a medical situation."

"You gotta give me more than that."

I took a deep breath. "I'm on interferon."

He looked wounded and asked—I think rhetorically—why I didn't come to him sooner. I don't remember if I even answered. Afterward, he made a point of asking how I was doing every day, and when Albany sent word that I'd been booted from work release before even starting it, he wanted to be the one to break the news.

"I'm sorry, Potter," he said when he pulled me aside to tell me during his cigarette break.

I felt a twinge of disappointment—but mostly a rush of relief as I turned and headed to my morning work assignment, and he strode inside for group.

"I bet you don't think I'll stay clean," I told him later. "I'll have to send you a 'Fuck you, I'm sober' card every year just so you know."

He laughed, then grew serious.

"No, I don't think that at all," he said. "I just think you're too smart for your own good."

It was one of the last times we talked, because not long after that, I got sent back up north, to the chaos of general population at Albion. It had only been eight months I'd been away, but so much had changed. This time around, I got put in a different dorm, a couple buildings over from The Jungle I'd been assigned to before. The unit was far calmer, though every morning we woke up to the sound of guards practicing to kill us as they fired off rounds at the shooting range just beyond the trees.

Stacy was still there, with updates on her latest lawsuits and petitions. But so many of the faces I missed had been transferred to other prisons, packed off to shock or let out on parole. Dani was gone, sent to a unit in Manhattan where she'd spend the last few months before her own release. And though Hailey was already at Albion—she'd beat me out of Taconic by a few weeks—I couldn't see her because she was in the separate work release dorm. She'd started a job at a nearby factory, but after a few weeks unwittingly came back with an extra pair of earrings, one more than the permitted number. For that, they sent her to solitary for an entire month, kicked her out of work release, and took her date. A year earlier I wouldn't have believed it. Now I understood that it was true, and I skipped over the shock and disbelief, instead mourning the loss of a fallen comrade.

Another thing that had changed was that now I was not one of the newbies. When people saw me on the walkway, they shouted in anger: "Harry Potter, why you back?!" They thought I'd already gone home and violated parole, wasting a shot at freedom. But the new girls, the ones with the freshly ironed name tags and bewildered faces, looked at my ID number and saw someone who'd been where they were going.

What should I know? How do I make my time go quick?

The woman who asked me during rec one day was in her early twenties, and at the beginning of a three-year bid. I paused and squinted, trying to put the past two years into words.

"I don't know, man," I said, still thinking out loud. "I think how quick the time goes in here comes down to who you are, or who you turn into."

I was so close to leaving that it felt like time had already stopped—but her question made me stand back and look again. And when I did, I could see how much the pace of life had shifted. For the me who came into jail two years earlier, every day was bitter and long. For the me getting ready to leave now, the days were calmer and went by more easily.

"I think if you can somehow figure out how to become a happier person, every day—not just the days in prison—passes more quickly. That's the only trick. It's like some of the tools you need to survive time in here are the tools you needed to survive life out there. And if you had them, you probably wouldn't be here in the first place. But now that you're here, it's just harder to find them."

She fell silent, and I realized my words must have sounded cryptic, like those of a Cheshire cat about to disappear.

"You did," she half said, half asked.

"Yeah. But in spite of this place, not because of it."

Two weeks later, I walked out the door.

It was a cool Friday morning. The sun was shining through the clouds, and Lee was there to pick me up. He stood in the parking lot as I struggled out with a cardboard box that held everything I owned: books, journals, letters. The bracelet from Dani, the zombie from Hailey, all the assorted detritus from doing time. As soon as Lee caught sight of me, he ran over to help.

Not caring what fell out, I dropped the box and threw my arms around him. It was the first time we'd ever touched outside the razor wire, and now I was the one all nervous and shaky. When we got in the car, our first stop was for coffee— real, brewed coffee with real liquid creamer—at a highway rest area with a Dunkin' Donuts. The building looked just like one on the other side, the one we'd stopped at eleven months earlier when I was in handcuffs, chains, and an orange jumpsuit. Instead of Reese's, this time I got a toasted everything bagel with cream cheese, something I'd been craving for months and have never craved since.

When we got back in the car, he asked: "What do you wanna do next, honey?"

"See Charlotte."

He passed me his phone, and I poked at it in confusion. When I'd gone in, most people didn't have smartphones—so I'd never used one before, and the fancy lock code and sleek touch screen felt like a piece of the future. With his help, I dialed the number—and heard Florianna's voice for the first time.

"Oh yes, Keri!" she said, rolling the *r*'s with a slight Costa Rican accent. If she had qualms about meeting a lady fresh out of prison, she hid them well. "Come over. We are so excited to meet you!"

I was nervous walking up the stone walkway of that ritzy home in Cayuga Heights, the suburb at the edge of Ithaca where rich professors like to live. Florianna and David had their own little forest out back, a stream on the side, and a beautiful garden out front with beds of flowers I could never identify or keep alive. Here I was with my jagged prison haircut and ill-fitting clothes my mom had ordered for my release, garments that felt awkward and foreign, their folds too soft and forgiving.

When I knocked, I heard the clickety-clack of dog nails on the floor, with the heavier steps of a human following behind. Florianna swung open the door. She had dark black hair and shiny dangling earrings, twinkling eyes, and a broad smile with dimples—one of the most joyful people I have ever known. Pulling at my skirt, I walked in and grinned as I saw Charlotte.

But she did not run toward me. She did not jump or bark. She barely wagged her tail. It had been almost two years— she had no idea who I was. In all the times I'd played this day through in my head, this possibility had never occurred to me: My dog had forgotten me.

We'd been through some of the worst moments of our lives together. She'd loved me when I couldn't love myself, and blindly accepted me when everyone else had judged. And ever since that first night in jail, I'd dreamed of her coarse black fur and musty hound smell, counting down the days till I could hear her familiar bark. Now, she didn't even know me at all. The truth sat heavy in my stomach, like a too-big slice of the saddest cheesecake ever.

"Maybe it's just your hair," Florianna said. "It used to be long, right? And you probably smell different now."

But if I was different, so was she; the dog who'd been so skittish and malnourished when we first met five years before was now sleek and calm, her soft fur sporting more patches of white than I remembered. She had her shit together. Fresh out of prison with no plan for the future, I still had a ways to go. For the next hour, I feigned normalcy as I sat on David and Florianna's beige carpet and played with Charlotte in front of the floor-to-ceiling living room windows. We all talked, and I tried to pretend that this didn't feel surreal, that I was not Alice stepping back through the looking glass. When Lee and I left, we did not bring Charlotte—she had a new home, and a new family. I hoped I could take her with me someday, but not yet. It was still before dark when we got back in the car and drove forty-five minutes out into the country to my new home at Lee's.

I think we both knew we were jumping ahead fast, moving in together on my first day out—before we'd ever even had a real date in the free world. But I didn't have any money of my own or any other places to live, so I could either go to a shelter or we could take a leap of faith. Despite my abysmal track record with leaps of faith, it seemed like this was not a difficult choice—especially when the parole office approved the arrangement with no questions asked. Plus, I reminded myself that unlike every single other person I'd dated, Lee was sober, working, and not breaking the law. He had a car and an apartment, an adorable dog, and a loving family nearby.

There was so much to be grateful for, and I knew that so many of my friends would get out to much less. But that night, I did not reflect on any of that. Instead, I was overwhelmed with vivid feelings of joy, confusion, hope, and relief for every second until I fell into a bed that now seemed so soft I woke up sore in the morning.

Then, I cried myself to sleep.

On the inside, it had been easier to ignore that the world had moved on. I'd been a fuck-up in the company of fellow fuck-ups—and together we could almost forget how much we'd derailed our own lives. But now that I was in the real world, I was surrounded by people who were not fuck-ups, people who spent their days doing more substantial things than simply letting time pass. They held down jobs, got degrees, bought houses, wrote books, lived their lives. I wanted all that, but it felt so far—familiar but unknowable, like dreams from a past life.

Chapter 24

My first year out of prison was a blur, a lost year. Lee and I lived in the middle of nowhere: Newark Valley, New York. Down a long driveway off a country road four miles from the nearest bus stop, we had a messy two-bedroom on the second floor of a small brick building a few hundred yards from a meth house that eventually blew up. Lee's extremely talkative older brother lived in the same fourplex, and his mother was twenty minutes away, close enough to stop by with food or have us over for dinner. She was chatty and welcoming and didn't appear the least bit fazed that I'd just gotten out of prison.

They were most of my world in the beginning, when I had nowhere to go and no way to get there. Occasionally, my own parents would come visit and we'd go shopping, or they'd take me out to dinner at our favorite vegetarian restaurant in Ithaca, like an imitation of some regular family whose kid never did time. We talked about parole and prison and Lee and whether

I'd ever be able to get back into Cornell, and I can only imagine how strange the waiters must have found our snippets of conversation. But my parents still lived in another state, so those dinners were the rare exception: Most of the time, the days blended together as I sat on the black leather sofa in Lee's living room, clack clack clacking on his laptop with the American flag on the back, emailing my mom to tell her everything and scouring Craigslist for jobs that didn't require a car or a background check. When he was home, Lee sat next to me playing Xbox or watching mindless shows like *Ancient Aliens* and *Pawn Stars* and *Tosh.0*. Sometimes, we went out to the mediocre Chinese buffet a couple towns over, or got groceries together—and I gawked at the rows and overwhelming rows of choices and colors and foods that hadn't been around two years earlier, like single-serving cups of oatmeal and drinkable cans of tomato soup.

When Lee was at work, I spent long hours alone, cleaning the apartment, trying to figure out basic appliances, and writing clandestine letters to the women who were still in prison, my words disguised as those of someone who was completely free and not on parole. It was one of those days on my own that I finally got up the nerve to log back into my email and my Facebook, still dreading the avalanche of unanswered messages from disappointed friends I'd let down two years earlier. Before checking my inbox, I scrolled through posts documenting photogenic lives, and I noticed which ones were missing, the people who'd unfriended me after my arrest as if I were too far gone for them to admit we had ever known each other. It stung, but it was something I'd at least expected. What I did not expect were the messages and emails from complete strangers who'd tracked me down after seeing the news and reached out to let me know how worthless I was.

"HAHAHAH," one guy wrote.

"Rot in prison!" said another. The one that stuck with me most, though, was the man who described in detail how he wished I would die, saying that police should have killed me to rid the world of another useless drug addict. A few years earlier, I might have agreed. But now I clicked through to the profile, scrolling up and down as I looked for answers. I wanted so badly to make a life worth enough that people somehow wouldn't say those things—or at least worth enough that I wouldn't believe them. From my spot alone on the couch in the middle of nowhere, that felt a long way off.

At that point, I had no income and was entirely dependent on my parents, my boyfriend, and government assistance. I was still working my way through the yearlong hepatitis treatment and didn't have a driver's license, a college degree, or any work history. There was no public transit, and the only places in walking distance—the gas station and Subway—were not hiring. After days of trawling the internet, I landed a gig writing trivia for a Korean quiz site. It paid twenty-five cents per question and came out to well under minimum wage, but it felt like some gesture at productivity, some sign that I was starting to rebuild.

In case you have ever wondered, a barnacle's penis is eight times its body length, bubble wrap was originally invented as 3D wallpaper, an earthworm has ten hearts, and almost a third of people released from prison end up right back there within a year. On the inside, we'd always judged those people so harshly. But once I got out, I realized: Parole isn't really designed for you to succeed.

When you're "on paper," you can go back to prison for something as trivial as getting a speeding ticket, getting caught out just a few minutes after curfew, or getting caught doing any mundane errand in another county. The rules are expansive and unexpected: There are required weekly meetings with your parole officer, required outpatient treatment every other day, and required self-help meetings at least twice a week. There's a monthly supervision fee to pay, along with the cost of the required counseling and any outstanding fines you have left. There are curfew checks and random home visits. You can't live in a house with guns, can't drink or set foot in a bar, and could go back to prison if your partner so much as leaves a beer in the fridge. You need permission to drive and to own a dog, and can't leave the county without approval. You have to get a job or at least show that you're trying to find work, cannot have any contact with police, and cannot have any contact with known felons—including all the women you just lived with for the past two years.

Failing to meet any of these requirements can—at the parole officer's discretion—trigger a "technical violation," which is when you get sent back to prison not for committing a new crime but for breaking a rule. That's exactly how 85 percent of New York parolees end up behind bars again, since the state locks up more people for technical violations than anywhere except Illinois. It's a lot easier to end up in that unlucky percent if you're poor and can't keep up with your fees, if you're mentally ill and get kicked out of your parole-approved housing, or if you're a person of color and you live in a heavily policed area where it's tough to avoid all contact with the law. The rules that are already hard to live by can be hardest on the people who are already closest to the edge. Even with everything that I had—a safe place to live, family to buy me a phone and some clothes, a boyfriend to drive me to appointments, a skin tone that didn't attract extra scrutiny from police—my two years on parole were drenched in a low-grade fear, as I perpetually waited for that knock on the door that would bring it all crashing down.

Although I knew that a first parole violation was usually only ninety days, I also knew that if I got sent back, the first stop would be the county jail in my new county, where I'd spend the two weeks in solitary. Then, I'd either go to Willard—a three-month version of shock camp geared toward parole violators—or back to Albion for a three-month-long walk of shame. Admittedly, my parole officer seemed like a nice guy, one more likely to be working tech support and answering computer questions than toting a gun and chasing parole absconders. Still, I knew the power he held, and I flinched whenever there were footsteps at the door—and sometimes when there weren't.

One afternoon when Lee was at work, a car pulled up in the long driveway and I panicked. It was white, with a dark stripe down the side: a patrol car. Surely, I thought, this was it.

I hid in the bathtub, almost in tears. Never mind that I hadn't broken any rules—I was convinced that if the cops were here, they were here for me. The blood thrummed in my head, and gray spots of anxiety clouded my vision.

I can't go back. I can't go back. I can't go back.

Crouched in the damp tub, I waited. When an hour passed and nothing happened, I hesitantly crawled out—then noticed my glasses sitting on the cluttered kitchen table and realized: I'd been walking around blind. I slipped them on and crept through the living room to the sliding glass doors, staying low and out of sight as I inched close enough to peer out from between the bent slats of the vertical blinds. Right away, I saw. The vehicle in the driveway was not a cop car; it was just a beat-up Honda Civic with a giant rust stripe. I sank down to the floor, laughing in hysterical relief.

The pounding rush of fear from that day is one of the clearest memories of my first year out of prison. The other is the last time I visited Charlotte. It must have been early November. Lee and I had been stopping by regularly, taking her for walks and hoping she'd at least get used to me—even if she never recognized me for the woman who'd loved her before, then disappeared. When we went out, she pulled at the leash and looked around nervously, searching for her owner, Florianna. She paid no mind to the spiky-haired stranger calling her name.

This time, we decided to take her to Collegetown, where I used to live. I was still banned from campus—just as I had been ever since the Cornell cop with the Looney Tunes tie had shown up at the jail days after my arrest—so we skirted university property, trudging up and down the hilly streets: Linden, Dryden, College Ave. We passed the laundromat I used for years, where Charlotte would sit in the corner and sniff the lint on the floor as I waited. We walked by the one convenience store that always let her in, as she padded silently behind me. We loitered in the parking lot I used to cut through when we walked to Alex's.

None of it seemed to click. Finally, we ended up on Eddy Street, in front of my old apartment in the adjunct sorority house. I stopped on the cracked pavement outside and gazed up at the green pillars and the three stories of brick, wondering who lived there now and hoping they were better off than I'd been.

I was lost in thought, and when I looked down, suddenly Charlotte was sitting at my feet, staring up at me with her eager dog eyes, eyes that said she knew: I was hers.

"Lee! Lee! Look, I think she figured it out!"

He looked at us, skeptical at first.

"Let's keep going and see for sure," I said.

But a few blocks later, she was still right next to me, and no longer scanning the street for her human.

Afterward, we brought Charlotte back to Cayuga Heights— but the next time we came by, we took her home. It was exactly what Florianna and David promised, but it had always seemed too good to be real, a second chance I did not truly believe I would get. I could bring her back for visits to show them I was giving her a good life, but I knew there was no way I could repay them. Fresh out of prison, I felt like I had so little to offer. But now I had my dog, and it seemed like the first thing I'd done right in a long time.

About a year after my release, I got a call from someone I used to get high with, a skinny, gray-haired British man with a penchant for poker, heroin, and philosophy. Three decades older than me, Jasper was the son of a Cornell professor, and a longtime Ithacan himself—though after years in and out of rehab and jail, he'd decamped further north to Watertown, away from the drug world he knew. We'd done so much self-destruction together over the years, but he'd been one of the safest, kindest people in my inner circle when I was getting high. Now, he was someone who was sober enough to remember the bad times for what they were. We caught up on our respective legal troubles and our hopes for the future, and then he got to why he called.

"My deeear," he said, "I have a friend who's an editor at the *Ithaca Times* and she's writing something about women in the jail, so I told her she should talk to you. I think you can be anonymous, but either way you two should meet—you'll love her."

A few days later, Glynis drove out to visit me in person, making the forty-five-minute trip from Ithaca to Tioga County, even though her job did not cover expenses. Her aging Volvo station wagon was a mess, with ceramic coffee cups and books scattered throughout, and two Irish setters in the back seat. She had a broad smile and looked every bit the part of a middle-aged Ithacan hippie, relaxed and natural. When she came inside, she sat on the coffee table with a notepad in hand and a pencil tucked behind her ear, held in place by a mass of curly brown hair.

The county was planning to expand the jail, she told me—in part so they wouldn't have to board out the women so much. She wanted to know what it was like to be a woman in jail and what it was like to get tossed back and forth from one lockup to the next. For more than an hour, I told her.

After I finished, we kept talking.

"So I Googled you before I came and I read some of your stuff—you're pretty good," she said. She must have meant pieces from the Cornell paper, but I didn't stop her to clarify because then she added: "You wanna work for us?"

It had not even occurred to me that this was possible. Sure, I'd majored in English and had been doing journalism since high school. And all the gigs I was looking for online involved writing. But a real, honest-to-goodness job—in journalism or anything else—wasn't even on my radar. I was still getting used to the idea that I was a real person, not a number locked away or a shadow flitting around the periphery of life.

"Oh my God, yes."

To start, the work would be on a freelance basis, covering assorted board meetings, parades, rubber duck races, and holiday festivals in the five-thousand-person towns just south of Ithaca. For $40, I'd type up a five-hundred-word story after sitting through a couple hours of slow conversations between old white men debating the merits of chicken ordinances or the cost of a new barn to store road salt.

"The pay is crap and you might think it's really boring—but I don't know, you might like it," Glynis said. "They'll love you," she added with a laugh.

I still don't know if she meant it. The rural parts of upstate New York can be as conservative as any Midwest backwater, and I stuck out with my black combat boots and face piercings, the ones preserved by all those comb teeth I'd used in prison. But people were friendly, or maybe won over by my enthusiasm for municipal code and regulatory nuance. It wasn't that I otherwise cared about these things, it was just that, for the first time in a long time, it felt like I was doing something that had value.

Sometimes, I'd get to cover stories for the main paper in

Ithaca, writing about the feuds in the county legislature, debates about the school budget, or controversies over the city's police. For months, I managed to avoid stories that required calling the department directly for comment, still nervous about talking to the cops in general and afraid that Ithaca cops in particular would hear my name and refuse to answer any questions from someone they probably saw as just a nosy ex-criminal. Eventually, I had to pick up the phone.

"Hi, I'm-I'm Keri. I'm a reporter with the *Ithaca Times* and Finger Lakes Community Newspapers."

"Keri? Are you Keri Blakinger?!"

My heart sank.

"I'm Jamie! Do you remember me?? I'm the one who was there when you jumped off the bridge!!"

I did not remember him, but he seemed unreasonably surprised at the thrill of talking to me.

"I stand out," he continued. "I have red hair—you'd recognize me if you saw me!"

"I, uh, I had a lot going on that day," I said, still fumbling for words. Suddenly I remembered. "I guess that means I gave you the finger, right? Um . . . sorry?"

"Yep, yes you did," he said.

Then he laughed.

It was not the reaction I expected. I was floored, then flattered. Then I thought about how rare it must have been for someone like him to talk to someone like me again, unless it was to put me in handcuffs. A happy ending is shocking, in part because the system isn't built for it.

At that point, I generally didn't hide my past—but I didn't

volunteer it, either. Sure, I mentioned it occasionally in blog posts, on a site that got so little traffic it hardly felt public. And sometimes I referenced it on Facebook, where I'd set everything to private after I got out. But somehow those seemed like small, safe spaces, and even though I'd always said I would write a book, now I was torn as to whether I really wanted to be so open about it or whether I just wanted to move on. What made up my mind was an email from a local reporter who worked for one of the same outlets that had splashed my mugshot across its pages a few years earlier. Now, he was writing a story on the resurgence of heroin in Ithaca.

To do that, he said, he'd need to interview me—the woman at the center of the highest profile drug bust in recent memory.

"I'd really like to hear your side," he said.

I demurred. I wasn't ready to be part of another front page story, I told him. Maybe someday but not yet.

"Can't you just leave me out of it?"

He explained that he could not: "My editors will never let me." He paused, and added, "If you don't want to interview, I'll still have to pull background from the clips, and if you don't want to send a picture, I'll probably have to use your mugshot."

He wasn't being a jerk; it was just the reality of the situation. But at the mention of the mugshot, that scabby-faced memento of shame, I caved immediately.

The interview itself must have been by phone, but I was so nervous I do not remember any of it, except that the reporter was polite and kind, and I think he might have felt bad. In the end, the story came out exactly the way he said it would, with no ugly surprises or gotchas.

But somewhere in the course of reliving it, I made a decision: I would not hide from my past. I would be relentlessly honest and open about it. If I told my story—on my own terms—then no one could use it against me. I would own it.

Chapter 25

Newark Valley, 2014

After prison, I didn't own things.

It wasn't because I just didn't have things to own anymore—though that was definitely part of it. Those looters who'd ransacked the basement apartment after my arrest had left me with almost nothing. Replacing all that I'd lost would have been costly, but that wasn't the biggest deterrent.

Behind bars, possessions represented a risk. There were so few of them, but each thing you owned was a thing you could lose—a thing the guards could take away. Pictures. Shoes. Books. Letters.

After I got out, it was hard to shake that mindset. Most of the time, prison still felt so close that after more than a year of freedom, I still owned no dishes or furniture and had never grown out my hair. Almost everything I owned fit in a car.

But among the things I kept were scattered remnants of prison, the part of my past I would not allow myself to forget. I still have the brown hoodie my parents ordered for me from the approved vendor at Albion, though I have never worn it since. I still have the bracelet Dani made before I left for Taconic, and my copy of *Orange Is the New Black* that I read when I went back up north to Albion, my name written in all caps marker on the side so no one could steal it. I also have a little pink composition book I brought along from prison to prison, listing everything I read along the way.

That's how I know I was in the middle of *The Keep* when I got moved to Taconic, had just finished *The Night Circus* when I started hepatitis treatment, and tore through *Miss Peregrine's Home for Peculiar Children* a few days before I got out. It's also how I know when I started working on those last two classes I needed to graduate from Cornell.

After the three-year minimum term of my suspension ended in late 2013, I sent my application for readmission to the university hearing board, along with an essay, letters of support, clips of stories I'd written for the *Ithaca Times*, and all the certificates that served as the requisite proof of what I'd learned in prison. Then, I had a short phone interview before I got the news in a crisp email from a university official: "I am pleased to report that you have been approved to finish your Cornell degree, starting in January 2014."

For as long as I could remember, this had been a measuring stick for my life, and my worth. Even as a kid, academic achievement seemed almost tantamount to moral value. I remember the moment when my parents suggested Harvard Summer School, the moment when Hootie's mom told me I should apply to Cornell, and that moment in the jail strip search room when I finally realized it had all fallen apart. But I do not remember where I was when I got that email. I can imagine myself on Lee's leather couch, probably alone while he was at work. I must have shrieked, then maybe cried, both elated and relieved for this second chance at something I had once taken for granted. Maybe that hole in my memory is a fluke—but maybe the fact of my forgetting is a sign I was finally beginning to see my own value, even without that measuring stick.

My first class was an independent study in memoir writing. Once a week on his way to the jail, Lee would drop me off in downtown Ithaca, and I'd wander around for a few hours, stop at the newspaper office, and then meet up with my professor in a pirate-themed cafe tucked inside a used bookstore. Even though I'd gotten back into the school and my parents had once again offered to pay, I was still banned from campus. That meant I had to figure out a way to finish without setting foot on university property. The bookstore was a safe distance away, downtown.

For the final paper, I cobbled together my journals into a messy memoir project, a blend of growth and gratitude with lingering stains of judgment and indulgence, as if a faint shadow of the person I had been still lurked between the lines. I told people it would be called *IV League*, the utterly cringey title we'd always joked about back in jail. I still don't think I fully understood how damaging prison had been, to me or all the women around me. But I did understand this: I wanted to pull something good from the wreckage, something to pay off the debt of all those radioactive years.

The last class I needed to graduate was a class about prisons. Until then, I'd only learned how broken the system was by witnessing it firsthand. But watching it from the inside, I had no idea how it got to that point. The professor who showed me that was Mary Katzenstein, a slight woman with short gray hair. I'd heard of her before only because she was so well-known on campus for her prison work—both teaching this particular class about prisons and teaching a handful of classes in prisons.

That semester the class I wanted to take was offered online, so I could actually do it without straying onto campus or even leaving the house. The first book we read, according to my pink notebook, was *The Punishment Imperative*. It showed us how, until the 1970s, the prison system was much smaller, and more focused on rehabilitation—and how that changed as part of a cynical political response to the crime spike of the decade before. Next up, we went back in time and read *Worse Than Slavery* to learn about convict leasing and America's long history of criminalizing Black bodies for profit once simply enslaving them was no longer an option.

We watched movies about the Angola prison farm in Louisiana, considered theories of deterrence and punishment, and learned how incarceration rates had gone up and up for decades, even when the crime rate went down. We wrote about reentry, and about mandatory minimums, and about the rise of determinate sentences, prison terms that were—like mine—a set amount of time instead of a range. As I took it all in, suddenly I saw the things I'd lived through in sharp relief, like turning on the light in a dark room I'd known only by touch.

My final paper was about racial control, and whether the system is racist on purpose or just happens to be racist. I typed up six pages to submit by email, and before hitting send I added: "I cannot believe I am finally finishing the very last thing I need to graduate. At many points along the way I really didn't think I'd live to."

I got an A.

"WHAT A moment," Mary wrote back. "Bravissima."

The actual graduation was on December 20, 2014, four years and one day after my arrest. It was below freezing outside, and thousands of twenty-somethings and their parents crowded into Barton Hall, the two-acre field house in the middle of campus. I was only able to be there in person because the police had finally rescinded my ban, a reversal that felt almost more miraculous than the decision to readmit me in the first place. My parents drove up from Lancaster, along with my brother and his girlfriend. Florianna and David came, and so did Glynis and her boyfriend, Bill. As I sat in the rows of folding chairs for graduates waiting to get up and cross the stage, I wondered what the kids next to me would think if they knew about the felon in their midst. Would they be shocked? Offended? Would they even care? If they knew what I knew, would it shape their world like it had shaped mine?

The photos from that day are terrible, blurry and washed out under the flood of fluorescent gym lights. My skin is off-color, and my hands look twitchy and nervous. But under the mortarboard cap and white tassel, my smile is unmistakable.

Afterward, a local news site called The Ithaca Voice posted a short story about it: CORNELL SENIOR ARRESTED WITH $50K OF HEROIN GRADUATES AFTER 21 MONTHS BEHIND BARS. The reporter, Jeff—an ex–*Cornell Sun* writer I'd known from before my arrest—interviewed me and Glynis, and pulled some background from old news clips.

"It does feel firmly behind me, but there are some memories that will always be very fresh," I told him. "I think there's some parts of both an active addiction as well as being in prison and jail that are traumatizing."

"Keri is one of the most dynamic—if not the most dynamic—reporters I have ever worked with," Glynis said. "She is a go-getter and has just incredible drive."

The story posted on a Sunday, and the response online was swift. "This is what happens to privileged white girls who 'misbehave,'" one person tweeted. Others griped that I'd only done "minimal jail time" and heroin had "helped" me. I was "sickening." A "nauseating example of white privilege."

The words stung—I wanted so badly not to be sickening or nauseating anymore. But I realized they were not wrong about the privilege. I thought back on all my interactions with the system over the years, the moments that could have gone differently if I were Black or did not have money. I thought of one time that I got caught shoplifting in Boston and wondered whether the security guard would have still let me go if he saw me as a troublemaking Black girl instead of a troubled white one. I thought of another time, the week before I moved to Ithaca, when a friend and I got pulled over after picking up dope in New Jersey. The cops started grilling us—until they saw the Cornell course guide on my lap and let us go.

I thought of all the close calls over nearly a decade of drug use and about how, by the time I got arrested, I might have already had a long record if I were a woman of color. With my priors, I would have qualified for a longer sentence, even in a liberal place like Ithaca. Then, just like that woman had warned me in line for the prison bus, I would have had a tougher time— maybe gotten more tickets, lost my date, waited longer to go home. When I finally got out, I would have been statistically less likely to come from a family with the means to help me get back on my feet—to get a phone and a used car. To pay for college. To start over.

For some people, privilege can be easy to doubt because at the most granular level it is tough to prove: I can't say for sure whether the university hearing board would have been so forgiving of a Black or brown student. But I can say for sure that the color of my skin greased the wheels of so many of the moments that made that forgiveness possible. Everybody should get the second chances I got, but most people do not. That's not to downplay anything or say that it was easy. Addiction and arrest, going to prison and getting back out—these are the sorts of things that are hard for everyone. But they are so much harder for people who did not have the advantages that I did. It took me a long time to really understand that, and to admit it.

Another, more intimate, thing that took me a long time to admit was that Lee and I would not work out. The people we'd become on the outside were not the people we'd been on the inside, and the threads that tied us together had frayed. So many of the things we enjoyed doing in the free world were not the things we bonded over when I was locked up: We didn't really like Scrabble, living on Reese's, or building snow pyramids. Our politics were different, and so were our pastimes.

At the outset I'd been so green and so dependent on him, like someone who needed saving. But as I built my own life, we began to fight. He got mad that I worked too much and didn't respect his beliefs about aliens or ESP. I got mad that he saw crime everywhere, from the quiet guy downstairs he was convinced was a sex offender to the children next door he was sure were involved in selling drugs.

But maybe more important—to me, at least—were the differences in how we thought of people in jail. Though he wanted to be the type of corrections officer who could make a difference in the lives of people behind bars, years of working for the jail had fostered a predictable skepticism about redemption. He'd seen people come in and out so much that he saw me as an exception, fundamentally different in my ability to stay off drugs and make good on a second chance. I saw that as exactly the problem: I wasn't different, I just had the chances.

By the end, every time we got in a fight he would remind me that I could just move out—even though we both knew that I couldn't because I was still on parole and this was my approved residence.

But then parole ended, and the next time he made that suggestion, I took him up on it.

At first we said we'd just live separately, but a few weeks later we split officially. It was not a dramatic breakup, and we stayed friends. It was the first time I'd been single in more than a decade—for almost my entire adult life I'd been in some sort of relationship, never standing entirely on my own. There was a sense of loss, but it was also a relief, a welcome pause in the medley of love songs I'd let play in the background behind drugs and prison. But those parts of my life were over, and the music was changing.

Chapter 26

After I moved back to Ithaca in the fall of 2014, I wound up downtown in a rented room right above a woman I knew from jail. Her name was Stephanie, but not the Steph I'd been sent to Chenango with. This was a woman I'd only known briefly—she hadn't been locked up nearly as long as I had, and whatever her charges were, they never landed her in prison. Now she was free again, living with her two adult daughters, and selling sex to pay for heroin. Her basement apartment was a revolving door of old men at odd hours, punctuated by the occasional visit from the police.

We were always friendly, and whenever I saw her outside we traded stories about where the people we knew in common had ended up. She asked about "that guy you married in the visiting room," and I told her I hadn't seen Alex since jail, though I heard he was in Arizona. Becca was sober, Steph had vanished, and Sam was locked up in a different county on a new charge that would ultimately land her in prison.

"Oh my God, girl," Stephanie said, wide-eyed when I explained: The newspapers said Sam and her boyfriend kidnapped one of her kids from her mother at knifepoint. It was a young boy, and Sam had lost custody—but I knew she had been allowed to visit whenever she wanted, so the alleged violence didn't make sense. Sam always said she had nothing to do with it but still ended up taking a plea rather than risking trial.

"Damn, that's fucked," Stephanie said, when I finished explaining. We stood when we chatted, usually on the sidewalk that connected my first-floor porch and her basement entrance. I think some of the other neighbors were unhappy about living around the drugs and the men and the sirens, but it all just made me sad. I understood her struggles too well: It was like living above the old me.

So one day when she informed me that she'd picked up some good stuff and whipped out a bag of heroin in front of me, I was not surprised.

"Ahhhh, yeah, it's fire," she said, opening her hand to reveal the little wax baggie in her palm.

"How much was it?" I asked, falling into that familiar druggie small talk.

"Twenty a bag. I'm so glad you're done with that, girl," she said, with complete sincerity. "Wish I could be."

She wasn't trying to tempt me so much as share with me a small victory in her hard life. I don't think she would have sold to me if I'd begged—but I wasn't begging, or even tempted. It was like a call from an old flame; I could be cordial and polite, but I wasn't interested. When I first picked up heroin over a decade earlier, there had been a hole in my life, the spot where skating had been. But now, I had found ways to fill it. There was no room for heroin anymore.

A few times a month I went to meetings for the two non-profit boards I was on, a rehab and a bail fund. My weeknights were eaten up by town and village board meetings, and my days spent filing stories. And every Friday afternoon, I went to the jail. Those weekly trips started after I'd been ranting to Glynis about the inequities at the local lockup, where there were so many programs for men and so few for women.

"I know there aren't as many women as there are men, but it's just fucked up," I told her.

"Well why don't you start a class for women? Like a writing class?"

"There's *no* way they'd let me back in as a volunteer." I paused. "Well, maybe if you come too and we co-teach."

We pitched the idea to jail brass and, after an awkward, stilted meeting with a lieutenant in a room tucked away in the back of the sheriff's office, much to my surprise we got the go-ahead. I put together worksheets and a website and a week-by-week curriculum on journalism—but I told all the women who showed up that it didn't matter what we did. If they wanted to write that was great, but if they just needed to vent or ask advice or spend an hour talking to someone who would treat them like a real person, that was fine, too. I wanted to be there for them however I could.

When I wasn't prepping for a jail visit or working for the paper, I did freelance writing on the side, constantly churning out stories for online news sites and addiction blogs. It was in the course of reporting one of those stories that I found a flimsy excuse to call Mr. S, ostensibly to interview him about the difficulties of providing meaningful treatment behind bars.

Assuming he was still at Taconic, I rang up the main number and asked to be transferred. When the guard who answered asked who I was, I said my name, and it meant nothing. Then I added, "Harry Potter. It's Harry Potter."

"Ohhhhhh, Harry P! Are you doing good? Hold on just a minute, let me put you through!"

The phone rang, then went to voicemail, but by the end of the day he called back.

"Potter! It's so good to hear from you. Did you just call to tell me to go fuck myself?"

I laughed and explained—and then he gave me his number to call him after work. "I guess it's alright since you're off parole now," he added.

When I tried him that night, we talked for an hour. He told me about his family and asked about mine, griped about drama at the prison, and asked if I was still sober. When I told him about how lost my first year out felt, he shared that he'd been struggling with depression. And when I told him about all the things I'd done with my life since I'd last seen him, he told me how happy that made him. For the first time, he talked to me like an equal.

Even though I'd come so far, on some level that still surprised me—just like it always surprised me when I found someone willing to treat me like a real person, instead of an object of suspicion or a number in a system. Over the course of a decade of decay, I'd grown so used to the worlds of addiction and prison that it surprised me when mistrust was not the default. So it surprised me when my parents invited me to come visit. It surprised me when the cop who'd arrested me saw me on the street and shook my hand. And it surprised me when David and Florianna gave me a key to their house.

At that point, they'd already become one of the constants in my life. On the weekends, we'd take Charlotte and Bailey on walks in the woods, go to the farmers' market, or spend the afternoon on the boat they kept on Cayuga Lake, stopping where it was deep enough that we could swim with the dogs. Sometimes, Florianna showed up randomly at my apartment with homemade meals or groceries. Sometimes, she invited me to movie nights with her friends or helped me plan community dinners. So at first it did not surprise me when she and David asked me to dog sit while they were away. But when I held that key in my hand, I marveled at the tiny hunk of metal with the red plastic on the top. It felt like a milestone: I racked my brain, but as far as I could remember no one had given me a key to their home since the day I'd left my parents' house.

Since my parents lived more than four hours away, even though they'd invited me to visit, I still didn't see them all that often. There were holidays, and even a few vacations in Florida, but most of our communications were—and still are—an extensive trail of emails and text messages. And after all the years of sparse contact, now my mom wanted links to all the stories I wrote. She read them all—or at least enough to develop an intimate knowledge of school board spats and planning board melees in tiny towns she'd never been to. Sometimes she tossed back a comment: "What a great last line!" Or: "How sad!" Between all the stories, I sent updates on my life: The things I learned, the places I saw, and the people I met—including the district attorney, who spotted me at a cafe in downtown Ithaca one day and unexpectedly beckoned me over to her table. She hadn't personally prosecuted my case before, but as the elected DA in a small county she must have known about it. So it was an utter shock when she introduced me to her friend as a "person who has been doing wonderful things." When I emailed my mom afterward to tell her about it, she wrote back within a few hours: "Five years ago it would be nearly unimaginable to think the DA would ever say that about you," she said. "You've certainly defied the odds."

But after a year back in Ithaca, I reluctantly started looking for jobs. I'd told Glynis I wanted to stay at the *Ithaca Times* forever, but she confidently assured me I would not and that I would go on to do so much more—then told me she was leaving, too. Despite my assorted freelancing and my time at the student newspaper, I'd never taken an actual journalism class and knew almost nothing about the media world outside of Ithaca. I didn't even know what jobs were realistic for a baby reporter, so my applications were scattershot and my expectations were low.

When I applied to the New York *Daily News* and heard back within a few days, I was shocked. The man who responded— Bob—was a newspaper veteran with a dark tabloid humor and explosive laugh. He talked fast and moved faster. After interviewing me for just twenty minutes on Skype, he explained: He was looking to hire thirty new reporters, fresh graduates who would work at the Jersey City office as a sort of B team doing aggregation and listicles. I don't think I knew what a listicle was or what a tabloid did—but I knew the *Daily News* was a big deal. And I knew they'd written about my arrest.

"The main thing is I have to have everyone in place by August 28," he said, making no mention of it. "Can you be here by then?"

It was three weeks away.

"Yes."

Less than two hours later, he emailed to say I was hired—without ever asking about my record. One of the clips I sent was a *Washington Post* essay I wrote that talked about prison and privilege, but I had no idea if he'd actually read my clips or searched the paper's own archives. As I packed and apartment hunted and tied up my life in Ithaca, I balanced excitement with utter panic, sure that I would get fired on the first day when Bob realized he'd accidentally hired a felon.

I found a rented room in a cheap apartment above an underground costume shop filled with princess gowns and villain heads, a twenty-minute drive from work. The Jersey office was actually a printing plant, and we took up one windowless room where long cafeteria tables served as shared desks. The building was just barely in sight of the Statue of Liberty—but only the backside, like New York was telling us to kiss her ass. The first day, I was so afraid I'd get lost on the way there that I showed up almost an hour early, overdressed and terrified.

Bob tried to set me up on my newly assigned computer, but the password wouldn't work, so instead he cursed extensively under his breath as I sat on pins and needles trying to guess whether he knew. Once the other new hires arrived—most of them much younger—Bob and his deputy, Joe, ran us through the basics before we could start the normal orientation routine. Just after lunch, Bob got up from his desk and turned to leave, then turned back and offered a casual afterthought: "By the way, I liked that essay you did for WaPo." Then he laughed, "What a terrible abbreviation, 'WaPo.'"

I probably laughed, then said thank you, but I can't remember my response over the flood of relief. By that point, I'd been out of prison long enough—three years—that I was beginning to understand the scope of all the things I couldn't do with a felony, all the ways it could restrict me in regular life. In some states I couldn't be a locksmith or a lawyer. In others I couldn't vote or buy pepper spray. In some places I wouldn't qualify for government assistance, couldn't adopt children, or get into a state school. And some private companies—like Airbnb and most dating apps—banned people like me from using their services. Over the years I would be rejected from countless apartments, a bank where I held an account, an animal shelter where I hoped to volunteer, and a slew of jobs.

Collectively, these restrictions are known as collateral consequences, extrajudicial punishments that last far longer than the court's actual sentence. Today they overwhelmingly impact communities of color, where a disproportionate number of people have been to prison. But they date back to a time, hundreds of years ago, when people didn't go to prison because the usual punishment for a felony was death. Before the state killed them, the condemned would lose all property and rights as they tied up their loose ends in the world. But those sorts of losses and limitations were never intended to last for decades on end. So once prison terms started to replace death sentences, these added punishments took on a new meaning, making it harder to come back from a bad past. Over the last couple decades, the number of collateral consequences has ballooned, buoyed in part by the internet and its easy access to criminal records. I'll never know how many jobs or life opportunities I've lost to the results of a quick web search. But at the *Daily News*, the only person who mattered saw those results and was willing to give me a chance.

The job wasn't providing the sort of service to the community that local reporting in Ithaca had, but I found that I loved the fast pace of the tabloid world. Every day, I'd write three to seven short stories for the web, mostly weird crime, D-list celebrity interviews, strange history, and occasionally salacious news-adjacent items. My most-read stories were not exactly impressive: a short post about a snow-day themed parody of an Adele song, a dive into the infamous Black Dahlia murder, a look at whether there really is a correlation between penis size and hand size—a tongue-in-cheek assignment lobbed my way after then-candidate Donald Trump insulted the size of primary opponent Marco Rubio's hands. (And, yes, a study showed there is a correlation—but it's to finger proportion and not hand size.)

But for all the weird things we could delve into for the most prurient readers, investigations and on-the-ground reporting were largely off the table, as those fell squarely in the purview of the A team in Lower Manhattan. For the most part, I was content to keep my head down and focus on what I was expected to do. Then a few weeks in, I found some data showing an uptick in the use of solitary in the state's prisons, even after officials had promised to decrease it. When I pitched it to Bob as a story, instead of telling me to stay in my lane he muttered, "I need to introduce you to Reuven."

Reuven Blau was in his late thirties and worked in the main newsroom. He wore glasses and a yarmulke and he'd been on the beat covering Rikers and prisons probably since before I'd ever set foot in one. When he called to talk about the numbers I had, he talked so fast I could barely make out the words.

"Okay-yes-I'll-get-it-skedded-and-we-can-do-twelve-inches-or-something."

He spoke with a tabloid slang I didn't even understand, but he was offering to work together. One story turned into another, and by December I was headed to the city jail. Reuven had gotten a tip about a woman who said she'd been raped by a guard in a storage closet, and he sent me to investigate.

On Rikers Island, the wait for visitation is brutal. It's hours of standing on line in the cold of the East River winds, waiting until stony-faced corrections officers search you again and again as you work your way further into concentric circles of correctional hell. If you're sneaking in to report, you go into the interview empty-handed, pretending to be a friend and not a journalist. With no notepad, you have to memorize the best quotes as they're spoken or, usually, whispered in the hope the guards don't overhear. I'd been in jails before as a free person— once to visit Sam and a few dozen times to teach the writing class with Glynis—but every time was like walking back into a bad dream, haunting and surreal.

That time it was Christmas Eve, and I was there to interview a woman named Jackie, who'd landed in jail on a robbery charge. And—unlike in most jail rape cases—she actually had hard proof. After the assault, she'd mailed her sister pieces of her clothes, covered in the guard's splotchy cum stain.

As we sat on opposite sides of the visiting room table and talked, we realized we'd already crossed paths: We'd been in prison together, sent through intake at Bedford the same month when she was in on her last charge.

We spent the hour in visitation flipping back and forth between trading notes on the whereabouts of all our common friends from upstate and discussing the details of her assault and the decision to save that sticky shirt.

"I wanted proof," she said. She'd been through the system enough times to know how much that mattered.

She went on to tell me how the man's face looked dead the whole time, "like he wasn't there," and how she was scared to report it through official channels, where the people in charge might just retaliate instead of helping her or investigating. But now that she'd decided to talk about it, she was ready to go all-in.

"Use my name," she said. She wanted it all out there, to make sure something happened to her rapist.

We didn't know it then, but eventually something would happen, an incredibly rare outcome behind bars. Even when there's evidence, only about 1 percent of prison and jail staff accused of sexually abusing people in custody actually get convicted for it.

That guard was one of them.

Afterward, Reuven commented that he didn't know if Jackie would have trusted another reporter in quite the same way, and I realized something: I could tell this story in a way that so few other people could, or even wanted to. I'd been there, I knew ten Jackies—and they all had stories to tell.

Chapter 27

Houston, 2017

On a warm evening in the fall of 2017, I sat down for tacos with two murderabilia dealers at a Mexican restaurant in a strip mall in southeast Houston. They were both scruffy, bearded thirty-somethings who traded in serial killer swag—fingernail clippings from death row, jail art from solitary, hand tracings from hands that had killed. But I wasn't there to talk about the market for death wares; I was there to talk about life in Texas prisons. From all their correspondences with the condemned, these men would know better than most.

"There's a guy on the row who said they're all getting dentures," one of them said, resting a heavily tattooed forearm on the cheap metal table.

"Wait, you mean before they weren't giving them *teeth*?" I was stunned. As questionable as the medical care had been in New York, teeth were never optional—and it never occurred to me that they could be.

"Naw, man. I guess they used to give 'em, but then they stopped, and this guy has like six teeth. He wrote me all hype that they're gonna start giving them dentures again."

He flashed a toothy grin, as if to demonstrate.

"Oh nice, that actually sounds like it's almost a happy story about prisons," I said. It wasn't the sort of investigative scoop I was looking for, but it seemed like something worth noting in print. "I can probably just get the spokesman to confirm and maybe talk to your guy, and then it should be a quick, easy story."

It was a story, but it was not easy or quick. When I called the Texas prison spokesman the next day, he told me the murderabilia man was wrong. There were no plans to start giving people teeth, at least not any more than they already did. He was vague on how often that was.

So I started to investigate.

I'd moved to Texas in the summer of 2016, almost exactly a year after I'd started at the *Daily News.* I hadn't planned to leave New York so soon, but four months after Bob hired us, the paper axed two-thirds of the Jersey City newsroom. Somehow I kept my job, probably just because I worked so obsessively that I'd published more stories than anyone else. But the deep cuts to such a new team seemed like a clear sign that we were indeed the "teetering tabloid" that the competing *New York Post* liked to call us.

As much as I liked the fast pace of that hardboiled world, in the slow moments I wondered about the point of it all. Between all the quick hits of sensational crime and outlandish gossip, I missed doing work that felt like it had value. Sure, it was a national outlet with millions of readers. And, sure, I had the occasional investigation with Reuven. But it did not feel like enough. Most of the time, I told myself that I should be happy I had come so far—and I was. But every night as I drove home on the slow curve of I-78, my thoughts wandered into dark places.

Just after the first sign for the Holland Tunnel, I'd glance to the left and stare out over the wasteland of my past. A few miles away was the Wendy's where I used to shoot up, and the IKEA where I used to wander around high. Beyond that was the house of a dealer who used to make me suck his dick for an hour at a time, and a few more miles south was the White Castle parking lot where I'd listened to Akon as I waited for the next trick. As my mind inched further and further down the state, the jagged skyline felt like a map of my mistakes. In Ithaca, I'd cleared the map, replaced the old memories with new ones: pirate cafes and writing classes and the field house graduation and slow afternoons at the *Ithaca Times* office. And then I'd left and come here, where I knew no one, and it was just me and my past.

I'd keep driving.

When I got to the steep slope of Paterson Plank Road, the part where it rises up out of Jersey City, I'd look to the right and catch a glimpse of the Hoboken treetops below. I'd take in the crisp reds and oranges, remembering that morning almost a decade earlier at the top of a gorge when the leaves were frozen and time had stopped. I'd think of all the lives I'd lived since then, and I'd wonder if everything I'd done was worth it—if I was worth it. If there are scales of justice, what do they take to balance? What is the weight of redemption?

At the top of the hill in Union City, I'd turn onto Palisade, and pass that one spot by Fourth Street where there's a vacant lot, and through the break in the dingy buildings of North Jersey you can suddenly see the Manhattan skyline: the Empire State, Hudson Yards, the buzz of a city that does not stop for time.

People say when you're in prison that you're doing time—like it is a thing you will do and it will be over. But then you get out, and you discover that there is more, as if the wasted hours and minutes follow you around and now your life is about reversing them, making good, undoing time. And when I looked at what I'd done with my time, I wondered: Was it enough? Would it ever be enough? Whatever enough was, it did not feel like a thing I would find in a printing plant in New Jersey.

So when I saw a listing online for a two-year fellowship at Hearst, I applied. The company founded by the American newspaper baron included a bunch of magazines, but it also included broadsheet papers like the *San Francisco Chronicle,* the *San Antonio Express-News,* and the *Houston Chronicle*—all major metro dailies, the sorts that did the on-the-ground reporting that changed lives. The whole application and interview process took half a year, so long that I managed to get promoted to the overnight A team at the *Daily News* in the meantime. But this wasn't like Reuven's job—this was covering mayhem in the middle of the night, writing quick hits about the worst things that happened across the country after dark, from mass shootings to sports scandals to police killings. So when a Hearst editor called to offer me a spot at the Houston paper, I took it.

At first it was just general assignment and breaking news,

but after the longtime death penalty reporter retired, my editor suggested I take over the coverage.

"And maybe you can throw in some stories about prisons, too," she added. It must have seemed like a natural fit to her—but I was skeptical, even though I didn't say it. Given my past, I worried that it was almost trite, an admission that this was the only thing a former prisoner could do well: *Of course the felon is covering the felons.* But at the same time, the idea stirred something in the back of my head, or maybe in my heart.

Even if the possibilities excited me, I had no idea where to start. I didn't know anyone who'd done time in Texas prisons, and I didn't know anything about how to start covering a beat. It was one thing to chase down a random lead every few weeks, file a few records requests to flesh out a particular story, or take care of an occasional jailhouse interview. But figuring out how to stay on top of something as big as the Texas prison system and as vast as the death penalty caseload in the killingest state—that was something else entirely. It would require trawling through the *Chronicle* archives to learn about the past, unraveling the twisting legal process for capital cases, finding guards who would give me the inside scoop on the state's hundred-plus lockup, developing a network of reliable sources among the 145,000 prisoners in the Texas Department of Criminal Justice. Since I had no idea how to do that, I called Reuven.

"Start-with-a-bunch-of-records-requests-ask-for-solitary-numbers-and-drug-testing-data-and-audits-of-their-prison-factories."

He paused.

"Death-reports-and-contraband-stats-and-settlementswe-got-such-a-huge-trove-of-lawsuits-settlements-from-the-comptroller."

As soon as we got off the phone, I started filing. Now that I knew what to do, I wanted to dive in. That first night, I put in enough requests that I got a call from a bemused prison spokesman the next day.

"I'm not sure we've ever gotten that many different records requests from one person in the same day," he said, with a dry chuckle. "Some of these could take a while." In the meantime, I followed Reuven's other advice: calling staff unions, finding advocacy groups, sifting through lawsuits, and tracking down people who knew things about the prison system.

That interview in the taco joint was one of my first, and afterward I started writing to the nearly toothless man on the row. When he responded, he explained this wasn't just about death row. *No one* could get dentures, he said. As we went back and forth, I realized: This was a bigger story than I thought. So I kept poking around, tracking down the source of the false rumor that started it all, talking to dental experts, and writing every prisoner I could, asking them to give my address to their toothless friends, waiting impatiently for their handwritten responses—and then asking them for their toothless friends and waiting for those responses, too.

While I waited, I found other stories to write about: Someone sent me a leaked email, and from it I uncovered a disciplinary quota system, where guards were ordered to write up prisoners a certain number of times per shift. After my story ran, officials tossed out hundreds of bogus disciplinary cases. Then, I found out about four officers who planted contraband screwdrivers in a prisoner's cell. I wrote about them, too, and a few weeks later they got indicted. When I wrote a story about a Houston public defender who'd started crowdfunding books to send to her clients in jail, people saw the story and started donating. She raised thousands of dollars, got a truck full of books, and started a monthly book club for women at the Harris County Jail. A few weeks later, I got a suicide note from a man who'd just killed himself there. He explained everything that went wrong, and when I wrote about it, the jail started a crisis hotline for people in their custody.

I wrote about wrongful convictions and hunger strikes and solitary confinement and drugs. I wrote about how there weren't enough guards to run the prisons and how they wouldn't turn the heat on in the winter. And in the course of it, I started to hear back from other toothless prisoners.

And in the summer of 2017 I visited a man named David Ford. He had a bald Black head and a grizzled mustache, and in my mind, I remember him stooping as if the years in a sweltering Texas prison had weighed him down. He wasn't the guy on death row that the murderabilia dealer originally told me about—but he was one of more than two dozen other men I talked to who had the same problem.

When he first got locked up, David had just enough molars to hold in place his partial dentures. But then he cracked a few teeth in a prison fight and lost the rest to a prison dentist. By the time I met him, his mouth was nearly empty. After five years of begging for dentures, he'd gotten nowhere.

At that point, the rule was that anyone with fewer than seven teeth could qualify—but only if it was considered a medical

302 | Keri Blakinger

necessity, and chewing didn't count. To make sure they could still eat, the prison would take regular mess hall food, puree it in a blender, and throw it in a cup.

"There's this misunderstanding that dentures are the only way to be able to process food," one of the head prison doctors told me later. "And our ability to provide that mechanically blended diet is actually a better solution than the mastication and chewing process."

When the story ran in September 2018, it was on the front page, just a little box in the bottom corner before the jump. With it was a picture, a close-up of David Ford's face, eyes watery as he held back his lips to show his toothless gums.

There was one particular state senator from Houston, John Whitmire, who was incensed by the whole thing. "Too many people don't care," he told me. Afterward, he called the prisons. I don't know what he said, but a few weeks later, I was sitting alone on my bedroom floor when I got a call. It was the prison medical director. They planned to change their policies, she said. They would hire a specialist and start a prison denture clinic. Now, she said, more people in prison could get teeth.

After we hung up, I leaned back against the wall and cried, smiling as the tears ran down my face. I knew it was a small thing in the bigger picture, but it was change. I'd done something that mattered, at least to the people who were in the dark places where I'd once been.

This was my enough.

A few weeks later, we ran a follow-up story, announcing the planned changes. And a few weeks after that, we ran another story. The headline seemed fantastical: TEXAS PRISONS TO START 3D-PRINTING DENTURES FOR TOOTHLESS INMATES. They'd ordered a 3D printer and there was a photo: David Ford, flashing an easy smile with a mouth full of teeth.

Afterward, I started getting letters. Letters and letters and *so* many letters—enough to fill the back seat of my car. There were short notes. There were handmade pop-up cards. There were lengthy missives of thanks. And they were all from prison. One guy commissioned abstract art from his neighbor and sent it. Another made a bracelet out of shoelaces and uniform threads and slipped it in an envelope. They sent me origami, cartoons of myself, lyrics to their favorite songs, and promises to keep me in their prayers. One unit sent a card signed by a dozen or so guys—all people I didn't even know. Sometimes they gave reasons: They'd gotten teeth. Had a disciplinary case tossed. Gotten off a lockdown. Sometimes, they said it was because of my reporting—but sometimes they didn't think they needed to give a reason.

"To Keri," one guy wrote. "Just because you care when others don't."

"We the Texas prisoners applaud all the hard work and your commitment to prison, and prisoner issues," scrawled another.

One of my favorites came in big block letters on the inside of an early Christmas card: "Thank you for giving US a voice. I haven't had one in 24 years. Bless you for all that you do for the incarcerated."

I teared up all over again reading every one.

That fall, I went back to Ithaca for a *Cornell Daily Sun* seminar for undergrads. It was not my first time back since moving to Texas, but it was the first time any of the former Sunnies had invited me to anything.

I stayed, of course, with Florianna and David. As I walked up the stone path through the garden, just like I had six years ago that month, I had none of the post-prison trepidation I had before. This time, it felt like home.

"Ker-ii!" Florianna exclaimed, spreading her arms in welcome.

When I walked in the door their dog, Bailey, ran up to greet me, wagging her tail as she strained to look for the dog she thought would be coming behind me.

But I was alone. I wished that I could tell Bailey in a way that she would understand: Charlotte was dead. She'd died just after I moved to Texas. She'd been there through the raids, and the robberies, and the late-night hallucinations. She'd been there when I got back into college, and curled up in my bed the night after I graduated. She'd barked at my parole officer and seen me successfully finish parole. She'd sat at my feet during long nights at the *Ithaca Times* office, then moved with me when I got hired as a reporter at the New York *Daily News* and again when I went to work at the *Houston Chronicle.* She'd seen the worst moments of my life and been there as I picked up the pieces.

As I turned over in my head the years of fur and love and mistakes, I started writing about that raw feeling of regret, but also about addiction and recovery and comebacks. I put it all in a Twitter thread—real tweets, not on paper like in jail. Someone at a criminal justice news website, The Marshall Project, saw my tweets and asked me to make them into a personal essay.

There were freelance gigs, speaking engagements, and interview requests—including one from Terry Gross, whose voice I'd once listened to on the way to skating practice, long before I knew anything about prisons or heroin.

And so, one afternoon in December, I drove to a quiet studio in Houston, slipped on a pair of headphones, and told her my story. I told her about skating, and about drugs. I told her about a lonely morning on the bridge, and two slow years in prison. And then I told her about books and teeth. And I told her about second chances, and I told her about hope.

"I was so lucky to come out of this," I told her. "And I've been so privileged in so many ways to end up with hope and second chances and a happy ending. And a lot of people don't have that."

Two weeks later, I emailed Mr. S. He wasn't great about answering the phone, but it was a few days before Christmas and I wanted to check in.

"Hey," I wrote. "You still hangin in there?"

An hour later, he replied. "Yeah barely. COPD is kicking my ass. How r u doing. Bring me up to date as to what's new with you."

"Oh my god I'm doing so amazing," I wrote. I sent him a link to my essay about Charlotte and told him I'd been on *Fresh Air*, and I told him about the stories I'd written. "And—this is the thing I am most proud of and the absolute highlight of my year," I wrote. "I GOT THE TEXAS PRISON SYSTEM TEETH."

The words still excited me every time I typed them in bold, shouty joy.

He responded on Christmas Eve.

"Damn way to go potter. I am truly proud of you," he wrote. "Believe me, life is measured in what we give & how we touch others. You have definitely touched many and someday you will think the stress and trauma was well worth it."

A few weeks later, I got an email from an editor at *The Washington Post Magazine*. She told me they were doing a special issue about prisons—and every story would be written by someone who did time. Was I interested in writing one?

And this is how I ended up where I will leave you: In California, on a sunny day. It is warm outside, but not yet hot.

The campus is beautiful, but the clanking chains remind me where I am, and I flinch. The walls of intake are a pretty sage green, and there are palm trees and a cement amphitheater outside for movie nights—but this is still a jail.

On a carefully landscaped forty-five-acre campus, the Las Colinas Women's Detention Facility in San Diego is considered the gold standard of "gender-responsive corrections." That's why *The Post*—one of the outlets that initially wrote about my arrest—sent me here to spend three days reporting. They have asked me to write four thousand words on jails and prisons tailored to women's needs.

The women here have a saying: "We don't count the days, we make the days count."

And they do. There's Melanie, who is taking a sewing class and ready to gush effusively about sobriety. Theresa, who stoically tells me about her unbelievably hard life—then cries on me afterward in the jail's greenhouse. And there's Tabatha, a former meth user who now spends her days taking math classes and doing crosswords. She'll probably be the focus in my story.

They've been told about me before I arrive.

"Are you the lady who was here a long, long time ago?"

"No, I did my time in New York."

"Oh."

They're skeptical at first, but still they have questions. How did I get clean? How did I get my job? What exactly does a reporter do? What sorts of stories do I write?

I tell them. I tell them about dentures and quotas and planted evidence and books. Their eyes are wide.

"There's, like, hope," one says, in a tone that could be either a question or a statement.

But I know—and they know—that most of them won't make it. Most of us don't. I came into this with a lot of trauma, but also a lot of privilege. Yes, I had the willingness to move on and to change, but also the tools to do so. Those aren't things I can give them. I can tell them my story, listen to theirs, and hope that one day they can bridge the gap. That's all that I can do, and hope that it is enough, for them and for me.

After today's reporting, I will get to leave. I will go back to the motel and run five miles. Not in circles around a cellblock, but outside on the street. I'll drink real coffee, not jailhouse instant. I'll turn in edits on a story about abuses in the New York prison system, write back one of the guys on death row, and check my email.

Then I'll go grab a drink with the photographer, Brian. Like me, he did time. Together, we head to the divey, New Orleans–themed motel bar, where a live band is playing Amy Winehouse ten times too loud. We listen and trade prison stories—and still none of this seems real. Not the band, not the gaudy masks on the wall in this bar, not the stories we're telling, not this moment.

Eventually, Brian and I decide to buy a pack of cigarettes—Parliaments—for old times' sake. We take out one each and leave the rest behind when we go out to smoke and talk about the reporting, the story, the trip. We don't know it yet, but this will win things. The entire November issue—the Prison Issue—will get a National Magazine Award, and my story will end up in the *Best American Magazine Writing of 2020*, one page after an essay by Piper Kerman, the woman who wrote *Orange Is the New Black*.

But right now, Brian and I aren't thinking that far ahead. We're thinking about what we've just seen, all the women and their lives and losses. The darkness of their pasts and the glimmer of their redemptions.

"Did you get anything out of it?" he asks.

"Yeah," I tell him, taking a drag. "I think I did."

Epilogue

My last real outing in the Before Times was dinner in bougie Rice Village, with the business columnist for the *Houston Chronicle*. It was technically the tail end of winter, but in
Houston that's easily nice enough to eat outside under the heat
lamps. We must have seemed an unlikely pair: Chris, in his
mid-fifties with some expensive haircut and fancy clothes. Me,
two decades younger with a lip ring and cheap athleisure.

We looked worlds apart, but what we had in common was
the bad shit we'd seen and survived. The scars we lived with,
and the way that we dealt with them: by writing. Chris was
never addicted to heroin and did not do time, at least not in
prison. He grew up poor in Texas and joined the army, then
went on to become a war reporter in Africa and the Middle
East, witnessing the worst the world had to offer—and writing
about it.

By the time we met, he'd been back in Texas for a decade

and had already written a bestselling book about his family and the sins of his slaveholding ancestors. For a year, I peppered him with questions about the logistics of reporting in a developing country conflict zone, before the era of cell phones and Wi-Fi hotspots. We gossiped about the *Chronicle*, and I asked for his advice on sources and stories and, eventually, on life—on living through trauma, and coming out the other side whole. Then, when book agents started approaching me after I went on *Fresh Air* and I had no idea what to do, he said he would walk me through it.

This book absolutely would not have happened without him.

When we had dinner that night in Rice Village, I was already thirty pages in. We must have talked about that and about the new book he was working on, and probably about my new job as a national reporter at The Marshall Project, covering prisons all across the country. But I don't actually remember anything from that night except the uncertainty, the gnawing fear of wondering if there were germs on the fork and whether it was safe to breathe the air.

It was March 8, 2020.

Three days later, Tom Hanks announced that he had Covid, the NBA canceled its season, and the whole world shut down. I sat on my best friend's couch and panicked. Gray spots of anxiety clouded my vision, and I started losing track of time. It wasn't the virus I was scared of so much as the lockdowns. The whole idea of forced seclusion awakened something in me that I didn't know was still there—that old fear of solitary, the feeling of being buried alive. I felt like I was teetering on the edge, almost losing touch in a way I did not think I still could. After ten years, the edge of lucidity, of reason, felt terrifyingly closer than I expected.

For the next few weeks—or maybe it was months, or days—I stopped working on the book, convinced this was the end of the world and there was no point in writing anything because there wouldn't be anyone left to read it.

Instead, I hunkered down with my best friend and her dog and threw myself into my work. In our quarantine bubble, this felt like the only thing that mattered. The news sounded so dire, and the news I heard from the inside sounded apocalyptic. Even after everything I had survived, and everything I had reported on, and everything you have read in this book, the first year of the pandemic taught me more about the casual cruelty of prisons than the ten years before it had. For months, I stayed up late into the night, texting with guards in California, messaging with terrified families from Florida, and talking to prisoners on their contraband phones. They sent horrifying pictures of the deteriorating conditions: moldy food you wouldn't feed your dog, decaying cells you wouldn't put an animal in, videos of sewage running down the walls, footage of fires burning in the common areas as men who'd unlocked their own cells fought each other, all while the guards—afraid of catching the virus or stretched too thin to respond—just ignored them.

So I wrote about it, publishing pictures of the unidentifiable food and video of the flames. At one point, I also wrote about myself—for *The New York Times*, a personal essay about isolation and incarceration. But when I started writing it, I began reaching out to the women I'd done time with. Some I'd kept in touch with over the years, and some I had to track down. And that is how I can tell you where they are now.

Some have beat the odds. Dani is sober and living near New York. She has a daughter now and finished parole five years ago. She started a dog-walking business and hasn't been back to prison.

Hailey relapsed early on, but stopped using for good a few years ago. She now has a son and a boyfriend and lives in upstate New York.

Stacy went back to prison for a few years on a new charge, but this time when she got out she stayed out and became an activist. She got a job at the College & Community Fellowship helping formerly incarcerated women get into college, and in 2021 got into a grad program herself, at Bard College.

Some people have had a harder time. Tawny the Cheshire Cat, from jail, has been in and out of rehab and prison many times, but as of this writing is all-in on her sobriety.

Susan—the woman in the Tompkins County Jail who suggested I keep a journal in the first place—started drinking again and kept doing so until it killed her.

Sam ended up doing seven years in prison, including long stretches in solitary. But we kept in touch the whole time, and somewhere in the last two years of it, something changed. Her last few years weren't as hard as the years before, and in 2020—in the middle of the pandemic—she got out. A few months later, she finished parole. She has not been back to prison.

Some people I haven't found or heard from. I have no idea what happened to Washington or the Steph I got boarded out with. And after I left the jail, I never saw Alex again. From time to time I'd hear a secondhand update on his life, like when he got in a near-fatal car wreck. Then, in the midst of the pandemic, a former heroin dealer messaged to tell me: He'd heard Alex had ratted out another man, then died of an overdose. A few months later, I got similar news about Todd: He'd died of an overdose, too—though he'd quit heroin in favor of meth.

After a few years of emails, I stopped hearing from Mr. S toward the end of 2019. After Covid hit, I got an email from his sister. "You don't know me," she began. She said she'd been following my work, adding: "He talked about you a lot (all good)."

For much of the past year, she said, he'd been deteriorating in a series of long-term care facilities. He had a variety of medical issues, including stage 4 cirrhosis—the hep C we'd bonded over was killing him. He died peacefully on June 24, at two in the morning.

"Keep writing, Keri," his sister wrote. "Keep advocating, and know that somewhere Santo is following all the good you are doing with your life."

And I do. Whether it is in a jail in California, a bustling newsroom in New York, or the parking lot of a Texas prison, I keep writing and rewriting and making corrections, not in pencil but in pen. I'm making my corrections in ink.

Acknowledgments

Writing acknowledgments is (surprisingly) hard—so I'll start with the easy one: I am so grateful for Charlotte, who will never know the ways she saved my life and made this book possible.

There are, of course, so many other people who made this book possible, so I'd generally like to thank everyone who put up with me and kept me alive during many self-destructive years.

I am grateful for the people who helped me get through prison—my parents—and the people who helped me rebuild after: Of course, Florianna and David and Bailey. But also my advisors Lynda Bogel, Barry Maxwell, and Tammy Shapiro, and some people in Richford and Newark Valley who would probably prefer not to be named.

I'm also deeply grateful to the people who took a chance and hired a felon: Glynis Hart, Bob Shields, Dianna Hunt, Nancy Barnes, and everyone at The Marshall Project. And I'm grateful for all the sources who've put so much on the line to talk to me again and again.

Thank you to the team at St. Martin's and my fabulous, fabulous editor: Hannah Phillips. I was so lucky to find someone who shared my vision for this book, and I will miss our weekly calls, though I am still available to rant angrily about prisons or the patriarchy at any time. Thanks also to my wonderful agents Christy Fletcher and Sarah Fuentes—and to Adam Thompson for introducing us.

Thanks to Annalee Gulley for her invaluable help on a title, and to all the friends and colleagues whose eagle-eyed reading on early drafts helped make this book what it is: Nicole Lewis, Pam Colloff, Shalini Ramanathan, and—most of all—Chris Tomlinson. There is nothing I can ever do to repay you for the edits, the guidance, and for letting me into your family in such a dark time.

Finally, thank you to all the prison officials whose lies and insults keep me motivated enough to uncover the truth. You know who you are.

Sources and Resources

What was the weather like on the morning of December 19, 2010? In my memory it was cold and sunny with a chance of handcuffs. After scouring the internet, I discovered that meteorology records agreed with me—at least on the first two.

That fact was what I planned to make the first entry in a thorough Works Cited section, beginning with the sites I used to confirm the temperature outside when I got arrested on page 1. But when I started writing, I realized most people reading this probably don't give a shit how I tracked down minor details like the time of winter sunrise in upstate New York or the exact distance to the gun range behind the prison dorm.

So instead I've pulled together a topical list of the sources I thought would interest people the most, along with some resources if you want to read more. Hopefully, if you've made it this far, you do.

Drugs

When digging into the disparate racial impacts of the Rocke-feller drug laws in chapter 4, some of the resources I relied on most were the Drug Policy Alliance website and the ACLU of New York's 2008 report "Rockefeller Drug Laws Cause Racial Disparities, Huge Taxpayer Burden." And I found a great take on the politics of why those laws were enacted in the first place in Jessica Neptune's summer 2012 paper in the academic jour-nal called *The Social History of Alcohol and Drugs*.

For the basic facts about the drug laws themselves, I re-lied on *New York Times* reporting, including a December 2004 article called "Changes Made to Drug Laws Don't Satisfy Advocates" and a 2009 article called "Albany Reaches Deal to Repeal '70s Drug Laws." For a deeper dive into drug laws and their fallout, check out Michelle Alexander's *The New Jim Crow*—if you have not done so already.

When I wrote about the medications used to treat addic-tion in chapter 4, I turned to journalist Zachary Siegel, who has written extensively about opioids and harm reduction. His 2018 Longreads piece, "Hating Big Pharma Is Good, But Supply-Side Epidemic Theory Is Killing People" is a good starting place.

Later on, in chapter 12 and elsewhere, I wrote about a controversial "treatment" option called "shock camp." Initially, I learned about shock in prison from the women around me. But after I got out, I spent a few months in 2019 investigating the program, which was by then one of the last in the country. The story that came out of that reporting offers far more detail than I could wedge into this book, and it was published on The Appeal's website in May 2019, under the headline: "New York Prisons Offer 'Tough Love' Boot Camp Programs. But Prisoners Say They're 'Torture' and 'Hell.'" For a much deeper dive into shock incarceration, check out the work of journalist Maia Szalavitz, who has written several articles about abusive treatment practices as well as a book, *Help at Any Cost*.

Race

The data in chapter 4 about national and local jail and prison demographics came from a 2017 Center for Governmental Research report to the Tompkins County Legislature and from the Prison Policy Initiative website, which is generally an invaluable resource for prison and jail research and statistics.

The passage in chapter 18 about the racial impacts of putting prisons in rural areas as an economic development strategy has been written about a lot, but for this I started with a 2003 report by The Sentencing Project called "Big Prisons, Small Towns: Prison Economics in Rural America" and North Country Public Radio's 2013 Prison Time Media Project. The first part of the *New York Times* investigation I referenced in that same section was published in December 2016 under the headline, "The Scourge of Racial Bias in New York State's Prisons." The second part ran that same month under the headline, "For Blacks Facing Parole in New York State, Signs of a Broken System."

The fact—noted in chapter 24—that 85 percent of New York parolees end up behind bars again for technical violations came from the Columbia University Justice Lab's March 2020 paper, "Racial Inequities in New York Parole Supervision." Some of the other parole-related data came from the Justice Lab as well. For further reading on the history of race and punishment, David Oshinsky's *Worse Than Slavery* is well worth your while.

Texas

Most of the things I wrote about the Texas prison system were things I learned from my own reporting. For more details on my investigation into prison dental care, see the September 2018 *Houston Chronicle* story "Toothless Texas Inmates Denied Dentures in State Prison"; the December 2018 follow-up, "Texas Prisons to Start 3D-printing Dentures for Toothless Inmates"; and the June 2019 story "Texas Prisons Start 3D-denture Printing Program."

The other stories I mentioned in chapter 27 are all on the *Houston Chronicle* website as well, but for newer stories, visit The Marshall Project at themarshallproject.org. It's a nonprofit news site that covers only criminal justice, and it's where I've been working since the start of 2020. It's also where you can find a video called "The Zo," an animated short based on a student project inspired by a California inmate's description of prison as The Twilight Zone. It's one of the best depictions of prison I've ever seen.

For more reading on the Texas prison system and how it came to be what it is, Robert Perkinson's *Texas Tough* is indispensable. For more about Texas death row in particular, try

Maurice Chammah's *Let the Lord Sort Them* or Michelle Lyons's *Death Row: The Final Minutes*.

Women

Throughout the book, most of the statistics I highlighted about women in prison came from things I learned in the course of reporting the *Washington Post Magazine* story mentioned in chapter 26. The piece ran in the November 2019 issue under the title, "Can We Build a Better Women's Prison?"

The statistics in chapter 19 about the number of young prisoners who spent time in foster care came from a 2014 article in *Labour Economics* journal called "Does Placing Children in Foster Care Increase Their Adult Criminality?" The numbers about poverty, literacy, and graduation rates come from the Brookings Institution, the Prison Policy Initiative, and a 2003 Justice Department report.

When I noted in chapter 22 that the New York prison system denied ever having a policy requiring women to pull out tampons for strip searches, I was referencing an October 2018 article by Lauren Gill on the website Shadowproof, called "For Wearing Tampon, Virginia Woman Says She's Barred from Prison Visits." After interviewing me for that story, Lauren asked a New York prison spokesman for comment and he (wrongly) claimed that no New York facilities ever had that policy.

The fact, mentioned in chapter 26, that only about 1 percent of prison and jail staff accused of sexually abusing people in custody actually get convicted for it came from a January

2014 ProPublica story titled, "Guards May Be Responsible for Half of Prison Sexual Assaults." The first assault I describe in prison—the one I heard about from the women who'd left Lakeview—was later detailed in an *Albany Times-Union* story written by Alysia Santo in 2013 under the headline, "Raped Behind Bars."

The assault on Rikers that I wrote about with Reuven Blau for the New York *Daily News* ran in December 2015 under the headline, "Female Inmate Accuses Rikers Island Guard of Rape, Mails 'Proof' of Attack to Friend and Family Member." A follow-up story in June 2017 ran under the headline, "Rikers Island Guard Admits to Sexually Assaulting Female Inmate, Avoids Jail Time." In 2019, another story—"NYC to Pay Ex-inmate $500,000 over Claims She Was Raped by Officers at Rikers"—noted that the city agreed to a large settlement over a lawsuit involving the same guard, though the former prisoner is not named.

For another book about women in prison—aside from, of course, *Orange Is the New Black*—check out Donna Hylton's *A Little Piece of Light*. If none of the books I've mentioned here interest you, please consider buying them anyway—to donate to the nearest Books Behind Bars or prison book project.